CUBASE 5

TIPS AND TRICKS

Keith Gemmell

PC Publishing

PC Publishing
Keeper's House
Merton
Thetford
Norfolk IP25 6QH
UK

Tel +44 1953 889900
email info@pc-publishing.com
web site http://www.pc-publishing.com

First published 2011

ISBN 13: 978 1 906005 191

British Library Cataloguing in Publication Data
A catalogue record for this book is available from the British Library

Printed and bound in Great Britain by Jellyfish Solutions, Hants

Contents

Introduction

Are you getting the best possible results from Cubase 6? It's certainly one of the most powerful audio and MIDI production suites you can buy. It's also a very large program with hundreds of features, sometimes lurking deep beneath the surface. For this reason Cubase sometimes baffles even the most seasoned audio professionals, let alone the inexperienced user. This is no surprise when you consider that the operation manual is almost 700 pages long.

However, if software instruction books are a 'turnoff' for you, fear not because this book is certainly not another manual. It was written with the sole purpose of helping you get the most from Cubase 6 with concise information, hints, tips and tricks on the many different aspects of using it creatively. It's the kind of book you can pick up and dip in to, at anytime, on any particular subject area that happens to interest you, be it audio recording, MIDI recording, using specific editors and so on. Of course, to really get the most from the book, you're recommended to read it from cover to cover.

Cubase has arguably reigned supreme among sequencers for over 20 years now and its popularity shows no sign of abating as it continues to attract hordes of devoted users. Looking back, it's easy to understand why.

1991 saw the introduction of Cubase Audio, the first sequencer to combine MIDI and audio recording. In 1996 Cubase VST, the first software studio with real-time EQ, effects, mixing and automation, was born. They're taken for granted now, but in 1999 VST Instruments completely revolutionized the world of audio production. Eventually, with all the add-ons over the years, Cubase VST became rather unwieldy and in 2002 Steinberg replaced it with a much-streamlined Cubase SX. This wasn't just another update but a completely new program based on Nuendo, Steinberg's already popular pro audio application. Then came Cubase 4, with a host of new plug-ins and SoundFrame, a revolutionary database-type method of managing your plug-ins, instruments and presets.

Cubase 5 contained many workflow improvements, new plug-ins and tools for making and mashing-up beats – LoopMash, Groove Agent ONE, Beat Designer, VariAudio, PichCorrect, REVerence and VST Expression. They are all covered in this book along with the exciting new features in Cubase 6 – the new drum editing and replacement tools, advanced tempo detection, audio quantization, track comping, VST Expression 2, guitar amp modeling and the brand new VST workstation, HALion Sonic SE.

Setup tips

Studio-ready computer

If you can afford it, invest in a computer that's been specially set up for audio. While making music on a computer may be very important to you it's definitely not on the average computer manufacturer's priority list. Many PCs are built for light office use and often unsuitable for music studio work. Audio recording is one of the most complicated processor intensive tasks you can ask a computer to do, so make sure your machine is up to the job.

Here are a few reputable companies that specialize in audio PCs:

- Carillon: www.carillonac1.com
- Music-pc.com: www.music-pc.com
- Millennium Music: www.millennium-music.co.uk
- dv247: www.dv247.com

Quick tip

If you are doing much audio recording consider adding a second, dedicated audio drive.

Info

Cubase 6 is a cross platform program with one version for Windows and another for the Mac. The obvious benefit of this is being able to transfer your projects between a Mac and PC.

Speed matters

Buy the fastest computer you can afford for the following reasons:

- You'll have more audio tracks to work with.
- You'll be able to use more effects and EQ.
- You'll be able to use more VST Instruments and plug-ins.

Which driver?

PC version

Most audio hardware is supplied with a specially written ASIO driver, and if you have one, that should be your first choice. Your audio sound card or interface will probably have its own setup page. If your audio hardware doesn't have an ASIO driver, use the Generic Low Latency ASIO driver (Windows 7). If that s not available use the ASIO DirectX driver instead. You select and make settings for your driver in the VST Audio System page (Devices menu).

Info

ASIO - Audio Stream In/Out technology is a software interface, which communicates between your music software (like Cubase) and your hardware, such as a soundcard or audio interface.

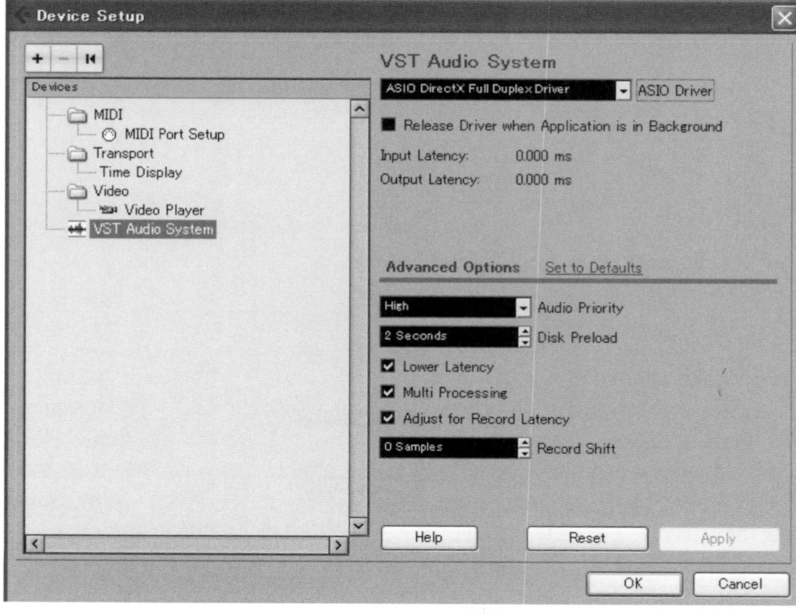

Figure 1.1
On the PC, ASIO drivers are selected in the Device Setup (VST Audio System window)

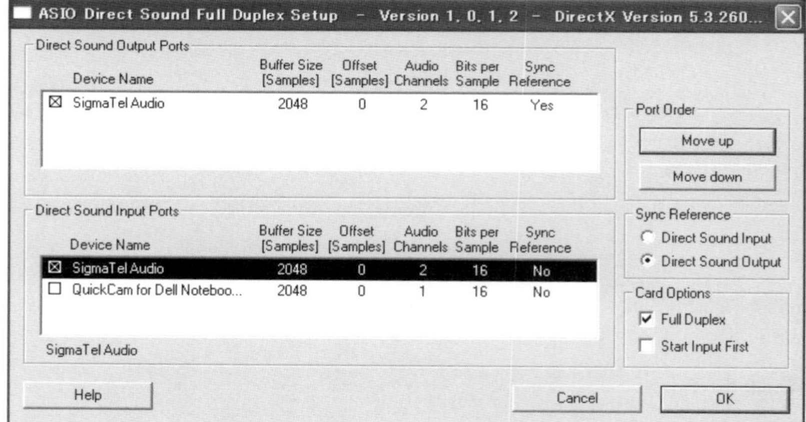

Figure 1.2
If your audio hardware doesn t have a specific ASIO driver and your version of Windows does not have a Generic Low Latency ASIO driver, use the ASIO DirectX driver instead.

Mac version

OS X saw the introduction of Core Audio and if your hardware has drivers specifically written for it they ll work fine and probably produce very low latency figures. However if your hardware has ASIO drivers, Steinberg strongly recommend that you use them as a first choice. Your audio sound card or interface will probably have its own setup page.

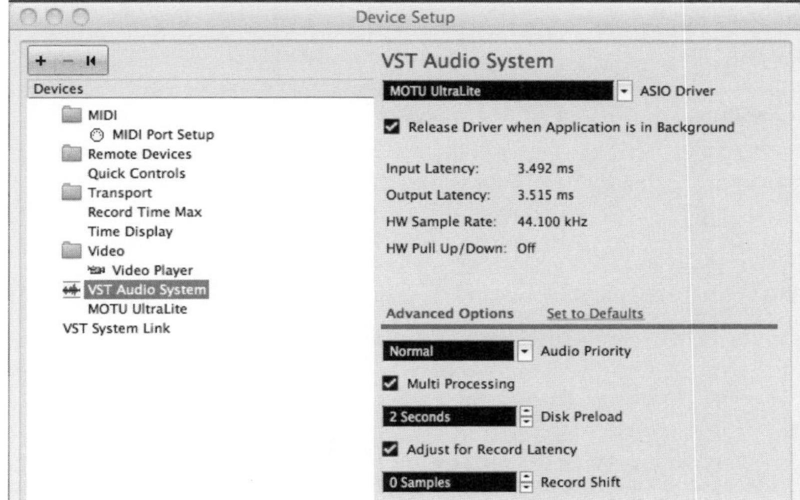

Figure 1.3
On the Mac, ASIO drivers are selected in the Device Setup (VST Audio System window)

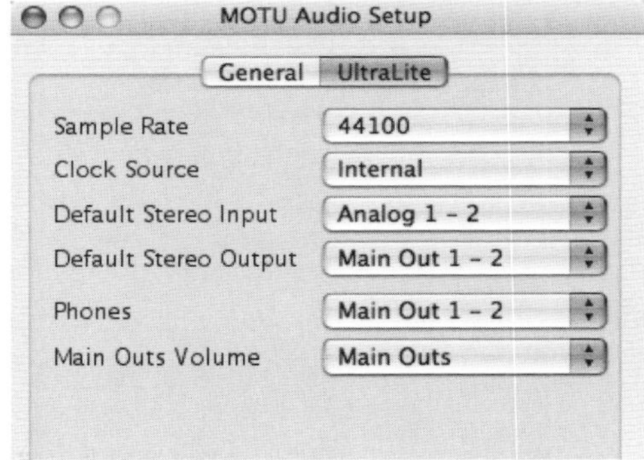

Figure 1.4
Your audio hardware will probably have its own setup page for setting sample rates, clock source, inputs and outputs

Quick tip

Check your audio hardware manufacturer's site on a regular basis and download the latest drivers for your sound card.

Setting a buffer size

Buffers handle the flow of audio to and from the audio hardware. Their size affects the latency figures and audio performance. Small buffer sizes mean lower latency. However, a small buffer size also means poorer audio performance. So it s a matter of balance. Be prepared to experiment until you find the best settings for your particular hardware setup. Buffer settings are made in the VST Audio System page.

Quick tip

Cubase 6 is updated regularly so check www.steinberg.net on a regular basis and download the latest versions and bug fixes.

VST Audio System, Advanced Options

If you have problems with audio playback, refer to the Advanced Options section (Device Setup > VST Audio System). Unless you're using a computer with more than one CPU the Multi Processing button will be disabled.

Information on the various settings can be found in the online help and may well solve your particular problem. Again it's a matter of experimenting. If you get in a mess, just click the Default button.

32-bit or 64-bit

Windows

Cubase 6 comes in two versions for Windows Vista and Windows 7 operating systems: 32-bit and 64-bit. So which one do you use?

The main difference between the two versions is the amount of RAM that can be addressed by both Cubase and the operating system.

Naturally, the 32-bit version of Windows Vista runs 32-bit applications only. These applications can only address up to 2 GB of available RAM. That applies to the 32-bit version of Cubase 6, of course.

However, the 64-bit version of both Windows Vista and Windows 7 will let you run 32-bit and 64-bit versions of Cubase 6. Cubase 6 x32 will be able to address up to 4 GB of the available RAM and Cubase 6 x64, much more.

Mac

Like the Windows version, Cubase 6 for Mac (OS X 10.6 or later) can be run as either a 32-bit or 64-bit application. Open the Get Info menu by right-clicking on the application icon.

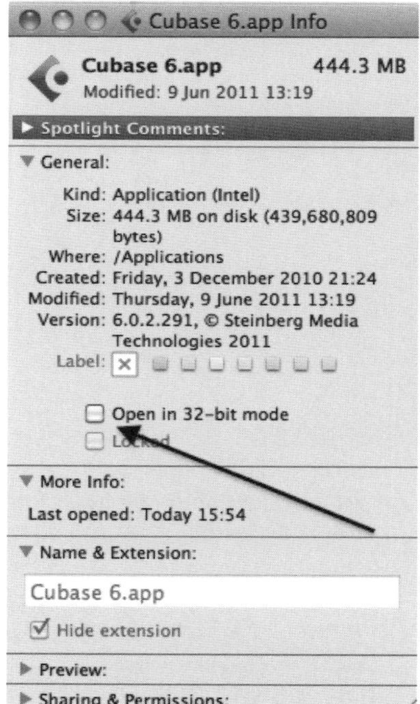

Figure 1.3
Open the Get Info menu by right-clicking on the application icon.

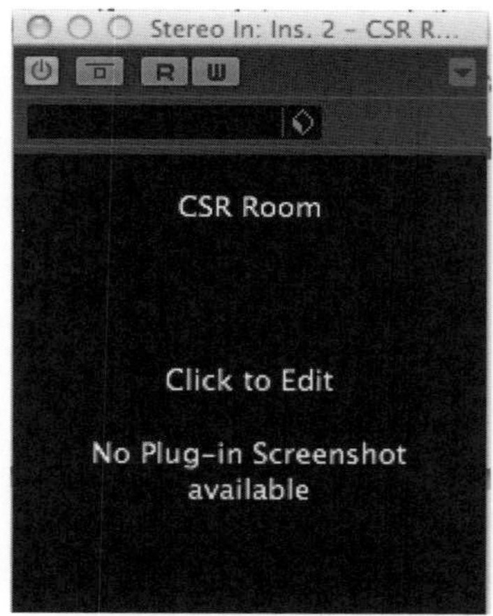

Figure 1.4
VST 2.4 32-bit plug-ins can be opened within Cubase 64-bit with the aid of the VSTBridge.

VST Bridge

All the VST3 plug-ins included in Cubase 6 are already 64-bit native and you'll get better system performance if you update your existing third party plug-ins to a native 64-bit version as well. However, to help you with the transition from 32-bit to 64-bit Cubase 6 includes a VST Bridge. It allows VST 2.4 32-bit plug-ins to be used inside Cubase 64-bit. The Bridge opens automatically when you select a 32-bit plug-in.

Some 32-bit plug-ins for Mac OS X might not work inside the VST Bridge. In that case, look for a replacement plug-in or keep working on the 32-bit version of Cubase 6. When the VST Bridge is in use, only the GUI of one of the plug-ins that are bridged can be displayed. The rest of the plug-ins inside the bridge will show a generic interface. More information on this can be found at https://www.steinberg.net/en/support/knowledgebase_new.html.

Working methods

Manual work

The Quick Start Guide supplied with Cubase 6 is excellent. Tip number one, then, is read it from cover to cover. If you're new to Cubase and MIDI and audio sequencing, the various tutorials will teach you the basics of recording, mixing, editing and using VST Instruments. It takes an hour or so to read but it's time well spent.

For anything beyond the basics you'll need the Operation Manual. However, it doesn't cover everything and four extra manuals can also be found in the Cubase Help menu.

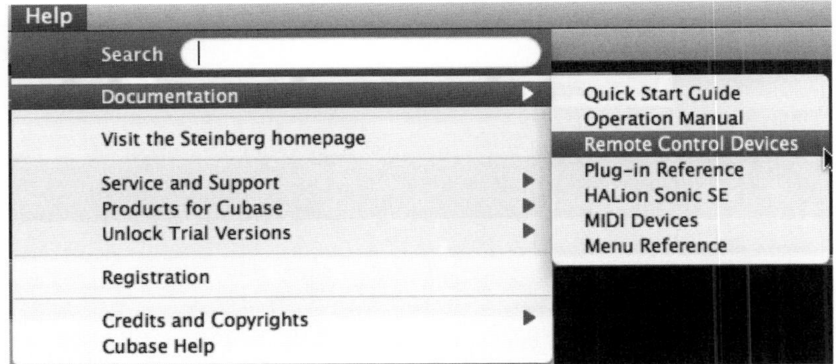

Figure 2.1
Help menu

- HALion Sonic SE – a manual for the VST workstation included with Cubase 6.
- Remote Control Devices – detailed information on controlling Cubase with various remote control devices.
- Plug-in Reference – detailed information on all aspects of the Cubase plug-ins including insert effects, send effects, using external effects, VST Instruments and MIDI effects. A valuable read if you want to get the most from the program.
- MIDI Devices – If you're into MIDI, read this book. It tells you, among many other things, how to use the MIDI Device panel to set up and build control panels for your hardware synths and VST Instruments. It also provides detailed information on system exclusive messages.
- Menu Reference – Do some of the many menu items in Cubase remain a mystery to you? Merge MIDI in Loop perhaps. Most of us need help with

the more obscure menu items from time to time. This mini-manual covers them all. Read it in its entirety and you may discover some features of Cubase that you never knew existed.

The Help section also has a search function. Enter a topic and two types of results appear, Menu items and Help Topics. Hover over a Menu item and you will be directed to a Cubase menu related to the topic you searched for. Clicking on a Help Topic opens a text screen with related information.

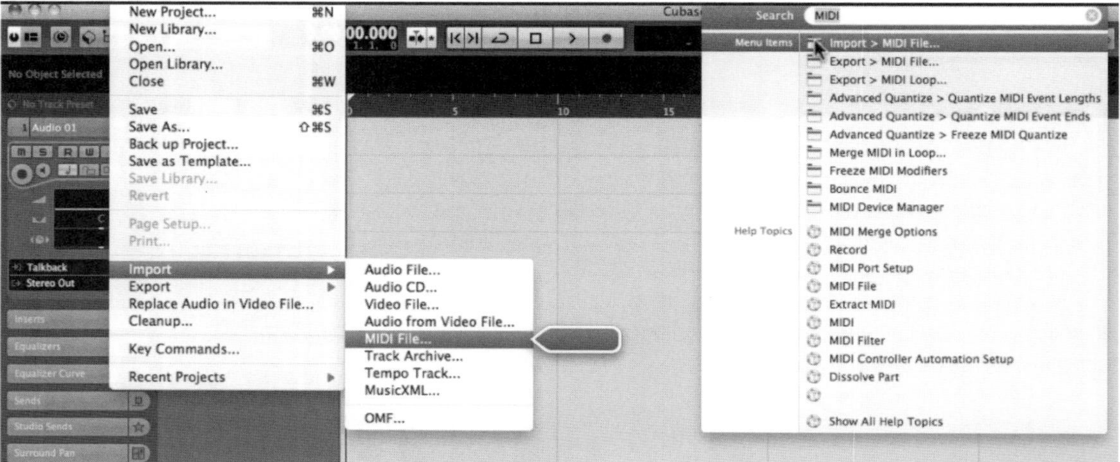

Figure 2.2
Help

Preferences

It always surprises me how many users remain seemingly oblivious to the Preferences menu. Make it your first port of call after setting up the program. It's a fair bet that you'll find at least one option that will speed up your workflow. Go to File > Preferences (on the Mac Cubase > Preferences) and tailor the program to suit you. Any changes you make are saved and loaded when you next start the program.

Preferences – Appearance

You can tailor the visual appearance of Cubase by using the Appearance Preferences. Three subheadings are available:

- General – for adjusting contrast, brightness and saturation.
- Meters – for adjusting the colour of the mixer meters.
- Work Area – for adjusting grid level intensity and suchlike in the project and editor windows.

You can also rename, save and store your preferences presets for later recall. That way, different projects can have different preferences settings.

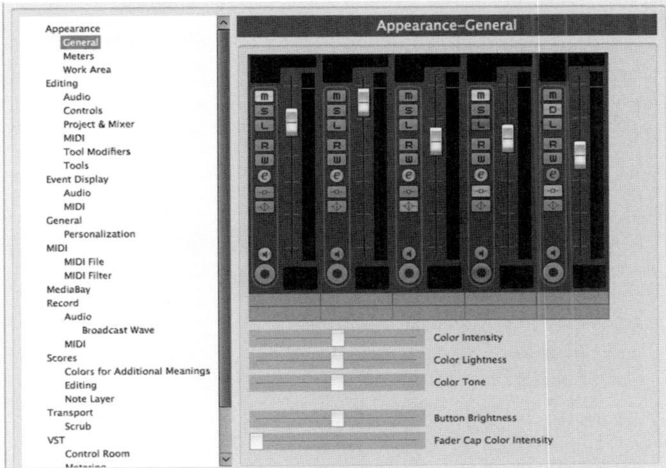

Figure 2.3
Preferences, Appearance – General

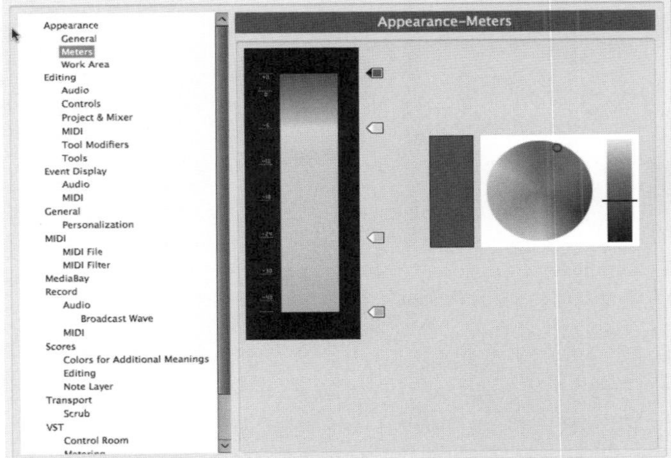

Figure 2.4
Preferences, Appearance – Meters

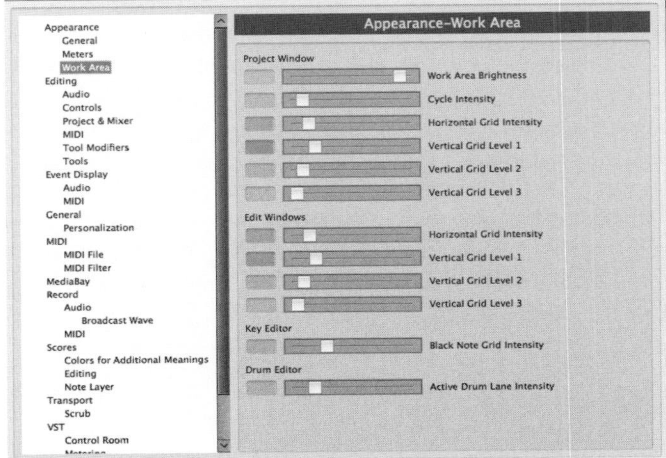

Figure 2.5
Preferences, Appearance – Work Area

Startup behaviour

On booting-up the program you may come across a blank screen by default. To alter this behaviour, go to Preferences > General and choose an option from the On Startup pop-up menu. Several alternatives are offered but perhaps the most useful is Open Last Project, which opens the last saved project on launching Cubase.

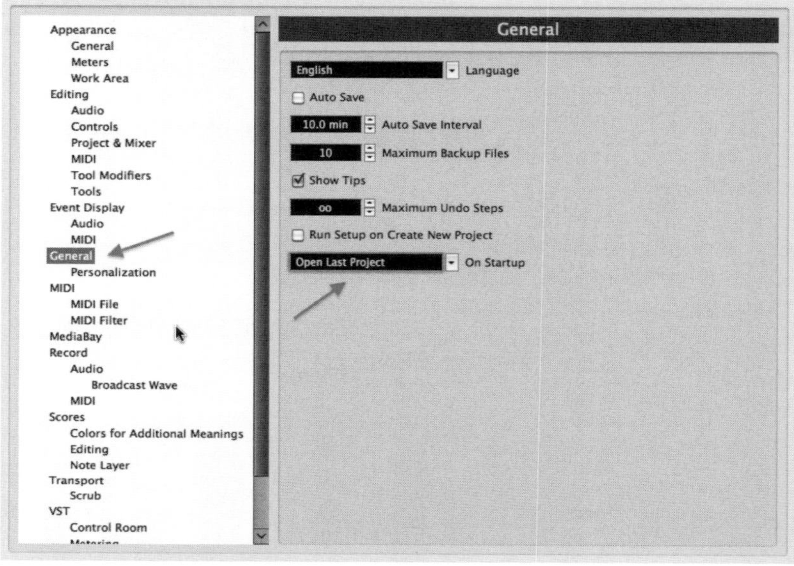

Figure 2.6
On Startup preferences

Here is a list of the available start up options:

- Do Nothing – Cubase launches without opening a project.
- Open Last Project – The last saved project is opened on launch.
- Open Default Template – The default project (the file default.cpr in the Cubase application folder) is opened.
- Show Open Dialogue – The Open dialogue appears on launch, allowing you to manually locate and open the desired project.
- Show Template Dialogue – The Template dialogue appears on launch, allowing you to create a new project from one of the templates.
- Show Open Options Dialogue – The Open Document Options dialogue appears on launch, allowing you to make a different choice each time you launch Cubase. For details, use the Help button in the dialogue.

Another useful option is Open Default Template. Of course you've got to save a new default template first (see Setting up a default template, page 51 in the Operation Manual). This feature is similar to the Autoload song that appeared in earlier versions of Cubase.

Quick tip

You can find detailed descriptions of all Preferences options in the dialogue help, opened by clicking the Help button at the bottom left of each dialogue.

Templates

Choosing File > New Project presents a choice of templates, which make good practical starting points for a number of potential projects. However, you may need a more personal configuration, in which case you can make your own. Your customized templates can be as elaborate as you want, containing VST Instruments, audio events and so on, just like regular projects. Save your template using the Save As Template option. You'll be prompted to enter a name before saving. Choose a template category in the Attribute Inspector section.

Figure 2.7
Saving a template

To open your new template, go to File > New Project and it will appear along side the others in the list.

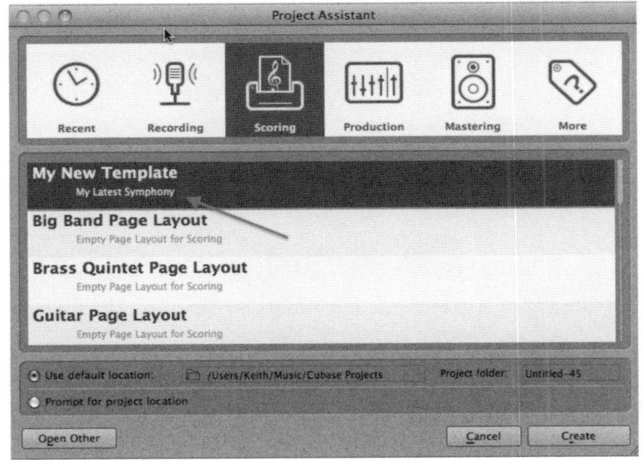

Figure 2.8
Opening a template

Quick tip

You can save any project as a template. However, if you decide to save just the track configuration, ensure the audio clips are removed from the pool first.

Toolsets and shortcuts

You can customize your own toolset and shortcut button sets by right clicking (control-clicking on the Mac) anywhere on the Toolbar and choosing what you want to see. This is useful because you may need quick access to different tools in different projects. Quite a few tools are available and precisely which items you can and cannot customize depends on which editor you are using. To view and select the available options, right-click on the Toolbar.

Figure 2.9
Control-click on the Toolbar to customize your toolset

You can select tools quickly in the project window by using the keys 1 – 9 (left to right) on the alphanumeric part of your computer keyboard. F10 selects the next tool and F9 the previous one. Another way is to right-click in the grid area to access the pop-up toolbox.

If you prefer not to see the pop-up toolbox when you right-click on the grid there's a preference setting (Editing > Tools page), which disables this behaviour.

Figure 2.10
Right-click on the grid for the pop-up Toolbox

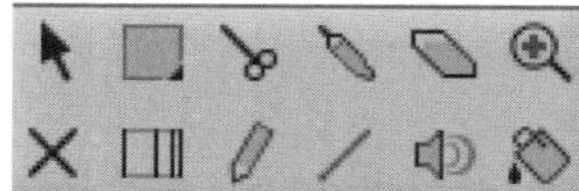

Quick Tip

Press 1 repeatedly to scroll through the object selection options for the Arrow tool; press 9 repeatedly to toggle between the Play and Scrub tools.

Quick Tip

If you re short on space on the Toolbar and you need to add more tools, consider removing the main tool buttons because you can have them as a floating box anyway.

Project Setup

Check out the Project Setup before you settle down to any serious work, particularly with audio. The Project Setup is where you set a sample rate, record format and file type for the project. Most settings here can be changed mid project but deciding upon a sample rate is best done beforehand. All the audio files in a project must conform to the same sample rate otherwise things will sound dreadfully wrong. Make a decision and stick to it.

Which file type? On a PC it's usual to choose Wave files (.WAV) and on a Mac, AIFF files (.AIFF). If you're recording live performances, which are likely to be very long, consider the Wave 64 option.

Which format (bit depth)? If your hardware only has 16-bit inputs there's nothing to be gained by selecting 24-bit except larger files with the same audio quality. The one exception to this is recording with inserted effects (see chapter 5, Audio recording). Of course, if your hardware supports it, choose a higher resolution but remember, the higher resolutions result in larger audio files, which means more strain on your computer.

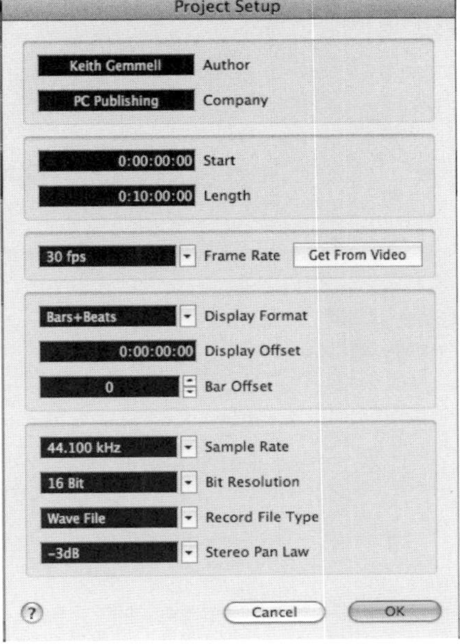

Figure 2.11
Project setup dialogue

MIDI Device Manager

There's a fair chance that you own one of the many MIDI controllable devices listed in the MIDI Device Manager. Trawl the Add MIDI Device list until you find your device. There's quite a selection. I even found one for my old Korg M1, which I've owned for the past twenty years.

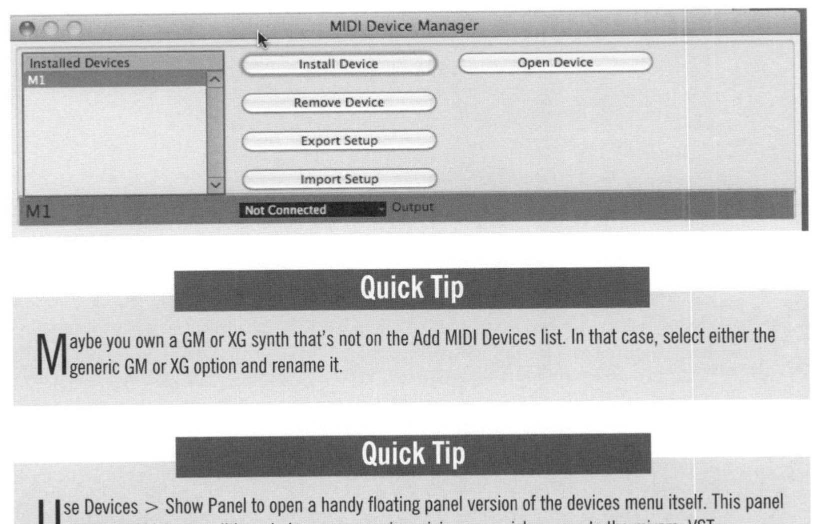

Figure 2.12 (left)
The MIDI Device Manager

Figure 2.13
Installing the Korg M1, using the MIDI Device Manager

Quick Tip

Maybe you own a GM or XG synth that's not on the Add MIDI Devices list. In that case, select either the generic GM or XG option and rename it.

Quick Tip

Use Devices > Show Panel to open a handy floating panel version of the devices menu itself. This panel will float, whichever editing window you are using, giving you quick access to the mixers, VST Instruments and so on.

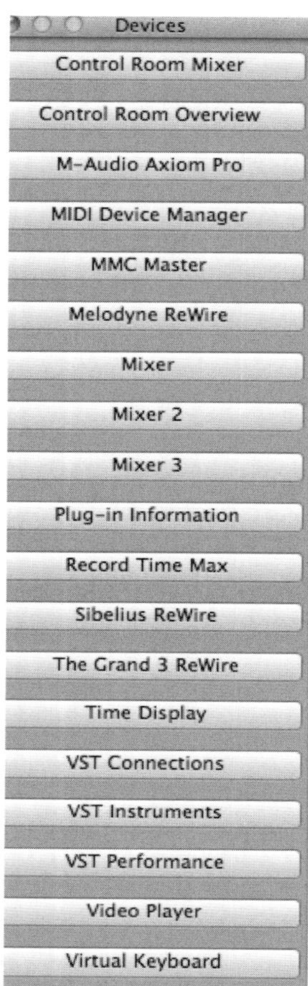

Figure 2.14
Floating the Devices menu allows quick access to the Mixers and so on

Renaming MIDI ports

Your MIDI inputs and outputs may have very long, technical names. To give them a nickname go to Device > Device Setup dialogue box, select the MIDI Port Setup, and type a new name in the Show As section.

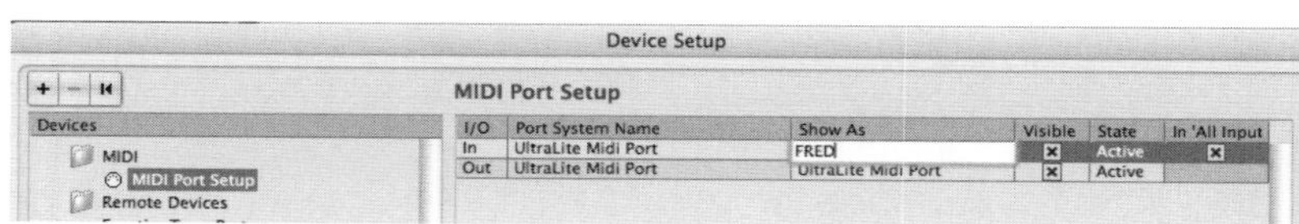

Figure 2.15
Rename your MIDI devices in the Device Setup

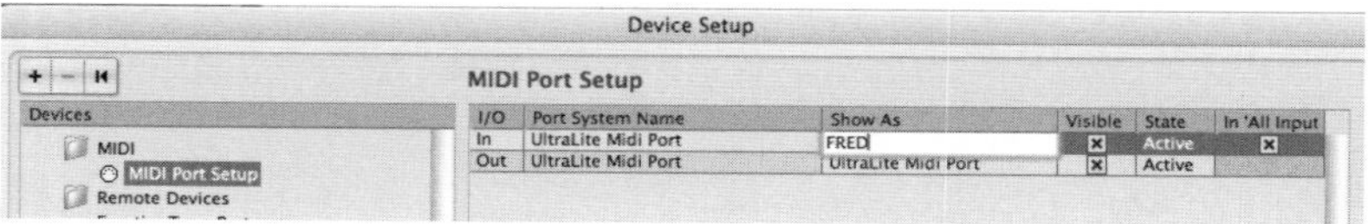

Figure 2.16
Rename your MIDI devices in the Device Setup

MIDI Thru

You've set up your MIDI connections properly but you can't hear the internal sounds on your MIDI keyboard. MIDI in and out are correctly set in the Inspector and you can see the MIDI in activity (although not MIDI out) on the Transport panel. What's wrong?

This is one of the most common problems asked by new users. It's most likely a MIDI Thru problem and easily solved by going to Preferences > MIDI and ticking the MIDI Thru Active box. Cubase will now send the incoming MIDI data to the MIDI Out socket.

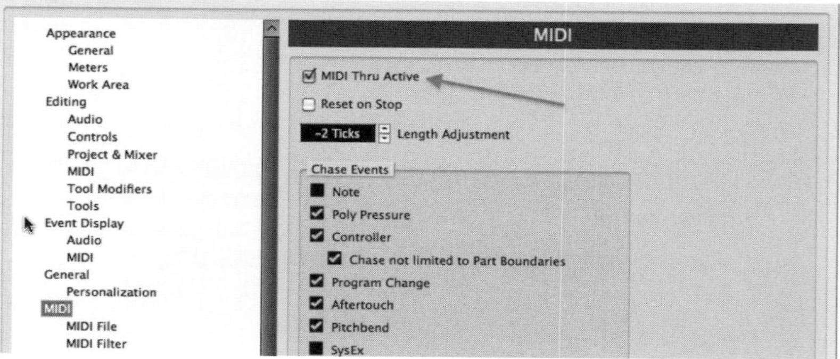

Figure 2.17
If you can't hear the internal sounds of your synthesizer, check MIDI Thru Active in the Preferences (top of MIDI page)

Info

Most modern synthesizers have a backup facility, commonly known as a System Exclusive dump, whereby you can save their settings to disk. You can do this using Cubase and record the dump on a MIDI track. Refer to your synthesizer manuals for details.

Remote control

If you don't enjoy using a mouse to operate mixer faders and knobs you can buy a remote control device such as a Mackie Control and use it to control Cubase. To set it up, choose Remote Devices in the Device Setup and select the Add/Remove tab (+). Select your device from the list (drivers for the device will probably have to be added first).

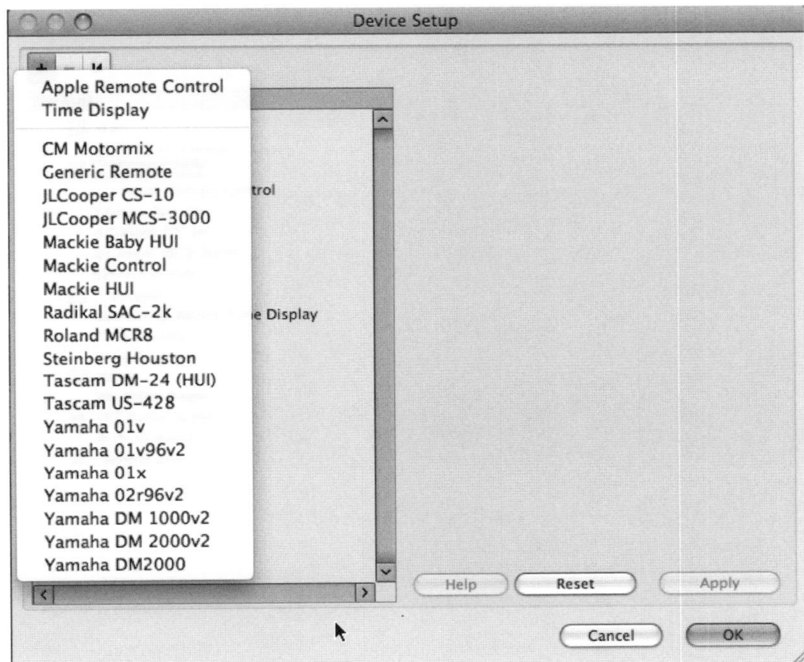

Figure 2.18
Installing remote control devices

Each device on the list has its own window where control buttons can be assigned to specific tasks. In Figure 2.19 you can see that my Apple Remote Controller has its Menu button (Quick press) assigned to Insert Cycle Marker.

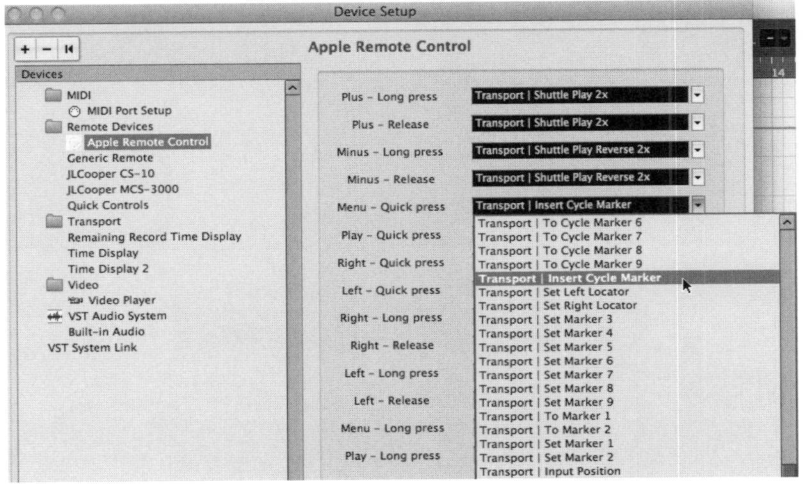

Figure 2.19
Each remote control device has its own window in the Device Setup

Quick Controls

A great way to speed up your workflow is to use the Quick Controls. Once set up, they can be used to control almost any parameter available in Cubase. For example, instead of opening several editors to access and adjust EQ, you can use the Quick Controls instead, right from the Project window. Click the Learn button (L) and turn a knob or move a fader on your MIDI controller.

Figure 2.20
The Quick Controls here are assigned to the Cubase EQ parameters

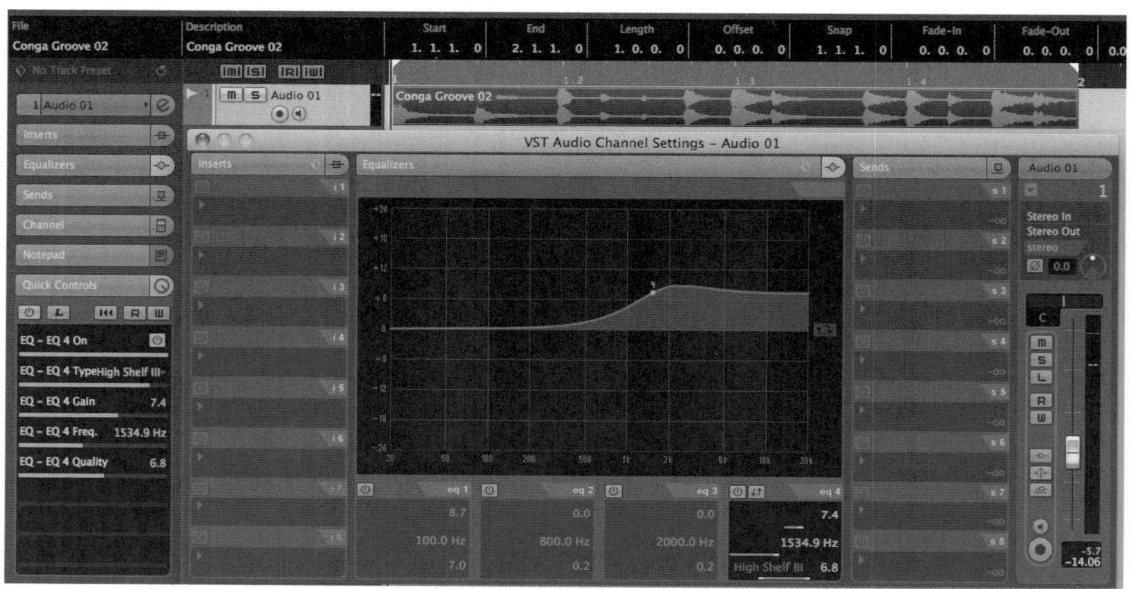

Figure 2.21
The Quick Controls here are assigned to the Cubase Amp Rack

Quick tip

Right-click a VST 3 plug-in or instrument control to assign it to a Quick Control set.

Steinberg CC121

For full remote control of Cubase, the Steinberg CC121 is hard to beat. It has dedicated controls for the Cubase channel settings, a full Cubase EQ section with rotary controls, and full transport controls with a jog wheel. There is a user assignable section and the 12 EQ controls can be assigned to Cubase Quick Controls for remote control of VST 2 and 3 plug-ins. A point-and-control AI knob is also provided. Just move the mouse over a parameter and it's placed automatically under the control of the AI Knob.

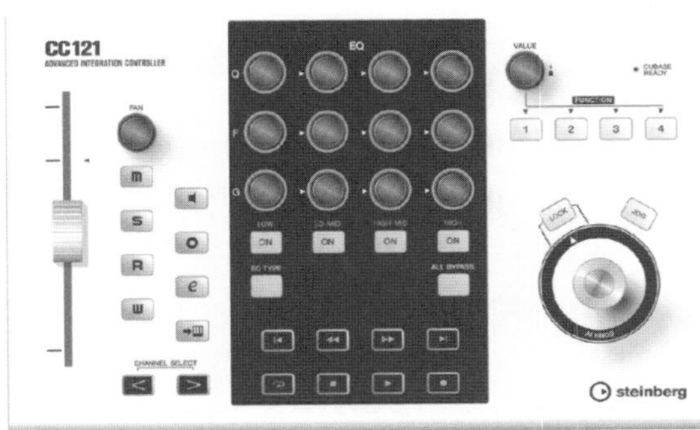

Figure 2.22
Steinberg CC121

Workspace layouts

A project is usually built in stages, something like: recording, MIDI editing, audio editing and mixing. Creating personal window layouts for the various tasks can make your work flow more efficiently.

First, arrange the various windows needed for a particular task. Press W and up pops the Organize Workspaces box. Now you can create and name as many workspace layouts as you need and remove those you don't. Switching between layouts is easy; just select one and press the Activate button.

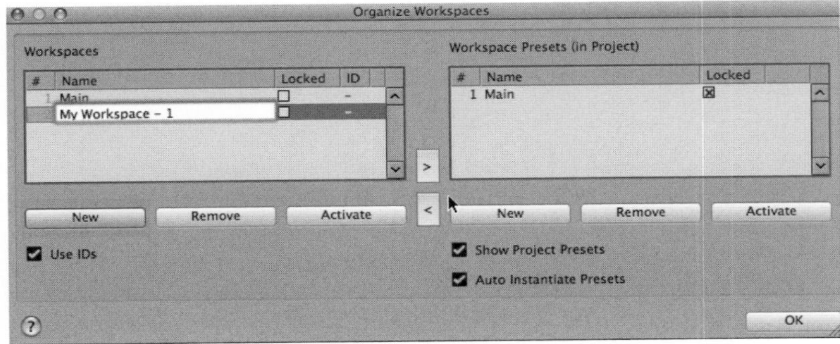

Figure 2.23
Organizing workspaces

Quick tip

In the Organize Workspaces box, double click in the number column to change layouts quickly.

Window box

Despite the larger monitors available these days the computer screen soon becomes cluttered when using Cubase. You'll find it easier to manage the open windows within the Windows box (Window > Windows). This replaces the first four items on the Window menu, enabling you to minimize, restore and close windows, all from one handy box. This box doesn t float so you'll have to close it before continuing work.

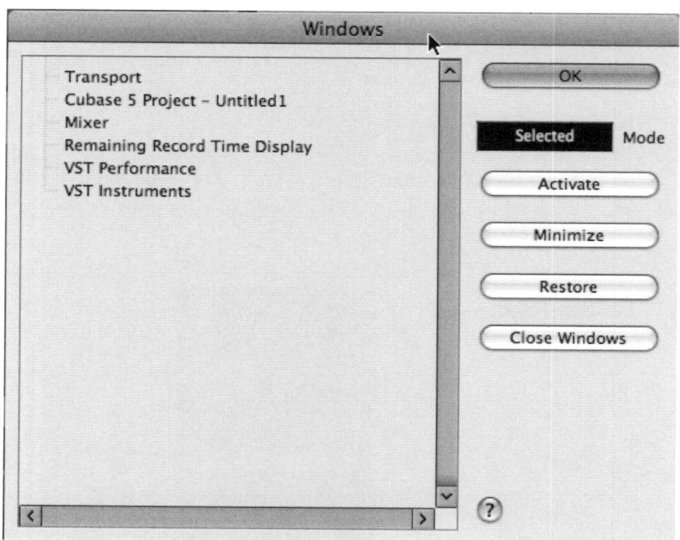

Figure 2.24
The Windows pane, for managing open windows

The Project Browser

Have you found the Project Browser? Some people don't seem to notice its existence. It's very handy though and provides a list-based representation of a project rather like Windows Explorer or OS X's Finder. Use Control+B (on the Mac, Command+B) to open it. From here you can view and numerically edit all events on all tracks using a value-based list. That goes for automation too. It's a great way of fine-tuning track data after first entering it with the Pencil Tool in the Project window, more precise and less clumsy.

Figure 2.25
Use the Project Browser for detailed editing

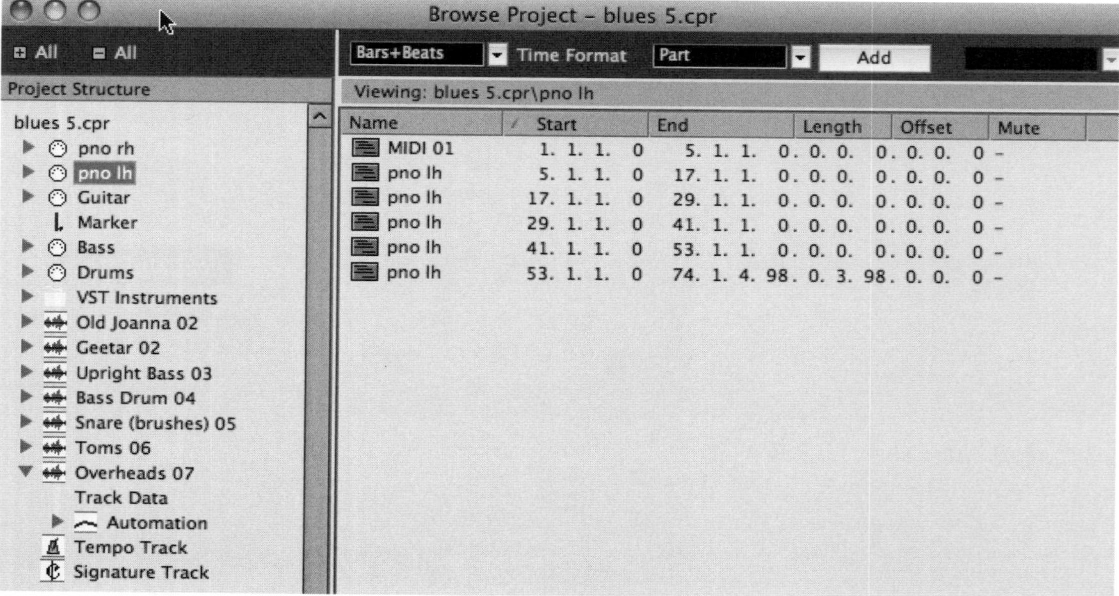

Key Commands

There are key commands for most menus and dozens more for various functions. Remembering them all, though, is a formidable task. You may find it easier to invent your own. Use the Key Commands dialogue (File menu) to add yours and customize the existing ones. Cubase SX 2 saw the introduction of stored key commands, saved as presets for later recall. In other words, different key commands for different projects.

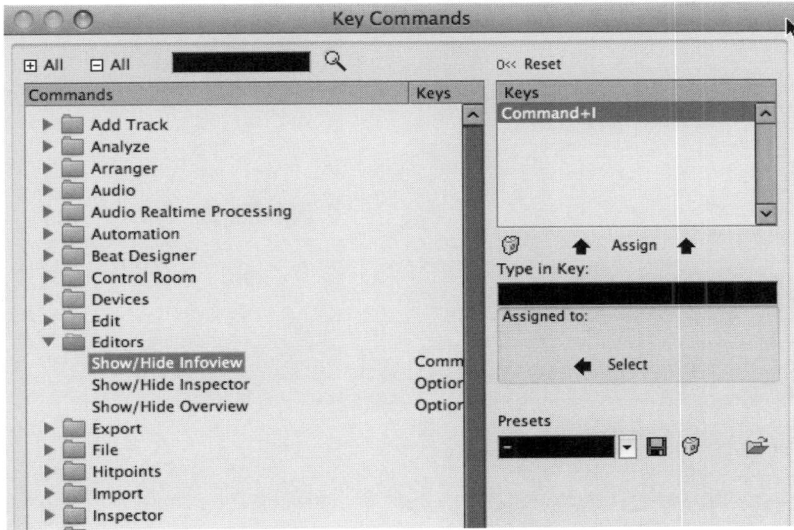

Figure 2.26
You can create and customize your own key commands

Here are a few of the most important key commands that you'll need.

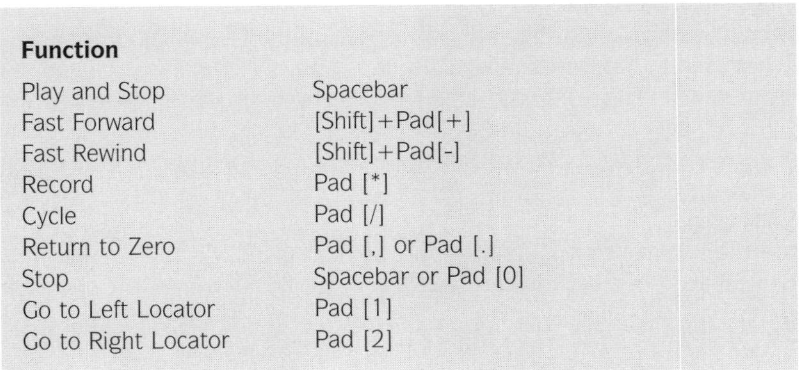

Function	
Play and Stop	Spacebar
Fast Forward	[Shift]+Pad[+]
Fast Rewind	[Shift]+Pad[-]
Record	Pad [*]
Cycle	Pad [/]
Return to Zero	Pad [,] or Pad [.]
Stop	Spacebar or Pad [0]
Go to Left Locator	Pad [1]
Go to Right Locator	Pad [2]

Info

There's a list of default key commands in Appendix 1 of this book.

Quick tip

Often overlooked: to close down an Editor - press the Enter key.

Switching preferences with Key Commands

You can assign key commands to toggle a whole bunch of switchable preferences. For example, you might want to switch a preference such as Enable Solo on Selected Track on and off whilst you are working on a project. A minute or two setting these key commands up will save you much frustration and unwelcome interruptions to your workflow. Check out the Preferences folder in the Key Commands section (File menu) (Figure 2.27).

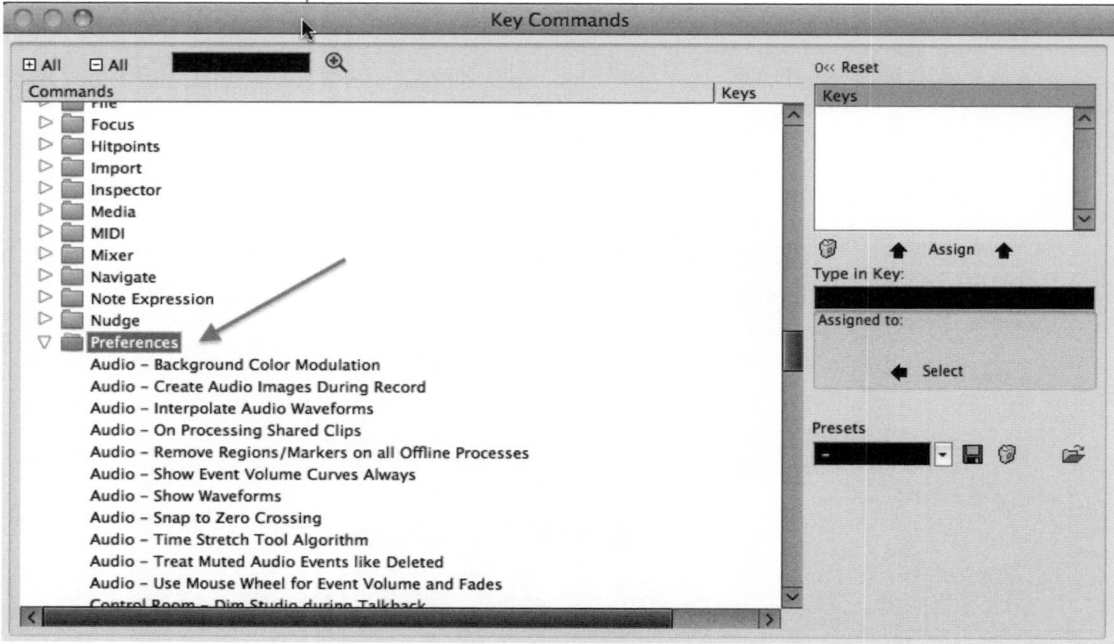

Figure 2.27
Key Commands Preferences Folder

Info

A Macro is a set of commands, which are performed one after another in one single pass.

Quick tip

Save your projects regularly, as you go, using Control+S (on the Mac, Command+S). It not only saves the project, but much angst too, if your computer crashes.

Key Command macros

If you have a multiple task to perform such as selecting a group of audio events on a single track, creating a fade in and exporting them as an audio mix-down you can make light work of it by setting up a macro in the Key Commands box.

Plug-in Information window

Keep tabs on your VST Plug-ins with the help of the Plug-in Information window, found in the Devices menu (Figure 2.28). Every installed plug-in will show up here. Press the Update button if you have recently installed one and you can't see it. Apart from specific plug-in information, you can see how many are currently in use and deactivate those you don't want on the menu.

Backing up

Use the automatic back up system if you're forgetful. Go to Preferences > General and tick the Auto Save box. Specify a time interval for the operation and a maximum number of backup files. Any open files will be backed up at the specified interval in the project folder, as you work. Your original files are unchanged. If things go wrong and you want to go back, select Revert from the File menu and you will be asked if you want to open the backup or the original file.

Archive back up

Before backing up a complete project to a CD use Media > Prepare Archive to tidy things up. Any stray audio files found outside the project folder will be returned to it. Use the Freeze Edit option and you will not need to save the edit folder.

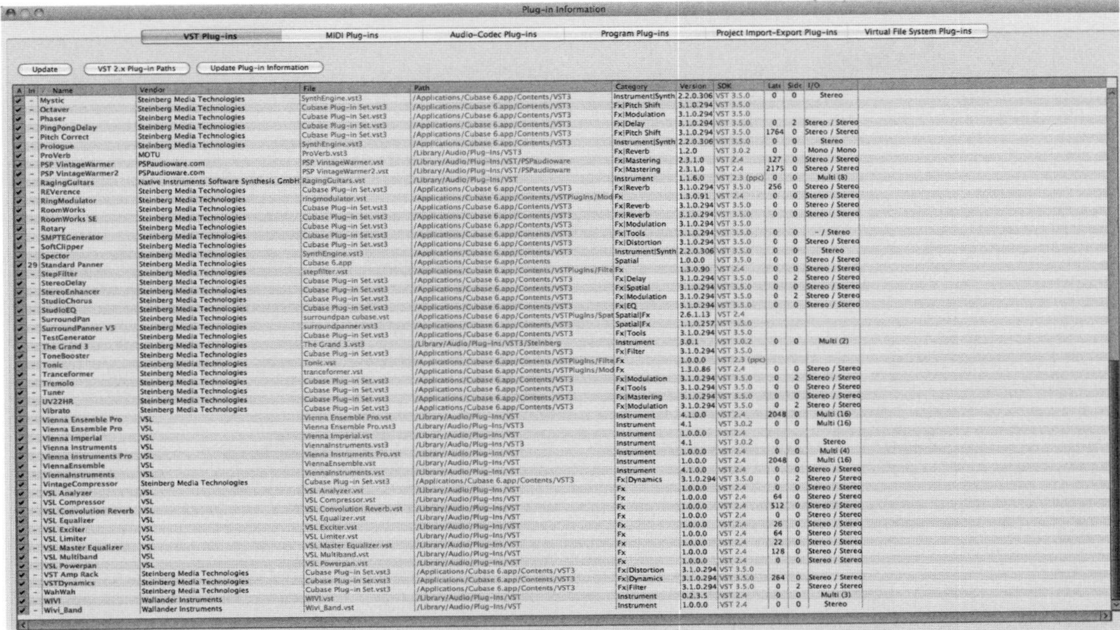

Figure 2.28
Keep track of all your plug-ins in the Plug-in Information window

Opening files

If you're opening a project containing audio files archived on a CD, perhaps created on another platform, it's best to copy the entire folder onto your computer desktop before opening the project file. Otherwise the audio files may not be referenced properly.

Importing audio

It's a good idea to have imported audio files copied into the project's audio folder and thereby referenced from there. This keeps things tidy. Go to Preferences > Editing-Audio and select Open Options Dialog. Now, when you import an audio file an Options dialogue will appear asking you if want to copy the file to the audio folder and convert it to the project settings. There are further options such as Copy and Convert. This will convert the files to the same sample rate and size.

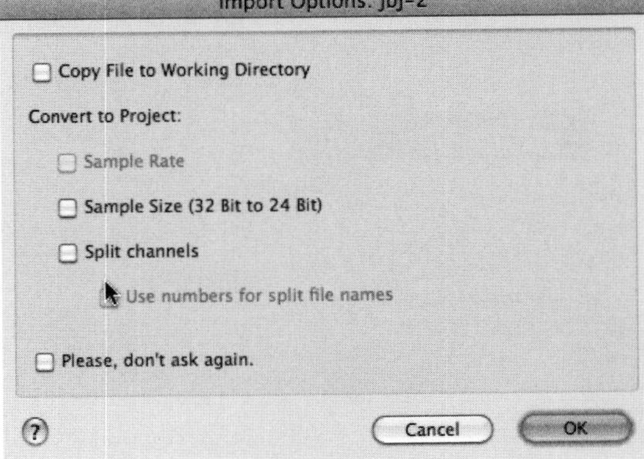

Figure 2.29
Audio file Import Options

Cleaning up

Save valuable hard disk space and use the Cleanup function File > Cleanup. Cubase will scan selected folders or entire hard disks for project folders containing wayward audio and image files that are not used by any project. These will be listed in a dialogue box awaiting your further action. Delete with extreme care. If you ve used any of these audio files in other projects, or moved or renamed them without updating their paths, Cubase will consider them unused.

Info

Image and Fade files can be safely deleted using the Cleanup function because they will be recreated again on use.

Slide control

How do you like your knobs and sliders? Go to Preferences > Editing - Controls. Here you can select your preferred ways of controlling knobs, sliders and value fields. For example, to have the mouse scroll value on the Transport panel, fader style, choose Increment/Decrement on Left Click and Drag in the pop up menu – very handy.

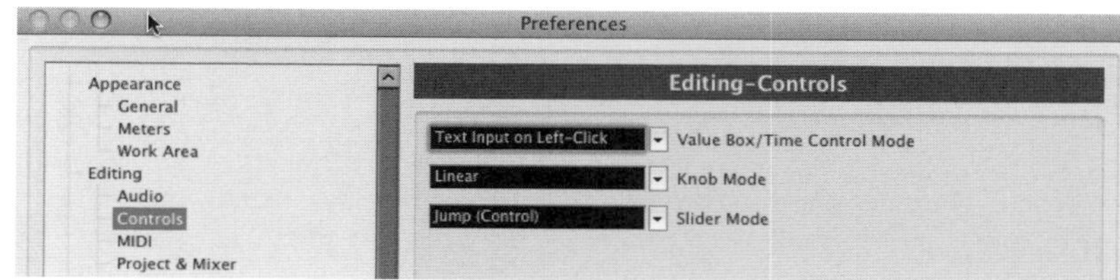

Figure 2.30
Customizing knobs and sliders

Quick tip

Throughout the program, all Mixer, Inspector, and VST Plug-in faders and knobs can be returned to their default settings. Simply Ctrl click (on the Mac, Command click) on the relevant object.

Edit History window

We all make mistakes and change our minds. You can use Undo and Redo repeatedly to get back where you need to be but it's quicker to use the Edit History window. Use Edit > History to open it. All your actions are recorded here and recorded in a list, the most recent at the top. A shaded curtain can be dragged down, using a blue divider line, to cover anything that you wish to undo. If you want to redo things, simply drag the curtain back up to a convenient point. This window floats and the changes are reflected in the Project window instantly. It's not saved with the project though, so get things right before you close it down.

Figure 2.31
You can undo and redo all your actions in the Edit History window

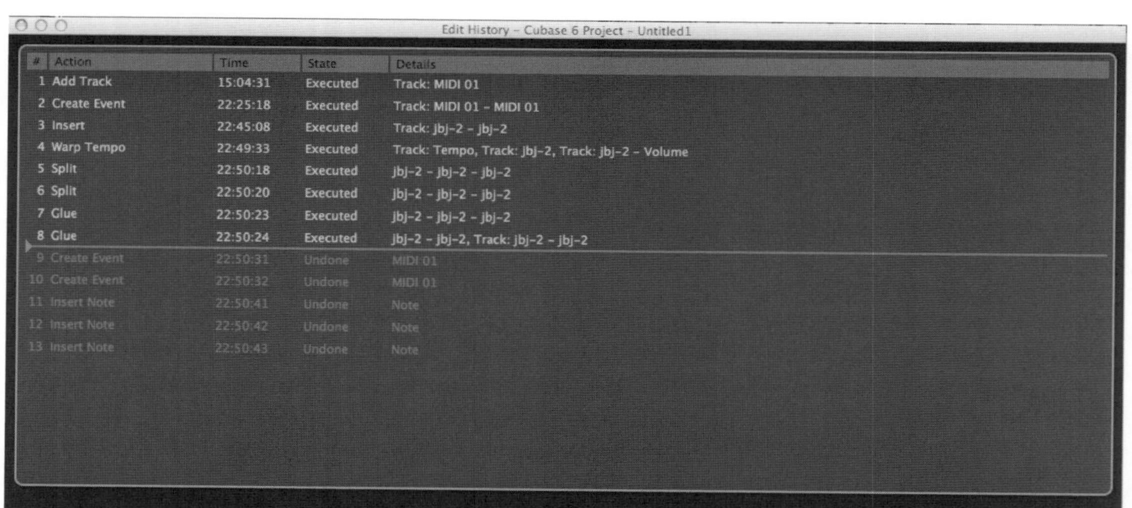

Quick tip

Jot down any project related memos such as ideas for the next session, a song lyric line, hardware settings and anything else you need to remember in Notepad (found in the Project menu).

Handy Edit menu key commands

- Undo Ctrl+Z (on the Mac, Command+Z)
- Redo Shift+Ctrl+Z (on the Mac, Shift+Ctrl+Z)

The Library

It's very likely that you already store your favourite loops, samples and even video clips in various folders on your hard disk. Accessing them might be made easier by using the Library feature. You can create as many Libraries as you need and drag and drop files directly into Cubase or use the Open Library, New Library and Save Library menu items. These files have the extension .npl .

Figure 2.32
The VST Sound logo

VST Sound

VST Sound appeared in Cubase 4.5, replacing the SoundFrame idea. It's a database-style management system that links the Media Bay, VST Sound Loops, VST3 Presets, Track Presets and VST Instruments. You can identify a VST Sound feature in Cubase by its logo, which crops up in several places including the Apply Track Preset box.

Figure 2.33
The VST Sound logo appears wherever the VST Sound features can be accessed, for example, the Load Track Preset box

Media Bay

An integral part of VST Sound, the Media Bay is a powerful media file management system that enables you to access and control all your media files from within Cubase. That includes audio files, MIDI files, video files, track presets, VST presets, pattern banks and project files.

Figure 2.34
You can access, preview and manage all your media files from within Cubase, using the MediaBay

Quick tip

Use your computer keyboard tab key to move between different sections of the Media Bay. Use the arrow keys to navigate the folders, files and tags.

Media management – which view?

The Media Management system has three preconfigured views to suit your working situation. Which one you choose depends on your working environment. All three are found on the Media menu:

- Open MediaBay (F5) – to view all available file types.
- Open Loop Browser (F6) – if you're working with audio files, particularly if they have been tagged by category and so on.
- Open Sound Browser – for managing presets.

Info

You can store loops and samples in your MediaBay on external USB hard drives, take them with you to another studio and call them up within another MediaBay. No further indexing required.

Track Presets

Track Presets are incredibly useful, especially if you need to recreate specific recording or work scenarios on a regular basis. They encompass all the usual tracks – audio, instrument, MIDI – plus a very useful multi track preset.

How to create a track preset is described in detail on 332 of the Operation Manual (Working with Track Presets section). Here's a quick summary:

1 Select a track (or tracks) in the Track list, open the context menu (right-click) and choose Create Track Preset.
2 In the Save Track Preset dialogue, enter a file name, open the Attribute Inspector (bottom left corner) and edit the tags (category, character, style and so on), click OK and you're done.

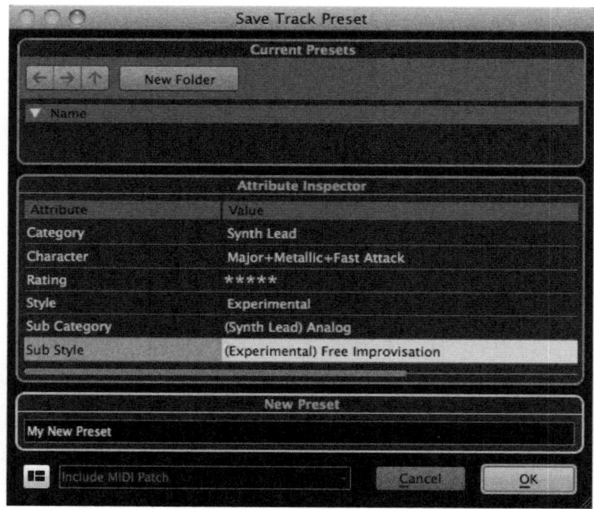

Figure 2.35
Saving a Track preset

Info

Track Presets can only be applied to tracks of the same type.

The simplest way to apply a track preset is to select it in the Sound Browser and drag and drop it to an appropriate track.

Info

When applying a Multi track preset, make sure that the target tracks are of the same type, number and in the same order as the saved preset.

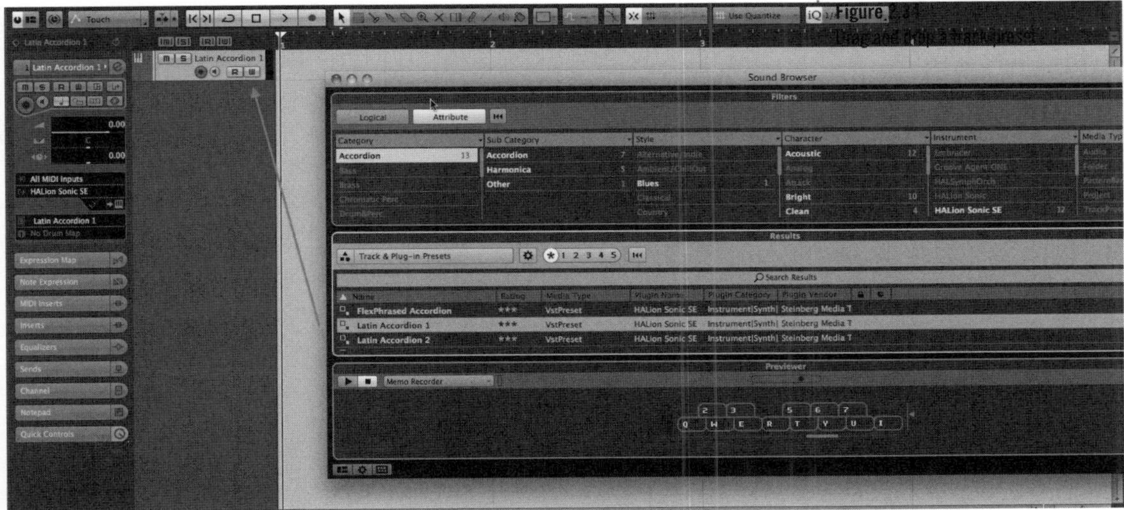

Figure 2.36
Drag and drop a Track preset

Track exchange

You may need to exchange tracks with a working partner who also uses Cubase or you may want to save a particular track configuration for later use in your own projects. You can do this by using the Import and Export items on the File menu. All track related information – mixer channel settings, automation sub tracks and so on – will be saved in a separate media folder and saved as an XML file.

- To export a track or a selection of tracks, use File > Export > Selected Tracks.
- To import a track, use File > Import > Track Archive.

Channel Batch Export

You probably know how to create a stereo mix-down of your projects – select the events you need between the left and right locators, leaving enough space at the end for any reverb tails, and use File > Export > Audio Mixdown.

However, you can also export the output of multiple mixer channels as audio files. Using the Export Audio Mixdown function, select the channels you want to export and tick the Channel Batch Export box (top left corner). Converting your files and VSTi tracks to audio tracks is an excellent way to free up system resources and save on CPU power.

Data dump

If you modify your synthesizer's presets, you can use Cubase to record and save the altered settings, along with your project data. It's a more convenient method than saving them to external media. For a start, everything is in one place, the project folder. Most synths and sound modules allow you transmit the settings. You'll probably find the information tucked away in the back of the manual.

Before you make the dump go to Preferences > MIDI-Filter and remove the tick from the Sysex box in the Record section. Leave the Sysex box in the Filter section ticked.

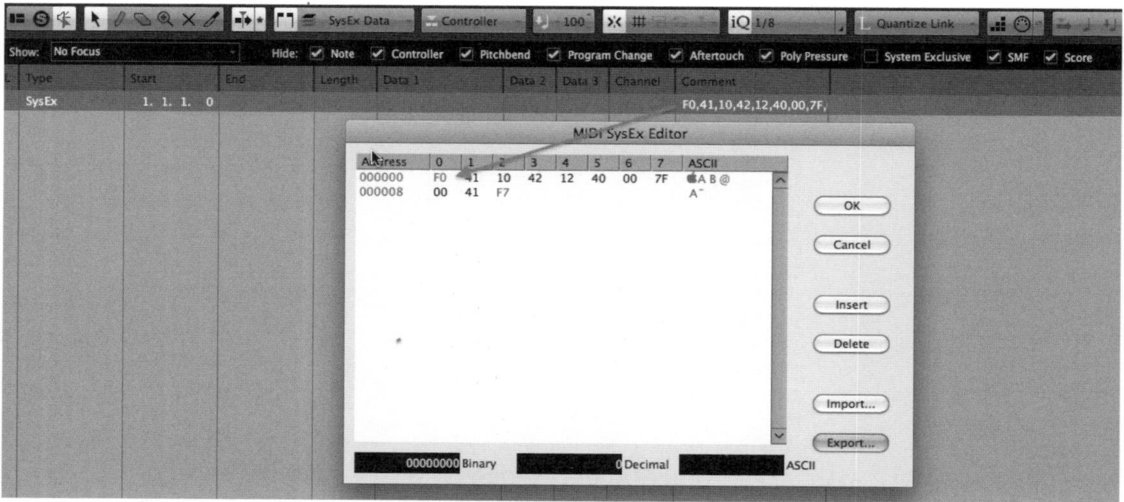

Figure 2.37
Data Dump viewed in the List and MIDI SysEx Editors

The data is recorded in the usual way, on a MIDI track and is best placed in a silent bar at the beginning of the project. When you transmit the data back to the synth, make sure that it is correctly routed. Again, check the manual because the device may receive the data on a specific MIDI channel. When you've finished the dump open the List Editor and check that the data has been recorded. Then click on the data itself, in the Comment column, if you intend editing the System Exclusive data.

Info

System Exclusive dump – term commonly used for transmitting a device's System Exclusive data and recording it to a floppy or hard disk drive.

Notepads

The Notepad in Cubase is easily overlooked but it's useful for jotting down all kinds of information about a project – song lyrics, song structure ideas, external equipment connections and anything you think might be forgotten when you return to the project later.

Did you know that Cubase has an additional Notepad, available for each track? You'll find it in the Inspector. Use it to jot down information related to a specific track.

Figure 2.38
Each track has its own NotePad

First choice Editor

Which MIDI editor do you use the most? To have Cubase open the editor of choice when you double click an event or part, go to Event Display-MIDI page in the Preferences and set it in the Default Edit Action menu.

Editing Tools

The little-known Crosshair Cursor is particularly useful for placing and editing events in Audio, MIDI and Instrument tracks lanes. So, too, is the option to Show Extra Info when using the Select tool. They can both be found in the Editing-Tools preferences.

Move To Front

When two audio events overlap, only the top one can be heard. To audition partly obscured audio use the Move To Front option on the Edit menu. As you would expect, Move To Back does the opposite.

Info

You can export notepad data as a text file (File > Export > Notepad Data).

Project window

Multiple projects

Having more than one Project window opened at a time enables you to copy and paste data between arrangements. Select the events in one window, press Ctrl+C (on the Mac, Command+C), switch to the second window, position the project cursor at the right spot and press Ctrl+V (on the Mac, Command+V). Completely new versions of a tune can be restructured this way and easily compared by switching window views.

Toolbar shortcuts

Speed up your workflow by making full use of the toolbar setup context menu (right-click on the toolbar). By default eight items are visible and seven are hidden. One of the hidden items is Media & Mixer Windows. Tick this if you need quick access to the Media Bay, The Pool (audio files), the Mixer or the Control Room Mixer.

To show or hide the Inspector, Info Line, Overview Line and the Status Line, click on the Set up Window Layout icon and tick their respective boxes.

✓ Constrain Delay Compensation
Media & Mixer Windows
Performance Meter
✓ Automation Mode
✓ Auto-Scroll
Locators
✓ Transport Buttons
Arranger Controls
Time Display
Markers
✓ Tool Buttons
✓ Color Menu
Nudge Palette
✓ Project Root Key
✓ Snap/Quantize
Show All
Default
Setup...

Figure 3.1
Right-click on the Toolbar for a list of visible/hidden items

Quick tip

Activate the auto-scroll button to have the project cursor permanently visible. Tick 'Stationary Cursors' in the transport preferences and it will remain centre screen, as events scroll by.

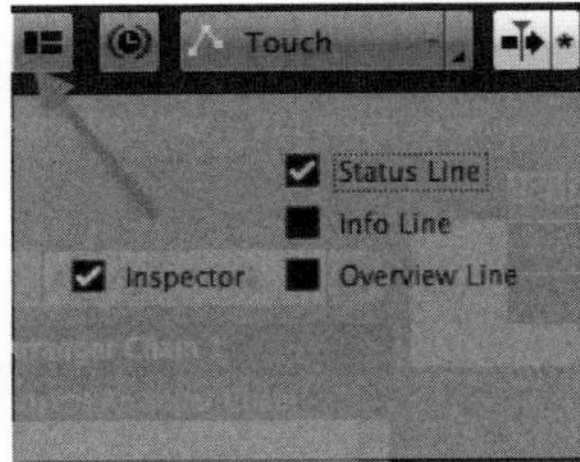

Figure 3.2
Access to Inspector

Quick tip

For a thick project cursor, change its width to '4' in the transport preferences.

Snap points

When audio events are moved with snap activated, it isn't always the beginning of the event that is used as a reference. Audio events contain snap points, which can be set in the sample editor.

You can also set the snap point of an audio event directly in the Project window:

- Select the event.
- Place the project cursor at a chosen point within the event.
- Select 'Snap Point to Cursor' from the audio menu and the Snap point will be

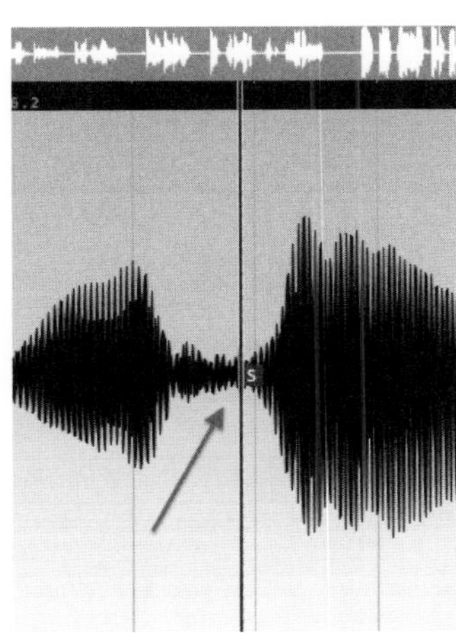

Figure 3.3
The Snap point is marked with an S

displayed as a thin line in the Project window. Move the project cursor afterwards to see it, otherwise it remains hidden

Info line

It's often said that knowledge is power. Well so is information! Keep an eye on the info line. You can view and edit precise details about any selected event here.

Figure 3.4
Stay informed and use the Info line

Project Overview

Do you find it difficult to find far-flung events in the project window? Use the Project Overview line to nip around your projects. A rectangle is used to navigate the project. Resize the rectangle - drag the edges - to zoom in or out.

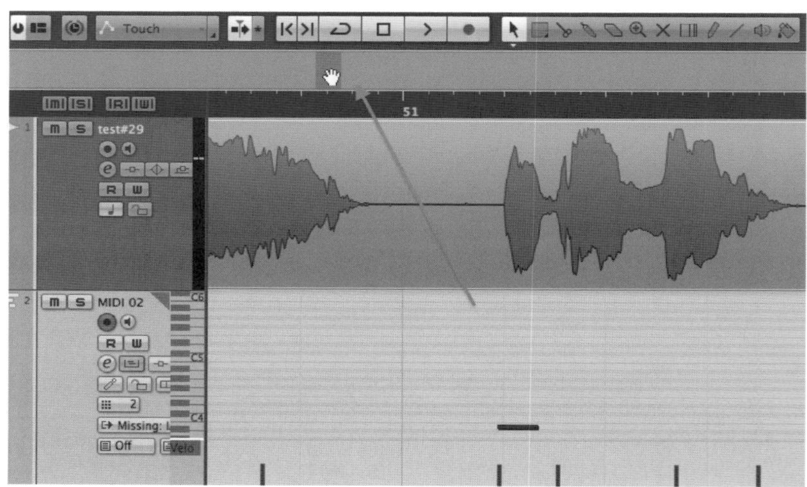

Figure 3.5
Use the Project Overview Line to move around projects

Grid display

To change the grid display, select a quantize preset and Use Quantize on the toolbar. Even triplet grids appear.

Figure 3.6

Ruler display

The display format chosen in the Project Setup appears on the Transport panel and the Ruler. However an independent display can be set for the Ruler. Click on the Arrow button (far right of the ruler), and select an option from the pop-up menu. This is useful if you are working with video and need Bars + Beats on the Transport panel and a frame rate in the Ruler.

Ruler Tracks

A peek at the Add Track menu reveals two recently added track types –Ruler tracks and FX Channel tracks. You can add as many Ruler tracks to a project as you like, and each one can show a separate display format, Bars + Beats, Seconds, Timecode and so on. This is very useful because you can position them adjacent to relevant tracks by dragging them up or down in the Project window. In this shot you can see three different Ruler tracks - Timecode, Seconds and Samples.

Figure 3.7
Choosing a Ruler display format

Figure 3.8
Three different Ruler tracks – Timecode, Seconds and Samples

Arranger Track

If you've ever used a hardware sequencer you'll be familiar with pattern-based sequencing as opposed to the linear approach used by Cubase.

In a linear sequence your parts are ranged along a timeline in an arrange page (in Cubase, the Project window). Generally speaking, you work in a linear fashion from start to finish.

Pattern-based sequencing is different. You program all your parts separately and assemble them afterwards as a series of patterns, commonly referred to as a pattern list.

Pattern-based sequencing is ideal for songwriters who compose conventional songs in sections; the verse, chorus and bridge format being the most obvious example. First you write the individual sections and then you experiment with the order of those sections and add an intro and ending (coda). This is how you go about it with the Cubase Arranger Track.

1. Create a Play Arranger Track, activate Snap and then draw a part for each section. The parts can be any length you want.
2. Rename the parts in the Info line.
3. Write and record your song's individual sections, verses, choruses and so on.
4. Open the Arranger Editor (click on 'e' in the Arranger Track or the Inspector). The individual sections are listed in the right pane of the Arranger Editor.
5. To arrange your song, drag the sections over to the left pane and arrange them in any order you wish. You can also repeat sections and alter their lengths.

Figure 3.9
Arranger Tracks are ideal for songwriters who like to compose their tunes in sections and rearrange them afterwards.

In the screenshot you can see that I decided to lengthen my intro by simply repeating it (I entered '2' in the Repeat column). I also repeated the last chorus three times.

Zooming

Lots of choice here. Apart from the comprehensive zoom options found in the Edit menu the horizontal and vertical sliders (bottom right) are very useful. The pop-up menus, found just next to the sliders, are often overlooked.

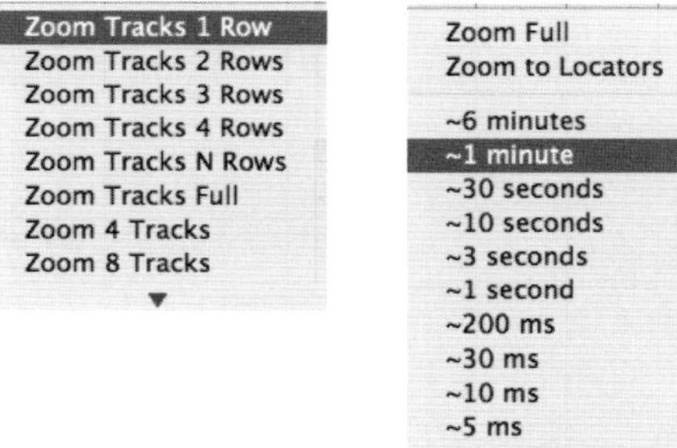

Figure 3.10
You can zoom in or out quickly, using the Zoom pop-up menu

Choose 'Organize' on the menu and you can devise your own zoom option presets and add them to the menu using a dialogue box.

Handy zoom key commands

H – zoom in
G – zoom out
Shift+F – zoom to full project
Shift+Zoom tool – zoom to full project

Track Controls Setting

You may prefer to work with a leaner track control list. To access the Track Controls Settings, click on the arrow in the bottom-right corner of the track list.

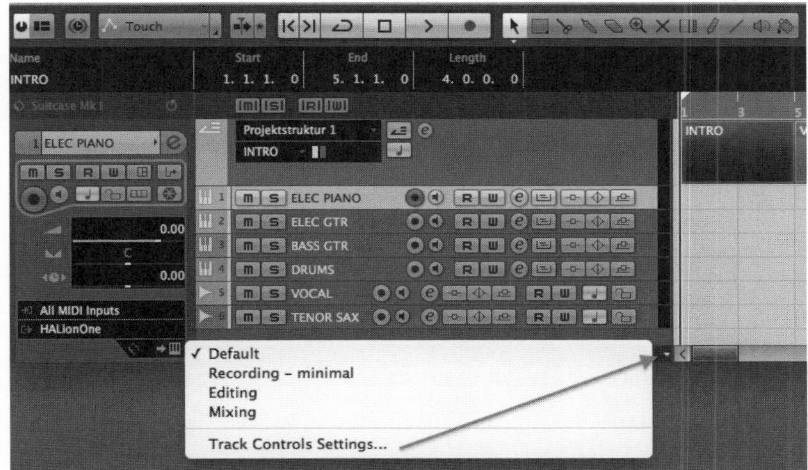

Figure 3.11
Click on the arrow for the Track Controls Setting

You can hide items by moving them from the Visible Controls list to the Hidden Controls list. Why would you want to do this? An example - if you're not using automation, Record/Write-Enable could be dispensed with. Or if the track is a purely conventional musical project, you could get rid of the button used for switching between Musical and Linear time base.

Another handy feature here is the facility to regroup the controls to various sets and number them 1, 2, 3 and so on. Now when you resize the track list the grouped controls will remain together (providing the Wrap Controls box is ticked).

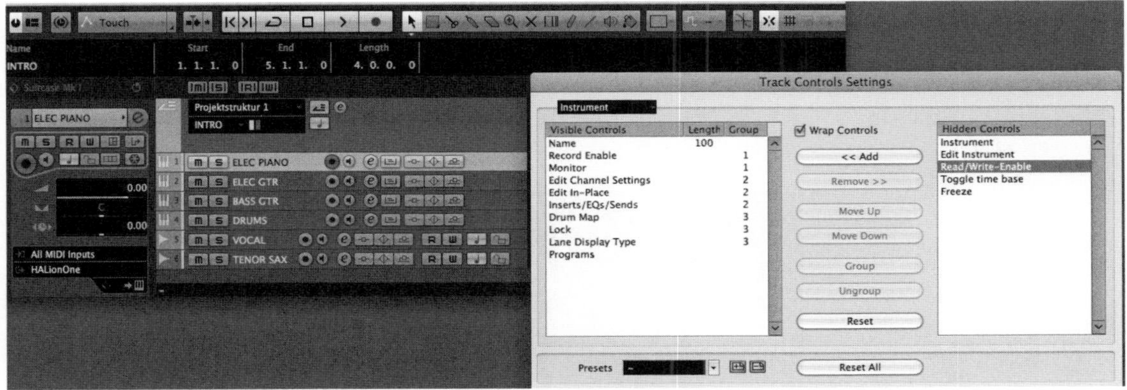

Figure 3.12
The Track Controls Settings. Record/Write-Enable has been disabled (moved to Hidden Controls)

Extending track lists

You can extend MIDI or audio track lists by dragging them to the right, across the screen. The further you go, the more information is revealed. Of course, this limits your working area in the event display, although hiding the

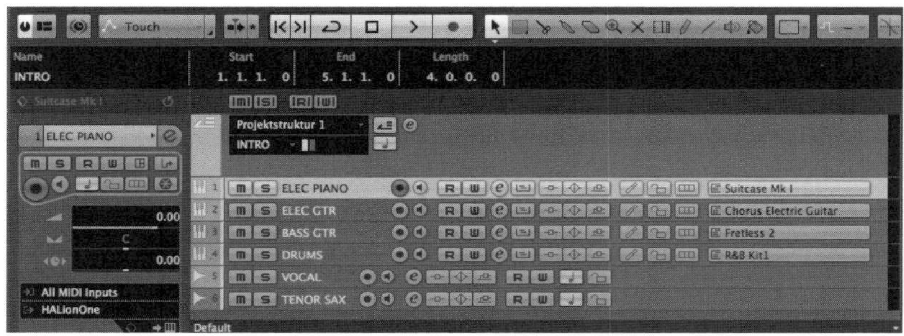

Figure 3.13
To extend the Track List, drag it to the right

Inspector will retrieve it (use the Show Inspector button). On the plus side, several Inspector settings are added to the list as well.

Handy track key commands:

- Ctrl+down/up (on the Mac, Command+down/up) - to resize selected tracks.
- Ctrl+click (on the Mac, Command+clicking) - to select multiple tracks.
- Shift+click - to select a continuous range of tracks.

Quick tip

Press Ctrl (on the Mac, Command) and drag up or down to resize the entire set of Project window tracks. Activate 'Snap Track Heights' on the track scale pop-up to change the track height in set increments.

Locking tracks

It's all too easy to accidentally move an event. To prevent this happening, lock the tracks. Click the Lock icon on the track list or in the Inspector. To unlock it, click again.

Quick tip

Double click in the empty space at the bottom of the track list to add a MIDI or audio track. Its type is determined by the last track already in the list.

Info

Exactly how the lock function behaves is defined in the 'Lock Event Attributes' pop-up menu in the Preferences dialogue (Editing page).

Folder Tracks

If you're working on a large project or just running out of screen space, consider using Folder tracks, Project > Add Track > Folder. You can drag several tracks onto the Folder track. A big band piece, for example, might have separate folders for saxophones, trumpets and trombones. Need the four trumpets repeated at bar 33? No problem. Just copy and paste them all in one go. You can easily open and close folders for individual editing on the different parts.

Figure 3.14
Big Band project with three Folder tracks: Saxes, Trumpets, and Trombones

Automatic fades

Having automatic fades activated will help smooth the transition between audio events. Apply it to a specific track by using the Auto-fades button in the Inspector to open the Auto Fades dialogue.

Figure 3.15
Auto Fades Settings button

Apply it to the project in general by using the Auto Fades Settings (Project menu). There's much to play with here in the form of fade curves and so on. However, there's a downside to all this. Because the fades are played back in real time and are not permanent, more processing power is used. Although a very useful feature, it's probably best used on a track basis rather than globally and only when necessary. Let your ears be the judge.

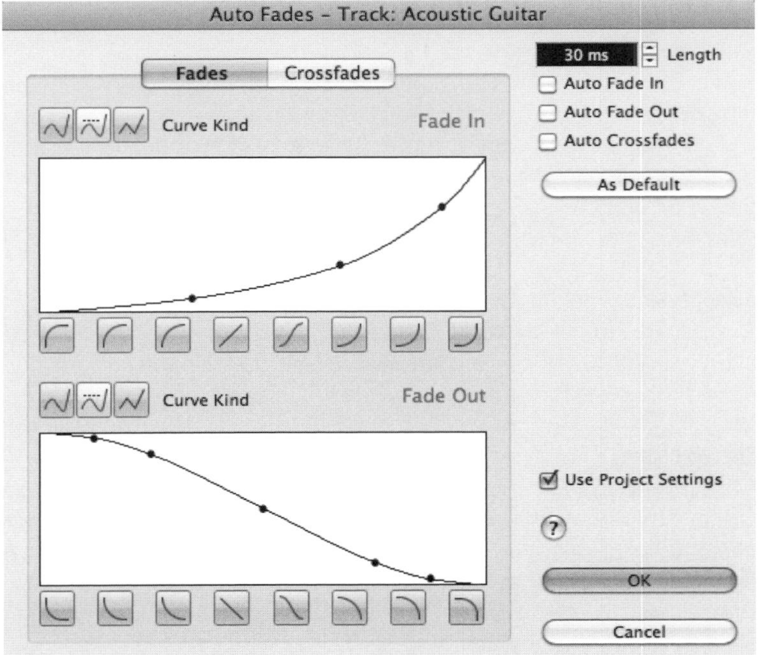

Figure 3.16
You can choose an automatic curve shape and edit it in the Auto Fades window

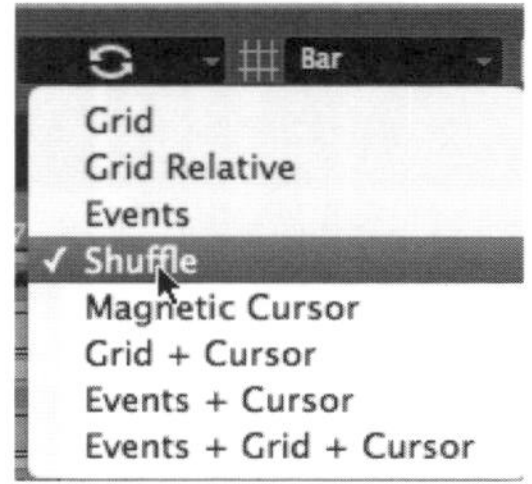

Figure 3.17
Selecting Shuffle from the Grid pop-up

Shuffle events

A handy way to exchange event positions: select Shuffle from the Grid pop-up menu. Now, with Snap activated, you can change the order of adjacent events. For example, if you have two adjacent events and drag the first one to the right, past the second event, the two events will change places. It works the same way with more events and is very useful if you want to move an event forwards or backwards. The other events shuffle along and close the gap.

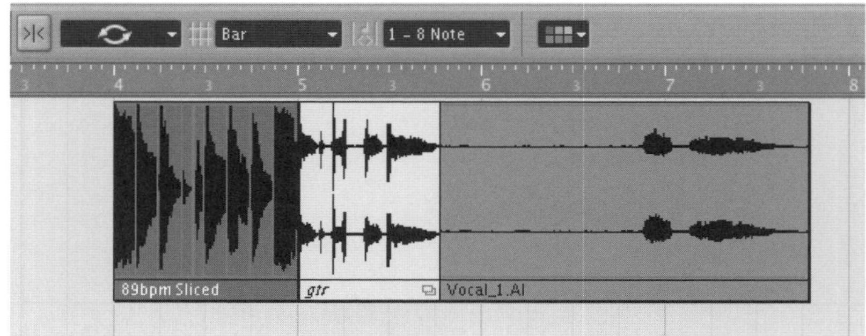

Figure 3.18
Events before shuffling

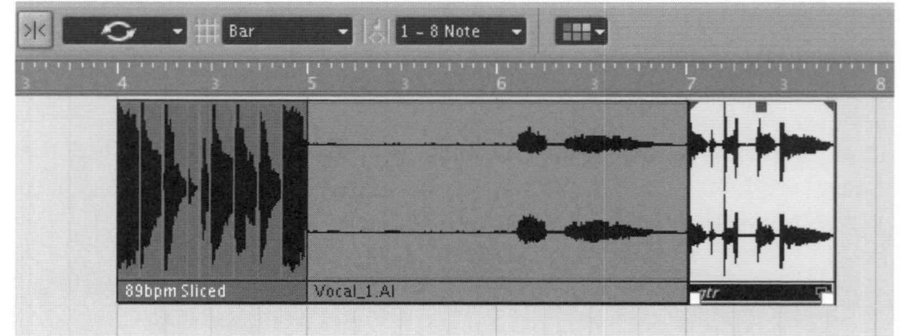

Figure 3.19
Events after shuffling

Drag delay

It's very easy to accidentally move an event when you select it with the mouse. If you find yourself doing this, use the variable Drag Delay setting in the Preferences > Editing page. It's set at 200 ms by default but 500 ms is safer. Mind you, it could irritate the more impatient user.

Select events under Cursor

A handy way to quickly select events and parts: go to Preferences > Editing and check Auto Select events under Cursor. Now, select a track and as you move the project cursor everything under it is selected.

Shared copies

A quick way to copy events - select them and use Ctrl+K (on the Mac, Command+K) or Edit > Repeat... If the Shared Copies option in the Repeat dialogue box is activated, and you are repeating audio or MIDI events, the new events will be shared copies of the original. If you edit the contents of a shared copy, all other shared copies of the same part are automatically edited in the same way. They're recognizable by italic text.

Quick tip

Press Ctrl+D (on the Mac, Command+D) to duplicate events.

Drag and repeat events

There was much wailing and gnashing of teeth among the faithful when Cubase SX was found not to include the handy Alt-Click and drag feature, used for repeating events. Steinberg must have got the message because it returned in SX 2 and remains a feature in Cubase 6. Just select the event(s), press Alt (on the Mac, Option), grab the lower right corner - the mouse pointer changes to the Pencil tool - and drag as far as you need. The copies will follow.

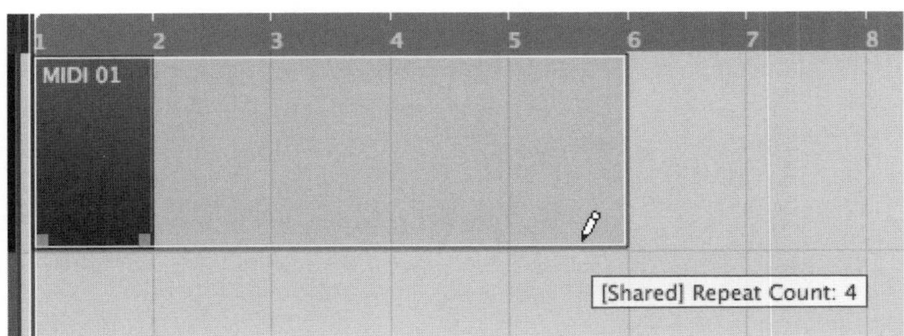

Figure 3.20
Repeating events with the Pencil tool

Use drag and drop

Although creating events is usually done by recording you can drag and drop material from the desktop, the Pool, another open project, the Audio Part Editor, and the Sample Editor. Get the habit and save time.

Quick tip

To create a part, between the locators, double click with the Arrow tool.

Range selections

Project window editing isn't just restricted to selecting whole events and parts with the Arrow tool; you can make selections with the Range tool as well. These are independent of the event, part and track boundaries. Once the Range tool is selected all the options from the Edit > Select menu become available as well as the Edit > Range menu. You can also cut, copy and paste ranges in the normal way.

Quick tip

To create a part anywhere in the project, double click on the grid with the Pencil tool and drag it to size.

Quick tip

To duplicate a selected range, hold down Alt (on the Mac, Option) and drag.

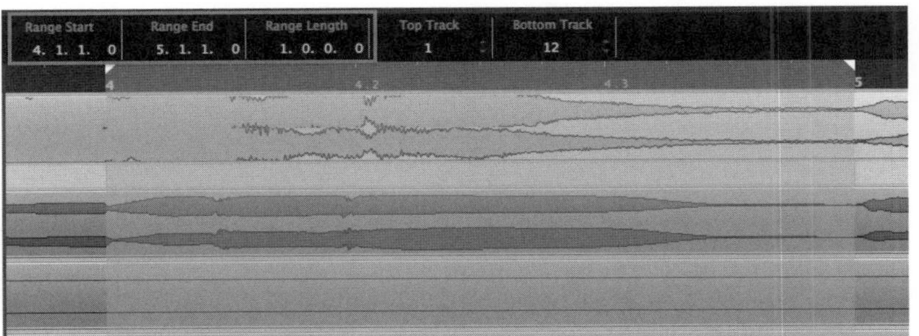

Figure 3.21
You can set a Range in the Info line

Info

With the Range tool selected, you can set complete ranges and individual track ranges in the Info line as an alternative method to using the mouse. Detailed editing can also be performed there.

Inserting silence

You've finished a piece and decided that it needs a bridge in the middle. Instead of going to work with the Scissors tool and splitting events on separate tracks, use the Range tool or the locators, it's much quicker. Make a

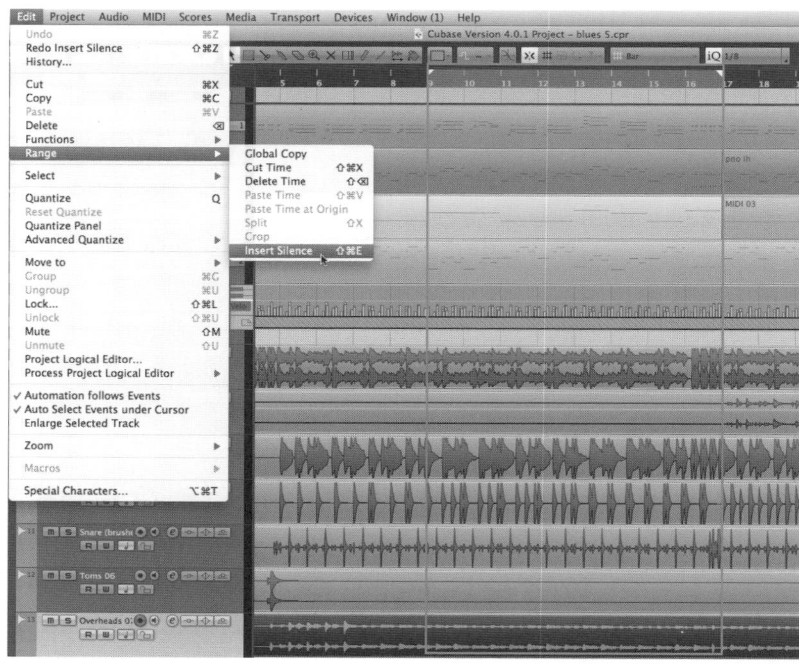

Figure 3.22
Before inserting two bars of silence

Figure 3.23
After eight bars of silence are inserted. All the events to the right of the empty space are moved along the timeline

selection and press Shift+Ctrl+E (on the Mac, Shift+Command+E). Silence is inserted in the selected area and all the split events are moved to the right, making the arrangement that much longer.

This is also useful for inserting space at the beginning of a project, to make way for MIDI file set-up data and so on. Repeating the keystroke will move the whole project by the same amount each time.

Quick tip

With 'Locate when Clicked in Empty Space' activated in the Transport Preferences, you can click in an empty space and the project cursor will follow on.

Transport menu

Make full use of the Transport menu options to get around a project quickly and easily. Handy locator key commands are:

P - send locators to selection
L - locate a selection
Alt (on the Mac, Option)+Spacebar - play a selected range
Shift+G - loop a selection

Info

You can adjust the width of the project cursor line in the Transport Preferences.

Transport panel configuration

A completely new Transport panel was included with Cubase SX 2 and opinions were divided on whether it was easier or more complicated to use. It remains similar in Cubase 6. One thing's for sure, the default version is pretty large and takes up a lot of screen space. As well as the usual things it now displays CPU usage and disk cache usage meters, markers, audio input level meter and an output level control slider. However, you do have the option to display cut down versions. There's a choice of seven and you can also customize your own. Ctrl-Click anywhere on the Transport panel to bring up a menu of options.

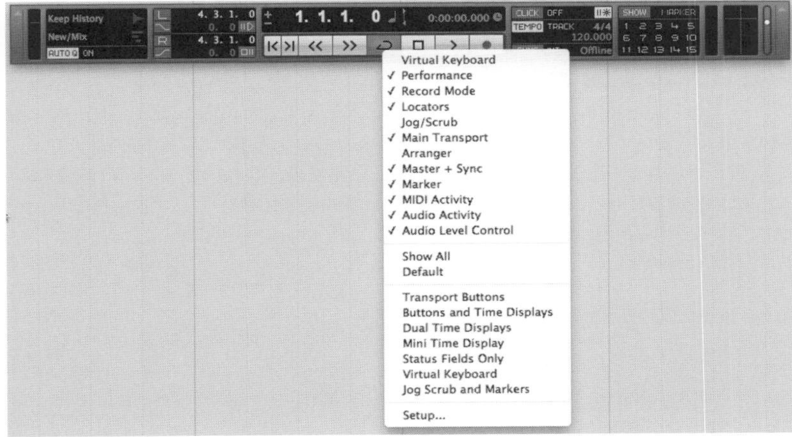

Figure 3.24 (left)
Transport panel options

Figure 3.25 (below)
Smaller transport

Open the Setup window and you can configure your own Transport panel by moving items between the visible and hidden columns. A particularly neat feature here is the ability to reposition items on the Transport panel by altering their position in the Visible Items list.

For example - if an item is at the top, it will be seen at the far left on the panel. Conversely, if it's at the bottom it will be positioned on the far right.

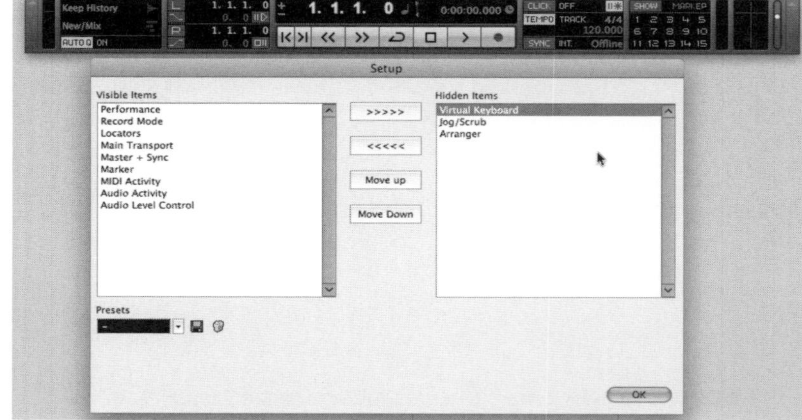

Figure 3.26
You can personalize the Transport panel using setup

> **Quick tip**
>
> Double click in the Ruler to move the cursor and stop or start playback.

Anywhere in-between and it will be positioned, of course, somewhere in-between. The changes are reflected immediately in the panel itself, so position the window so that you can see the Transport panel as you make the alterations.

The Jog Wheel

Visually, the most striking thing about the Transport bar is the large scrub dial. You can use the outer wheel (Shuttle Speed control) to play the project at any speed, forwards or backwards, to quickly locate or 'cue' to a specific position in a project.

The inner one acts as a jog wheel. You use it to move the playback position manually, forwards or backwards, much like scrubbing on a tape deck. In the days of analogue-only recording, engineers would manually adjust the tape spools on a tape recorder. Whilst rotating the spools backwards and forwards, they would listen intently until exactly the right spot for editing was found. Then they would mark the tape and finally, splice it with a razor blade. You can use the inner jog wheel in the same way, to pinpoint editing spots.

In the centre of the dial you'll find two nudge buttons for moving the project cursor left or right. This is useful for working with film or video. Each time you click on the nudge button it moves by one frame. The default frame rate is 24 fps (frames per second) the traditional frame rate of 35 mm film.

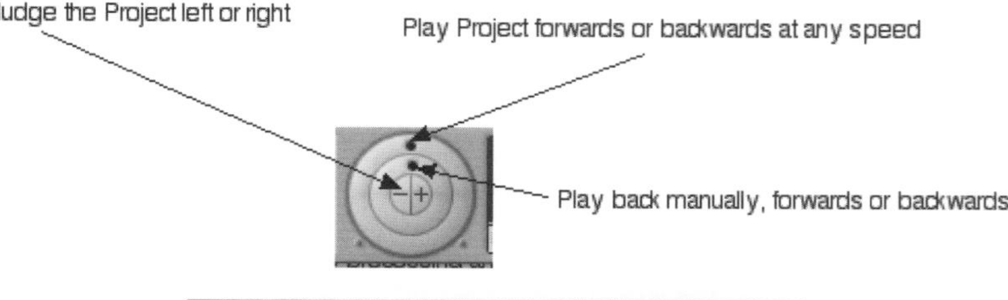

Figure 3.27
The Scrub Dial

> **Info**
>
> A source of irritation to many, turning Cycle on and off during playback wasn't possible in earlier versions of Cubase. This issue has now been rectified and the sequencer even continues uninterrupted playback as the cycle is edited in the ruler or transport panel.

Markers

Setting up a Marker track (Project > Add Track > Marker) may seem a bit of a fiddle at first but it's worthwhile in the long run and saves time when navigating a large project.

They're best managed and edited in the Marker window (opened from the Project menu). There, you can change their positions and name them as verses, choruses and so on. For quick access, set up a Marker track and use the Inspector.

> **Quick tip**
>
> For high speed fast-forward and backward operations press the computer shift key as well as the transport buttons.

> **Quick tip**
>
> If the transport panel is in the way, hide it. Use F2 on your computer keyboard to toggle it on and off.

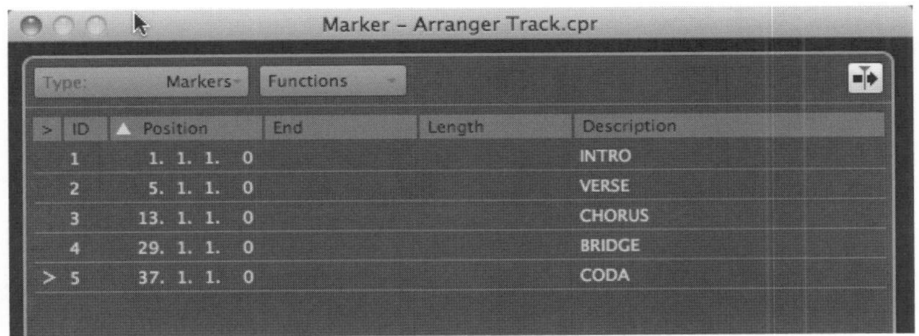

Figure 3.28
You can edit Markers in the Marker window

Figure 3.29
Opening Markers

> **Quick tip**
>
> You can open the Marker window using the Show Marker button on the Transport bar.

Cycle Markers

It's tedious isn't it, having to keep setting up the locators each time you want to cycle record in a new location? Do it the easy way and store all your cycles as markers, for easy recall.

Set the left and right locators and select Add Cycle Marker from the Functions menu in the Marker Window.

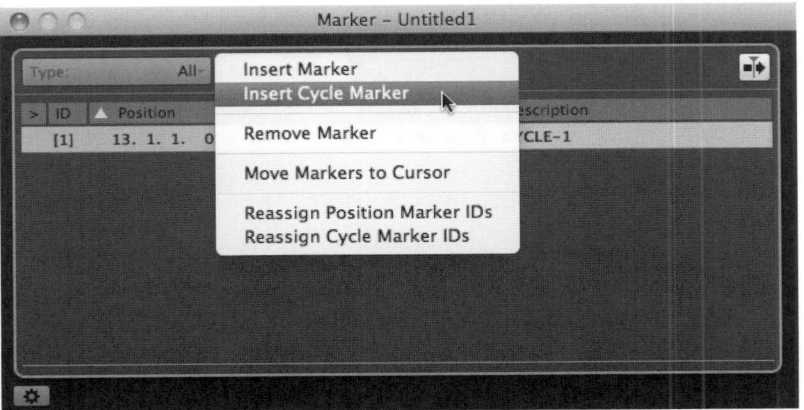

Figure 3.30
Adding Cycle Markers

Alternatively, if you have set up a Marker track, use the Add Cycle Marker button on the Track list.

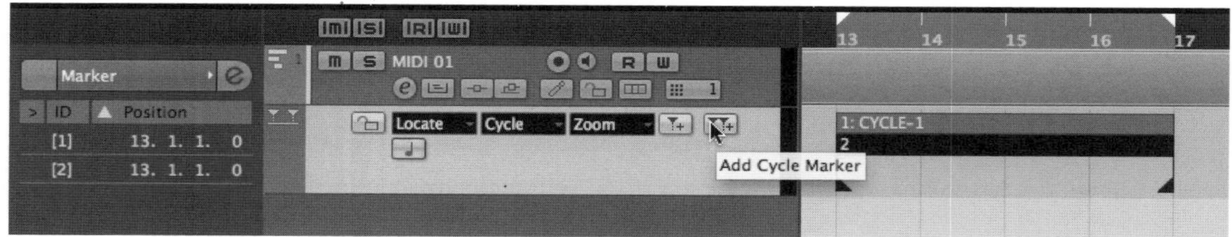

Figure 3.31
Set up a Marker track and use the Add Marker/Cycle Marker buttons to insert Markers, on-the-fly or in stationary mode

Handy key command: Open the Marker window using Ctrl+M (on the Mac, Command+M).

Reverse locators

You're not sure if that bridge passage in your song works well or not. You can of course, cut it out and see how it sounds, safe in the knowledge that you can use the History list to undo things if it doesn't work. But there's a quicker way.

Set the right locator at the beginning of the bridge section and the left locator at the end. In other words, set them back to front. You'll notice that the ruler turns from blue to a reddish brown colour. Press the cycle button; start playback and the project cursor will skip the bridge section.

Quick tip

You can add markers 'on the fly', at the cursor position, during playback or in stationary mode. Use the Insert key (Win) or the Add Marker button in the track list. Use the Add Cycle button for cycles.

Colouring parts

Colouring tracks makes them easily identifiable. So, why not colour individual parts within a track as well? This is useful for marking out verses, choruses and bridge sections within a song as a visual alternative to the marker track. Use the Color pop-up menu. You can customize the colours by choosing Select Colors... in the menu.

Quick tip

You can drag markers - use the little handles.

Figure 3.32
You can colour parts and tracks using the Color pop-up menu found on the toolbar

Importing MIDI files

If you've bought or downloaded a MIDI file from the Internet use the Import command in the File menu to open it. If it's a type 0 MIDI file, ensure the MIDI channel is set to 'Any' for correct playback. This is because type 0 MIDI files have only one track containing up to 16 different MIDI channels. Setting the track to a specific MIDI channel would result in everything being played back with the same sound - not what you want at all. To unravel the channels on individual tracks use MIDI > Dissolve Part.

Exporting MIDI files

Working with MIDI took a step backwards when Cubase SX first appeared and preparing data for export became awkward using the Merge MIDI in Loop feature. Steinberg quickly addressed this shortcoming.

You can now export projects as MIDI files, without freezing the parameters and so on. The inspector settings such as patch, volume and pan are automatically inserted into the file. If you like, MIDI plug-in settings can be saved in the files as well. Similar options are available when you import MIDI files - the first patch, volume and pan settings are detected and displayed in the track inspector.

Project activation

A common scenario: you've selected a track in project one, copied it ready to paste into project two and on switching windows project two refuses to come to life. The reason for this is that the project isn't yet active. In the project window, press the first button on the toolbar, the 'Active project indicator'. The area surrounding the button will turn white and the project will spring to life.

Figure 3.33
The Active project indicator (first button on the left)

Renaming parts

You used to be able to name parts in Cubase by selecting them and using Alt+click. That doesn't work in Cubase 6 but you can rename parts in the info line. Select an event; open the info line and type a name under 'File'.

Figure 3.34
Use the Info line to rename parts

If you move parts from one track to another, you can have them renamed, automatically by going to Preferences > Editing and ticking the Parts Get Track Names box.

Renaming events

You can rename all events on a track with the track name itself. Double click on the track name and type a new one. Press any modifier key such as Ctrl (on the Mac, Command) and press Enter. Upon closing, all the events are named.

Track List division

You can split a track list into two sections; an upper and a lower, each with its own zoom and scroll controls. Just press the Divide Track List button.

This is very useful when running a video track and multiple audio tracks together because you can scroll specific audio tracks to line up directly beneath the video track, for easy reference. It's also a handy place to store marker and ruler tracks.

Quick tip

To import a MIDI file just drag it from the desktop (or where ever) and drop it into Cubase.

Info

There are two types of MIDI file - Type 1 files, which have separate tracks for each channel and type 0 files which have just one track containing all the channels.

Quick tip

With the arrow tool selected, press Alt (on the Mac, Option) to split parts and events.

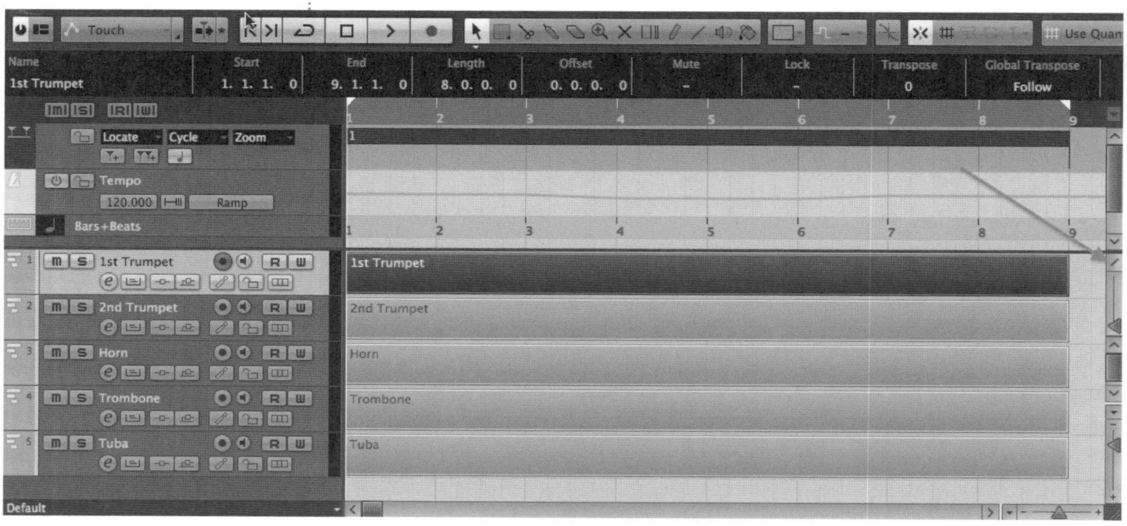

Figure 3.35
Marker, Tempo and Ruler tracks have been placed in the upper part of a divided track list

Group events

It's sometimes handy to group several events together for editing operations such as moving or duplicating, resizing, adjusting audio fades, splitting, locking, muting and deleting. Select the events and choose 'Group' from the Edit menu. All the selected events receive a group icon on the right.

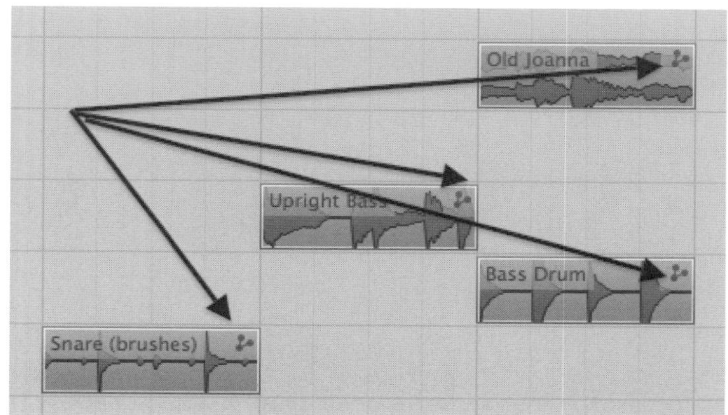

Figure 3.36
Grouped events share a 'Group' icon in their top right corner

Mixer tips

The Mixer only contains tracks that are set up in the Project window. This way you only have used tracks, or those you are going to use, appearing in the Mixer. To keep the Mixer to a manageable size, set up your projects track by track instead of using templates. This will increase your screen space.

Figure 4.1
The full Cubase mixer consumes a large area of screen space even with a modest number of tracks

If you do load a template and it contains more tracks than you are likely to need, then delete some. The Cubase 6 RnB Production template, for example, is a great starting point but comes with both electric piano and synth tracks plus three FX tracks with settings. The chances are that you will not need all three FX tracks and maybe only one keyboard so, to save screenspace, delete the unecessary tracks.

Of course, if you think you might need those extra tracks and FX channels later, you can temporarily hide them. To hide a channel, simply change its 'hide' status.

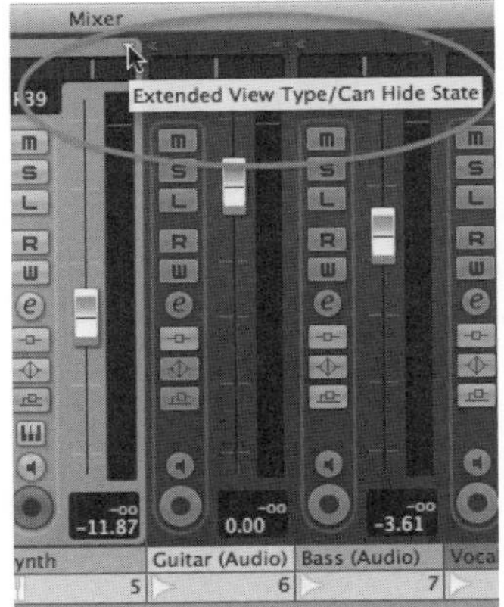

Figure 4.2
Change the 'hide' status

Then, in the Common panel (far left panel of the mixer), toggle the 'Can Hide' button to hide or show the channel.

igure 4.3

Hiding channels

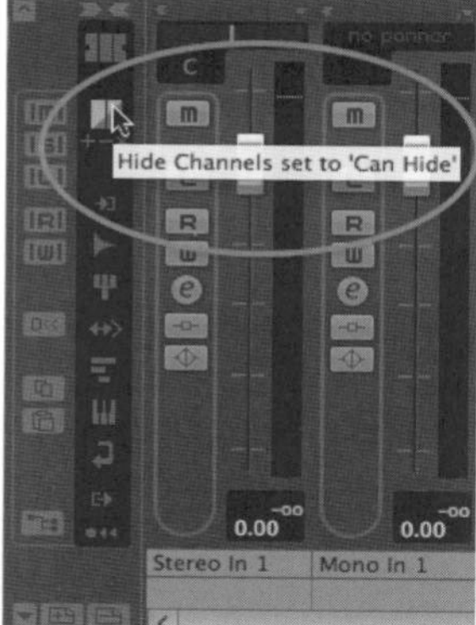

Another way of saving space is to narrow all or just a selected number of mixer channels.

Figure 4.4
Narrow the channels

Mixer 2 and 3

You have a choice of three mixers in Cubase 6. They're not really separate mixers, just separate views of the same one. Each one can be configured to show different combinations of channels, channel types, inserts and so on. For example, you could configure a 'MIDI only' mixer if you wanted to, and perhaps another for just audio channels. Although the configurations for each mixer are different, any changes you make in one mixer (settings) will be simultaneously mirrored in the other.

Quick tip

Hold down the Shift key for fine control of volume and pan settings.

VST Channel window

If you're working with a laptop, you may find that the extended mixer - EQ, inserts and so on - takes up too much screen space. Click the button marked 'e' in the Channel Strip and the VST Channel window appears. Everything is there - inserts, sends and EQ. You can't have knobs on your send effects however; you'll have to make do with sliders. The only real disadvantage is not being able to see all the channels at once.

Figure 4.5
The Channel Settings window

Inspector Channel strip

You don't actually have to have the Mixer open when recording or editing a single track. Use the Inspector instead. Inserts, equalizers, sends and a fader are all available here, plus fast access to the VST Channel window. Your settings are reflected in the Mixer.

Figure 4.6
Inserts, Equalizers, Sends and Channel Fader are all available in the Inspector

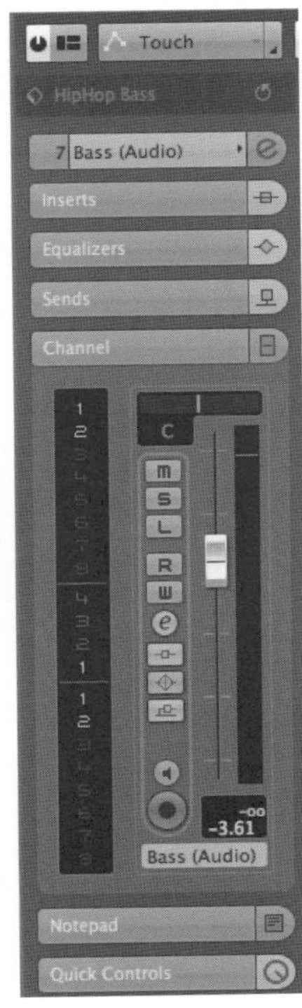

Channel Select menu

When you change channels, in the Channel Settings window, it isn't necessary to close down one window and open another. A quicker way is to use the Channel Select pop-up menu. A new window opens and the old one closes.

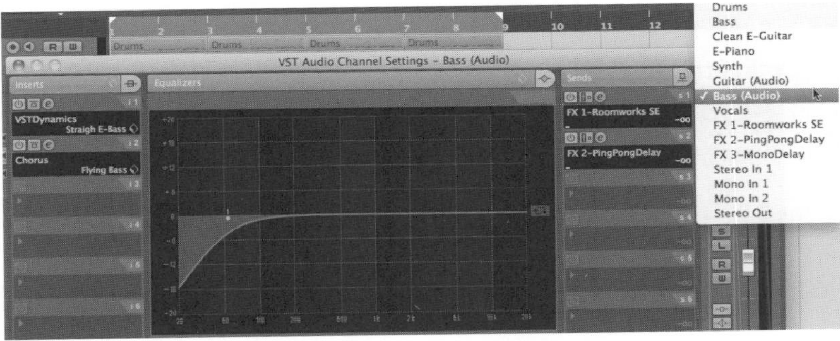

Figure 4.7
The Channel Select pop-up menu

Quick tip

Activate 'Sync Project and Mixer Selection' in the Preferences (Editing-Project & Mixer) to have the Channel Settings window follow your track selection in the Project window and vice versa.

Mixer Setting files

You can save complete mixes or individual channels (audio only) as Mixer setting files. They have the extension '.vmx' and you can recall them at a later time or reload them into new projects. Right click (on the Mac, Control click) anywhere in the Mixer (or the Channel Settings window) to bring up the Mixer context menu.

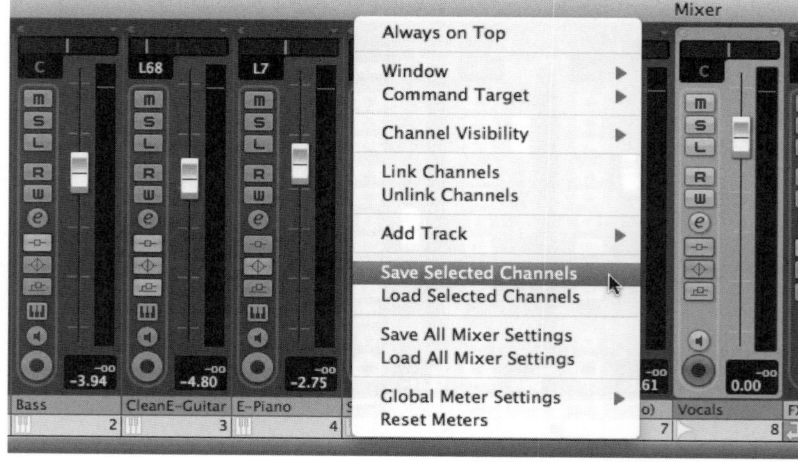

Figure 4.8
You can save your Mixer settings as .VMX files

> **Quick tip**
>
> Hold down the Alt key (on the Mac, Option) to alter settings separately for linked channels.

Linked Mixer Channels

You can 'gang' as many channels as you like with 'Link Channels', found in the Mixer context menu. This is particularly useful for linking faders when mixing. For example, three brass tracks could be ganged this way. Watch out though; make new channel settings (i.e. EQ) on a linked track and they will be applied to the others as well.

Figure 4.9
You can copy settings between channels using the Copy and Paste buttons

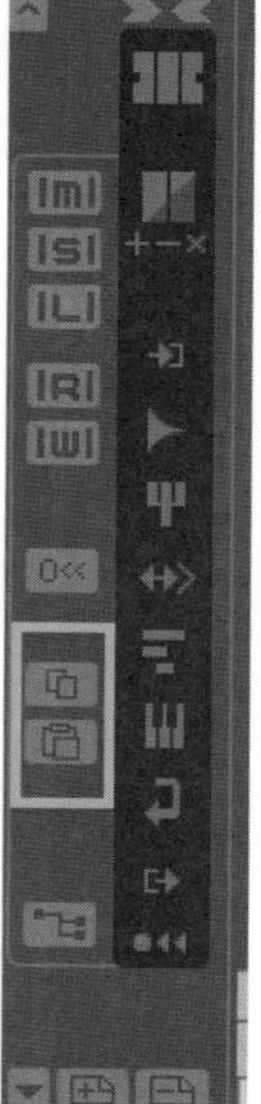

Copy and Paste settings

Use the Copy and Paste buttons in the Common panel to transfer settings from one channel to another. Just select a channel, click the Copy button, select the destination channel and click the Paste button.

Channel View Sets

Once you have a mixer configuration for a project all set up you can save it as a Channel View Set. Click the Store View Set button and type a name for the preset in the resulting dialogue box.

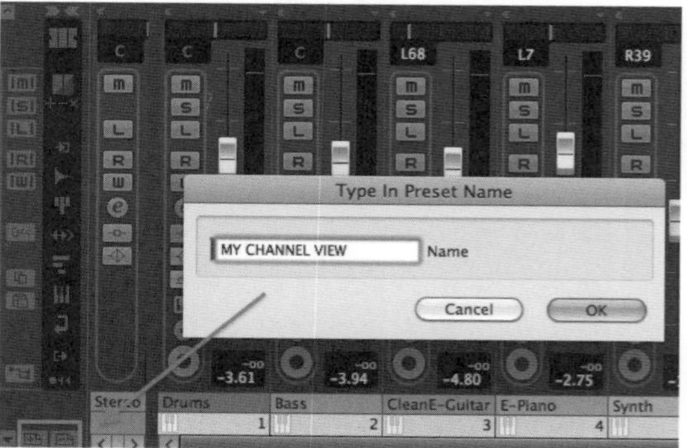

Figure 4.10
You can name your own Channel View Sets (buttons, lower left corner)

Initialize Channel

You can reset everything on a channel, including EQ, insert and send effects. Click on the Initialize Channel button in the Mixer. Press it and you'll be asked if you want to reset all the channels or just the selected one.

Figure 4.11
The Initialize Channel button – click to reset channels

Automation data

You can record and play back all your mixer actions as automation data when you activate the Read (R) and Write (W) buttons, before you start playback. An automation track is created in the project window and the data can be edited from there.

> **Quick tip**
>
> Hold down the Shift key for extra fader control.

Figure 4.12
Automation data is recorded and played back in the Mixer with the Write (W) and Read (R) buttons respectively

Group Tracks

Just like hardware recording consoles, the mixer has group channels for controlling and treating a defined set of channels. You can add groups to the mixer using the Project > Add track menu. A corresponding group track is created in the project window.

The most obvious use for group channels is for controlling a sub-mix, such as a drum kit. For example, you have recorded kick, snare, high-hat, high toms, low toms and overhead ambience mics on separate tracks. After setting up a volume balance for the individual tracks it makes sense to combine them in a group. This will enable you to mix the entire kit on to one stereo channel.

> **Info**
>
> The record button on the transport panel is not used for recording automation data. Activate the Write button (W) and start playback.

In Figure 4,13 seven mono drum tracks are balanced individually and then routed to a group track, renamed Drum Set. The routing is done in the track inspector.

Figure 4.13
Seven drum tracks assigned to a stereo Group track (DRUM SET)

GM/GS/XG control

If you own a GM/GS or XG sound module of some kind you can control it in real time from within the Mixer: Open the MIDI Channel Settings window.

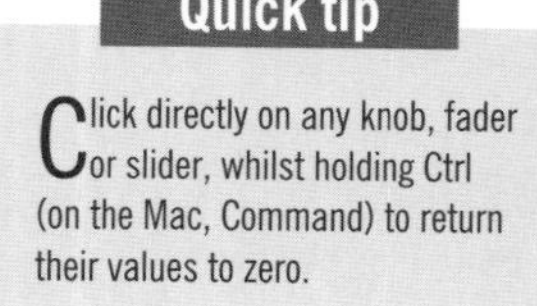

Quick tip

Click directly on any knob, fader or slider, whilst holding Ctrl (on the Mac, Command) to return their values to zero.

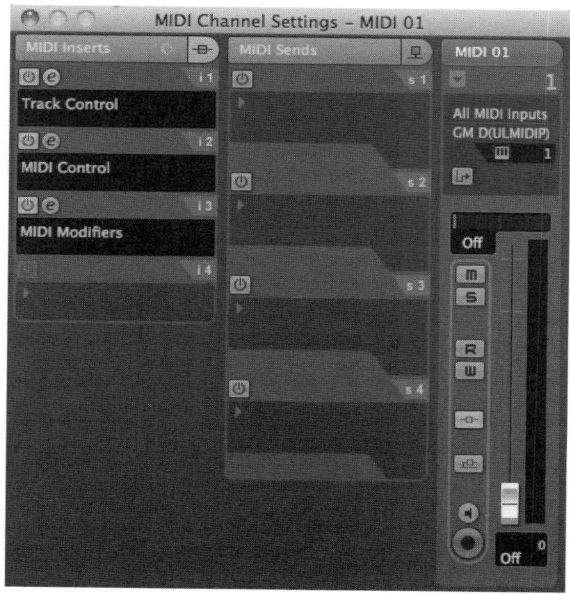

Figure 4.14
MIDI Channel Settings

Quick tip

Rename your Group Channels, in the Project window or Project browser, for easy identification.

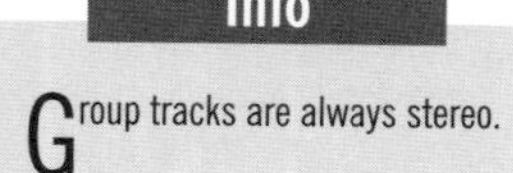

Info

Group tracks are always stereo.

Click in the Insert section and load the Track Control plug-in from the pop-up menu.

Now you can address your sound module's parameters and effects here and tweak the controls (Figure 4.15).

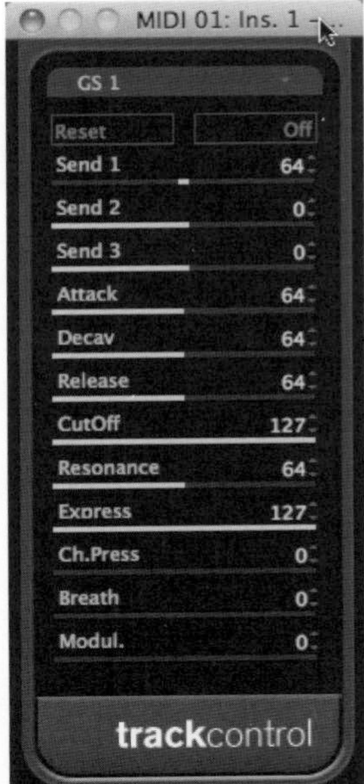

Figure 4.15
You can use Track Control to address your GM/GS/XG sound modules

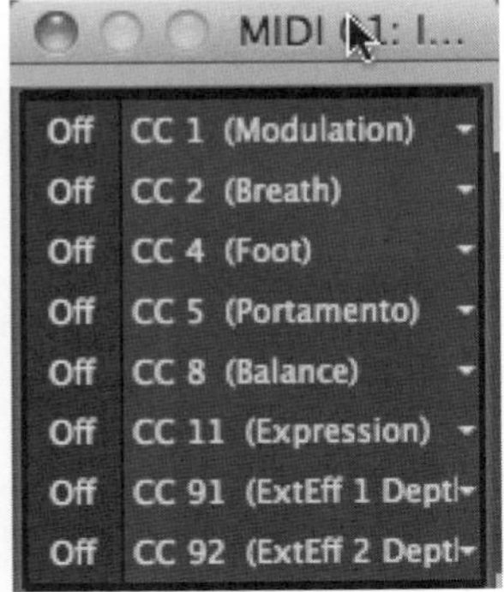

Figure 4.16
MIDI Control gives you access to eight different controllers

There's another 'generic' control panel that you can select from the MIDI Insert pop-up called MIDI Control (Figure 4.16).

By selecting the correct MIDI controller types, you can use this plug-in as a control panel for adjusting the sound of any MIDI instrument that receives them.

Handy Mixer key commands:

- Hold Ctrl (on the Mac, Command) and click on the slider to centralize pan.
- Hold Shift to increment and decrement the pan slider in single units.

Instrument tracks

In previous versions of Cubase, using a VST instrument necessitated the setting up of two tracks in the Project window, one for the MIDI data and another for the audio output. And that also meant two corresponding channels in the Mixer, one with MIDI inserts and MIDI send effects and the other providing EQ and audio inserts and returns. In a large project with many tracks, this arrangement could be very confusing. In Cubase 6 we have an alternative, the Instrument track.

Instrument tracks combine both aspects of a VST instrument, the MIDI data and the audio output, which is far less confusing and much more convenient than the previous arrangement. You can now bypass the VST instrument rack completely and simply add an Instrument track using the Add Tracks menu.

Figure 4.17 shows four Instrument tracks in the Project window: Prologue, Mystic, Spector and HALionOne. The first track (Prologue) uses in-place edit-

Figure 4.17
Instrument tracks

ing, and the MIDI data (Key Editor) can be clearly seen. The Mixer is also open and now, unlike some earlier versions of Cubase, only four channels (audio) are displayed, not eight - no MIDI channels.

However, there are situations where the old two-track system is the only method available. They are:

- When an instrument has only a mono output.
- When an instrument never sends on the first channel
- When the instrument concerned is a multi-timbral device and you need to use more than one voice.

The two-track setup is also necessary if you need to:

- Use MIDI send effects
- Apply MIDI volume and pan settings

Info

VST Instruments that are added via the Add Track method (Project menu) are not added to the VST Instrument window (Devices menu). Only the instruments that are actually created in this window are displayed there.

VST Instrument setup

If you opt to use the two-track VST instrument setup, for one of the reasons mentioned above, you would need to set up a VST Instrument track first.

- Choose VST Instruments from the Devices menu
- Select a VST Instrument. A VST Instrument track is created. You may be asked if you want to create a MIDI track assigned to the instrument. If so, choose 'Create.' If not, create one yourself using Project > Add Track and assign its output to the newly created VST instrument.

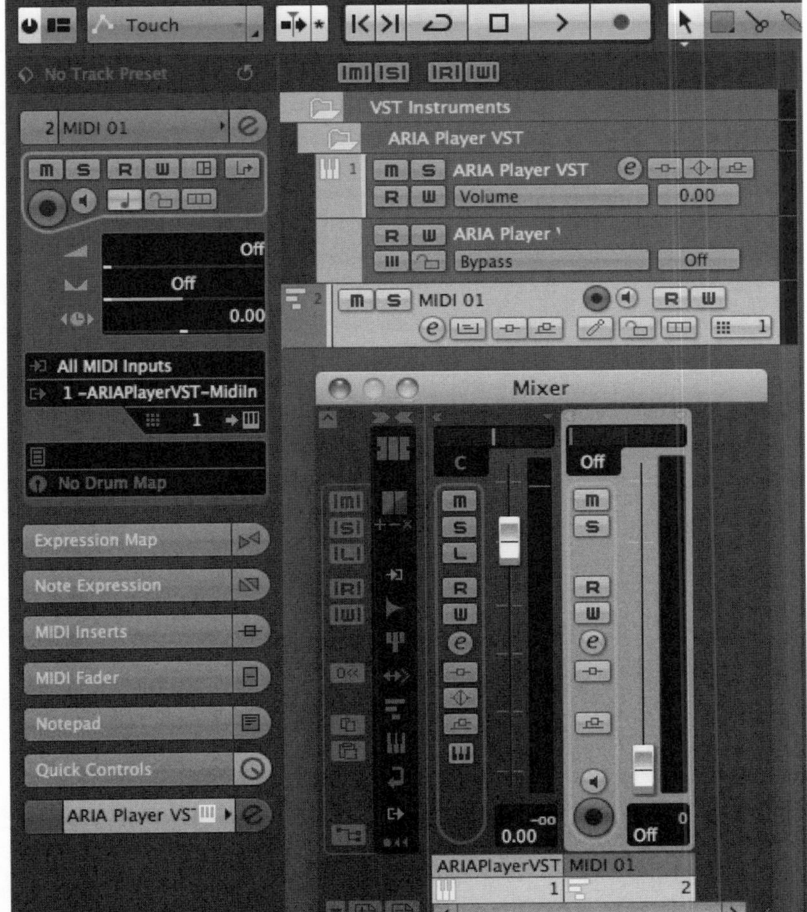

Figure 4.18
If you set up a multi-timbral instrument several channels will appear in the mixer alongside the MIDI track. Click the tiny button to the right of the 'e' button to view the output options.

If you set up a multi-timbral instrument several channels will appear in the mixer alongside the MIDI track. Click the tiny button to the right of the 'e' button to view the output options.

Group Channel routing

You can route Group channels on to other groups. It can't be done in the Mixer, though, you have to do it in the Inspector. In previous versions of Cubase, group outputs could only be routed to another group with a higher number (to the right). This was changed in Cubase 5 and group outputs can now be freely routed to other groups.

Info

When recording automation data, you can watch and listen to already recorded data whilst recording further actions on another channel. Activate the Read and Write buttons simultaneously.

Info

You can't record on a group channel because it's never connected to an input. That's why there are no record enable or monitoring buttons on group channels.

Figure 4.19
Group Channel 3 is routed on to Group 1

Moving inserted plug-ins

An irritating pre Cubase 4 scenario: you've set up a series of insert plug-ins on a mixer channel and you decide to change the order. But you can't do so without blanking the inserts and starting over. The problem has now been solved.

You can move inserted plug-ins from slot to slot by grabbing the insert number tag (i1, i2, i3 and so on). And if you drop a plug-in into a slot already occupied by another plug-in, they exchange places. You can also move insert effects from channel to channel this way.

REVerence

It was a long time arriving but Cubase 5 saw the inclusion of a high-quality convolution-based reverb. However, in common with most convolution reverb plug-ins it's inclined to drain your computer's resources. It's wise, then, to set up a single instance of REVerence as a send effect (as opposed to using channel inserts). You can then route as many audio and instrument tracks as you wish to that single instance of REVerence, preserving valuable CPU usage in the process (Figure 4.20).

Figure 4.20
Two Audio Tracks and an Instrument Track are set up as sends and routed to an FX Channel Track containing an instance of REVerence

Audio recording

Events, clips and files

Audio recording on a computer hard disc can be a confusing business to the uninitiated. Of course, it's easier to understand if you are moving across from dedicated hardware recording, either digital or analogue. Before you record any audio it's important to understand exactly how Cubase handles the process. Basically, three things happen:

1. An 'audio file' is created on the computer's hard disk.
2. An 'audio clip' is also created in the Pool. This 'audio clip' is a direct reference to the 'audio file' itself which is created in your Project folder.
3. An 'audio event' is created on an audio track, in the Project window. This 'audio event' plays back the 'audio clip'.

In other words, events play the clip, which communicates with the audio file. As if that isn't complicated enough, specific audio regions can be created from clips and events.

Inputs and outputs

Getting music in and out of Cubase is very flexible these days because you can configure as many inputs and output busses as you like. Mono, stereo or surround format are all possible. Configurations are made in the VST Connections window and saved along with your projects.

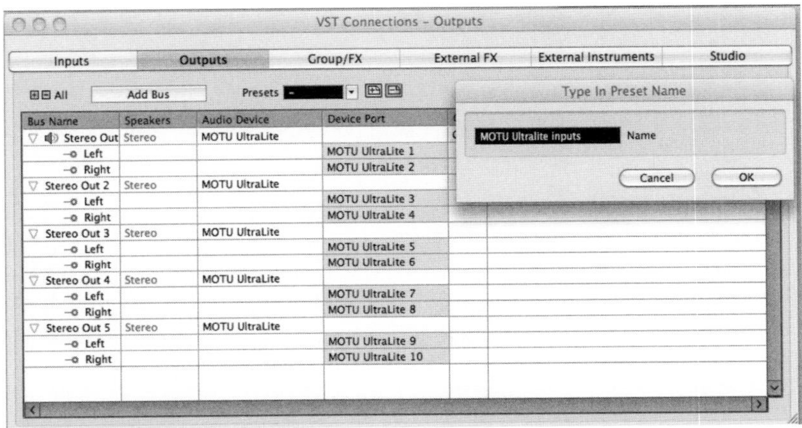

Figure 5.1
Busses are configured in the VST Connections window

For this reason it makes sense to first set up your busses and then save them as templates. If you need different busses for different projects you can also save them as presets for instant recall.

How many busses do you need? It depends on your hardware and the number of inputs and outputs you have. If you have selected your audio interface's ASIO driver in the VST Audio System (Device Setup) these will show up in a separate window as a list, named after your interface.

Figure 5.2

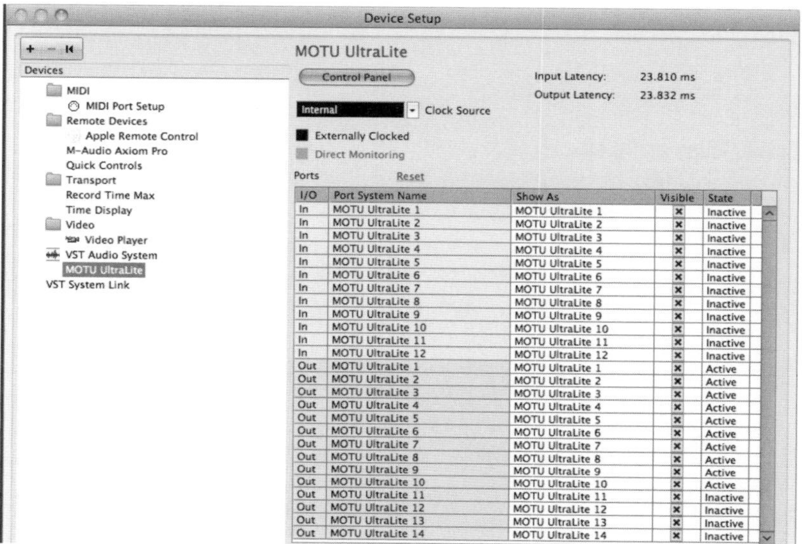

All available inputs will be checked in the Visible box and if you have made them available as busses in the VST Connections window (see above) they will be marked Active.

Surround sound bus naming

Before you set up a surround sound bus, name the inputs and outputs on your audio hardware - Left, Right, Centre and so on. That way, if you're working with a colleague, you can both have the same names for the set-up, regardless of different hardware. It's a time-saver because Cubase will automatically locate the correct inputs and outputs when your projects are loaded on either computer.

It's also a good idea to name your input and output busses. Something simple like Stereo in, Mono in and Digital Out will do.

Sample rates

Basically, the higher the sample rate the better the sound quality. What's actually available depends on your audio hardware. Depending on the type of interface you use, you could have a choice of anything between 44.1 kHz and 192 kHz. Most people work with 44.1 kHz and if your project is destined for a CD, that's how it will end up anyway. By all means use 96 kHz or higher if you have the capability, but remember, it will use more disk space and processing power. Setting a sample rate is done in the Project Setup (Figure 5.3).

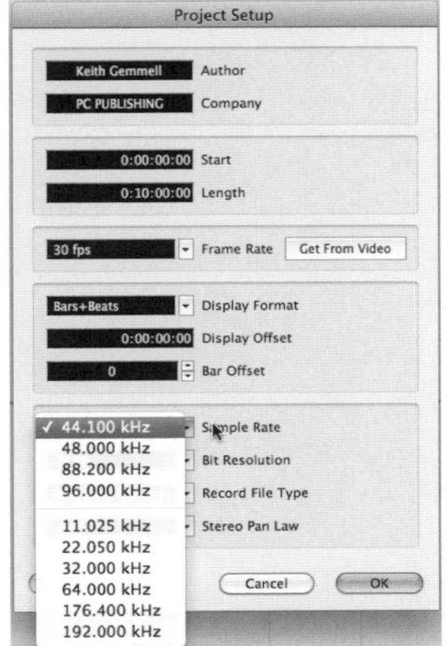

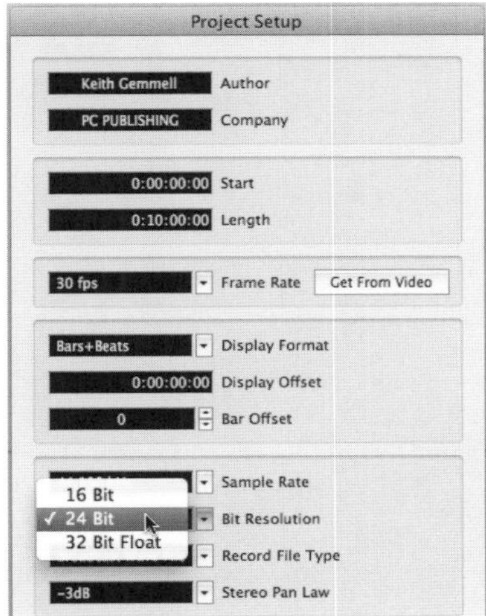

Figure 5.3 (left)
Sample rates are set up in the Project Setup

Figure 5.4 (right)
Bit Resolutions are chosen in the Project Setup

> **Quick tip**
>
> Once you've decided on a sample rate, stick with it throughout the project.

Bit Resolution

Cubase supports 16-bit, 24-bit 32-bit and 64-bit recording (Figure 5.4). If your audio hardware only supports 16-bit there's nothing to be gained by selecting 24-bit except larger files with the same audio quality. However, if your hardware supports it, choose a higher resolution. Bear in mind though that higher resolutions result in larger audio files, thereby putting more strain on your computer. Setting the record format is done in the Project Setup.

> **Info**
>
> Although the sample rate must remain fixed for a project you can change the bit depth (sample resolution) at any time.

File types

You have a choice of four file types when you record: AIFF, Wave, Broadcast Wave and Wave 64. Which type you choose depends largely on whether you use a PC or Mac computer. Choosing a file type is done in the Project Setup.

Generally speaking choose 'AIFF File' if you're working on a Mac (although you can record Wave files) and 'Wave File' if you're working on a PC.

If you wish to embed details such as author, description and reference

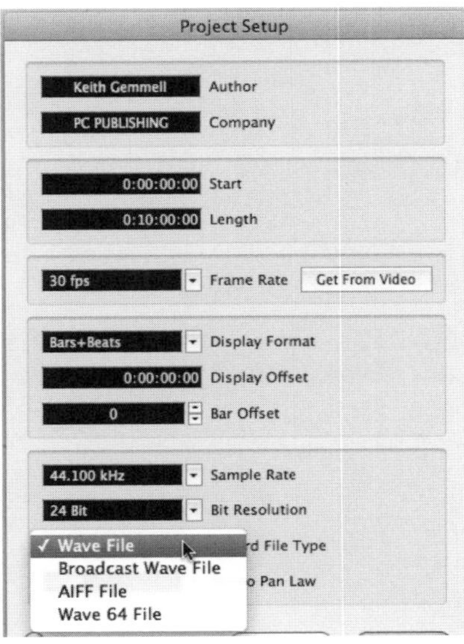

Figure 5.5
You set the file type in the Project Setup

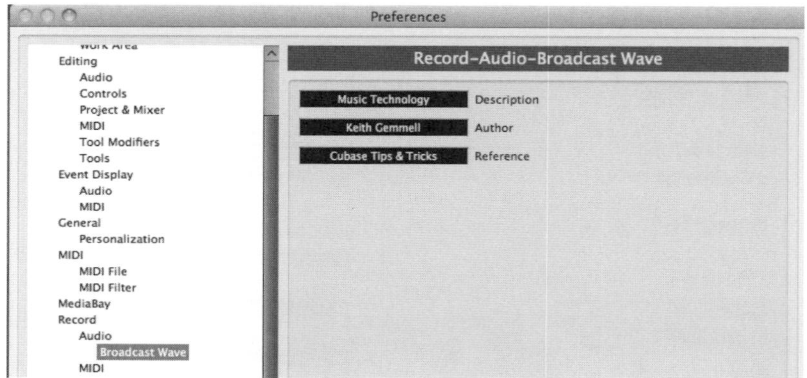

Figure 5.6
You can embed copyright details in Broadcast Wave Files

text into a file, choose 'Broadcast Wave File'. This is useful if you intend transferring the files to another computer. Adding the text is done in the preferences section.

In fact, you can export any file type as a Broadcast Wave File when you export an audio file (File > Export > Audio Mixdown). On choosing the 'Broadcast Wave File' as a file type you are given the option to add the text before completing the process.

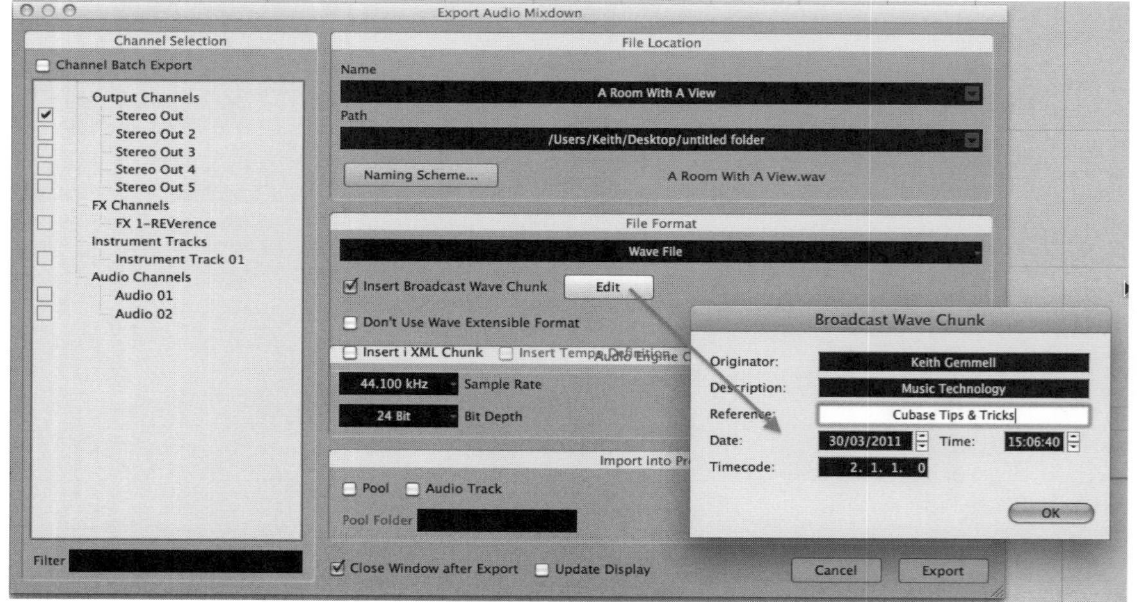

Figure 5.7
You can export any file type as a Broadcast Wave File

You can also specify a time code position here as well, for use in video projects and so on. This is set by default to the start position of the exported audio in the project (the left locator position), but you can alter this to whatever you want.

Input/Output channels

The busses you first set up in the VST Connections page appear in the mixer as input and output channels (only the output channels appear in Cubase Studio). They look much the same as regular audio channels but have their own dividers and horizontal scroll bars.

The input channel is placed to the left of the audio channels and the output channels to their right. Visually they're identical twins, except that the input channel doesn't have a solo button.

Figure 5.8
Left to right: 2 Mono Input Channels, 2 Stereo Input Channels, 2 Audio Channels and 4 Stereo Output Channels

When recording in Cubase, you check the signal levels using the Input channel - in 'Meter Input' mode (in Cubase Studio the input levels are checked in the channel strip that's being used for the recording).

Figure 5.9
Checking the Input level

When that's done, still working with the Input channel, you switch to 'Meter Post-Fader' mode and check the output level - the signal being recorded on your hard disk.

Figure 5.10
Checking the output level of the input bus (the level to be recorded)

Only the output bus is visible in Cubase Studio and the input levels are checked using the channel strip on the audio track itself.

Clipping and distortion

If you've ever used an analogue tape recorder you'll know that it's possible to occasionally drive the record levels into the red without fear of distortion. On analogue tape this amounts to a form of compression and can provide a bigger, warmer sound. However, try it on a digital recorder and you'll end up with nothing of the sort, just distortion. By all means keep as close to the red area as possible but be careful not to exceed it. That said: you can sometimes break the rules, read on...

Maximizer plug-in

If digital recording is too cold and clinical sounding for you, try using the Maximizer plug-in as an insert effect.

This feature (available only in Cubase, not Cubase Studio) can be used to raise the loudness of audio material without the risk of clipping. There is also a soft clip function for removing short peaks in the input signal. This lends a warm tube-like distortion to the signal.

Figure 5.11
The Maximizer plug-in raises the loudness of audio without the risk of clipping

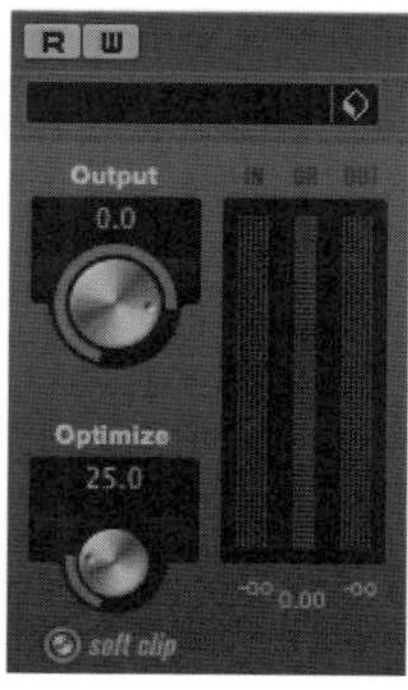

Warming up audio signals

Try recording vocals with the Maximizer inserted in the input channel (post-fader mode), for a warmer 'tube-like' effect. Alternatively use the DaTube plug-in instead. It's located in the Distortion VST plug-ins section. DaTube makes a luscious job of warming up vocals too.

Figure 5.12
The DaTube plug-in 'warms up' audio signals

32-bit float record format

For obvious reasons we usually record audio signals 'dry', without reverb effects. But sometimes it's desirable to compress or warm up a vocal performance as you actually record it. If you do record this way Steinberg recommend that you take advantage of their 32 Bit Float record format, to avoid digital distortion. The reason for this is that the effect processing in the input channel is done in 32-Bit Float format anyway. If you record at 16 or 24-Bit, the audio will be converted to this lower resolution when it's written to file and might result in a poorer signal.

Quick tip

Keep your signal levels as high as possible (without exceeding the clipping level of 0.0 dB) at all stages of the recording process - sound source, external mixer, sound card mixer, Cubase inputs and so on.

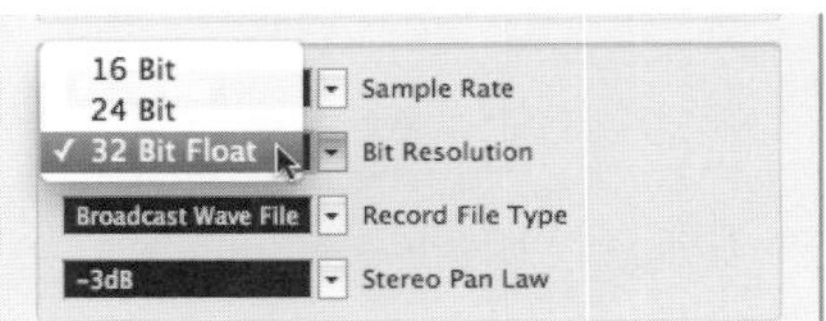

Figure 5.13
32-bit Float Record selected in the Project Setup

Input levels

Many beginners mistakenly assume that when recording, they should set the input levels using the channel strip fader. Of course, if you think about it this can't be so. The fader only affects the playback of the audio once it's recorded. So when recording, remember, the level meters show the signal level at the 'input' selected for the audio channel. You can adjust this level in one of the following ways:

- By adjusting the output level of the sound source (synthesizer, or whatever) or your external mixer.
- By using your audio hardware's own software mixer to set the input levels, if this is provided.

Figure 5.14
Many audio interfaces, like the MOTU Ultralite, include a software mixer where audio input levels can be adjusted.

Quick tip

Remaining Record Time – a Project's remaining record time is displayed below the Track list. However, if you would like it to be displayed in a separate window, select Remaining Record Time from the Devices menu.

Record Enable (manual v automatic)

You've probably noticed that enabling tracks for recording is automatic (by default) whenever you select a track. You can switch this off in the preferences (Editing-Project & Mixer page) by un-checking Enable Record on Selected Track. Having it on all the time can be irritating, particularly if you are used to using a conventional hardware recorder.

Multitrack recording

A frequently asked question - I thought that Cubase recorded several tracks of audio at a time, like a conventional tape recorder. I can't get this to work. How's it done?

You can record on as many audio tracks as your computer's processing power can handle. The main limitation to this is your audio hardware. If you have a stereo sound card, then only two inputs will show up in the VST connections window.

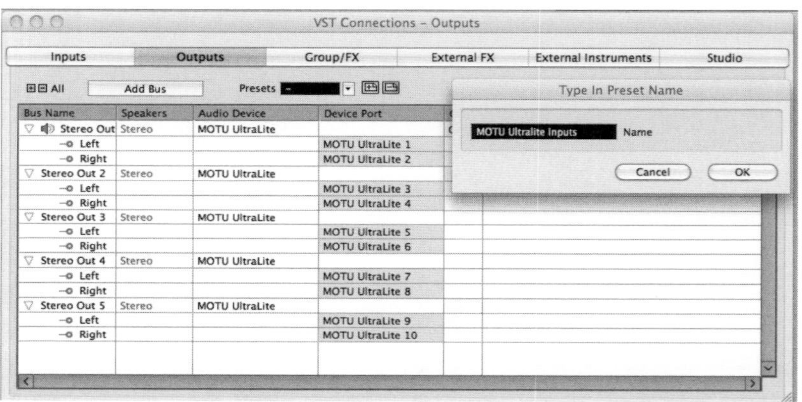

Figure 5.15
The VST Connections window

> **Quick tip**
>
> Key commands are available for arming and disarming all audio tracks at once (Mixer category).

> **Quick tip**
>
> If you find yourself occasionally dropping out of record mode by accidentally pressing the Space bar, you can set up a Lock Record key command (Transport section). Details on page 107 of the Operation Manual.

In this case you can only record two sound sources at once (although a single source may contain a mix of different instruments) and further overdubbing will probably be required.

If you have a multi-input card, any amount of inputs (depending on the card) will show up in the VST Inputs window. They can, of course, be routed to different audio channels.

Recording vocals

To record vocals properly you'll need a directional microphone. If you can afford it, a condenser model is best. Companies like AKG produce a range to suit most pockets but there are also quite a few cheap, decent Chinese condenser models around. Failing that a quality dynamic microphone such as the trusty Shure SM57 or SM58 will still produce good results.Although many vocal microphones have built-in windshields it's still a good idea to use a pop screen. Apart from preventing sudden pops, if you are recording a vocalist other than yourself, it will also prevent them getting too close to the microphone.

A distance of between 15 and 60 cms between the mouth and microphone is usual with the microphone tilted slightly, either up or down, away from a direct line with the mouth. A greater distance is fine but bear in mind the fact that more gain may be needed if the vocalist has a quiet voice. Problems with background noise could arise. Keep the microphone away from reflective surfaces, walls being an obvious example.

Recording electric guitars

Small practice amps are ideal for recording guitars but the sound is reflected off the floor and colours the tone. The answer - place the amp on a chair, half a metre or so above the ground.

A dynamic microphone such as a Shure SM 57 is the usual choice for the job. To begin with place it between 15 and 30 cms from the centre of one of the speakers in the amp cabinet. Experiment by moving it off centre from there, to alter the tone. Try using two microphones, one further away or at the side, or even behind the speaker cabinet. Use a similar method for bass guitar, but place it further away to avoid a boxy sound.

Alternatively, you can record them using the VST Amp Rack included with Cubase 6. There's a choice of virtual guitar amplifiers plus an effects suite. Use it as an insert on the mono audio track you are recording your guitar onto. After selecting an amp, cabinet and any effects that you want to record, you can experiment with the virtual microphones.

Both a condenser type and a dynamic are shown and you can crossfade between the two using a dial. Extreme left or right will provide just a single mic signal. Click on a red ball to position them.

Figure 5.16
AmpRack-1

Info

You can tune your guitar strings with a pedal-style tuner found in the Master section. If the LEDs are red you're out of tune. If the LEDs are green you're in tune.

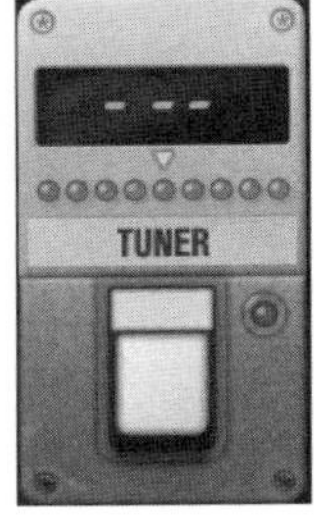

Info

Hover controls (small up and down arrows) are provided for switching between compact and default views. They can be found top-centre on the amp frame by hovering around with the mouse.

You may also like to try the AmpSimulator, a distortion plugin that also emulates various guitar amp and speaker setups. It's not as sophisticated as the Amp Rack but does a fine job just the same.

Figure 5.17
AmpSimulator

Recording acoustic guitars

Nylon string guitars are not loud instruments. You'll need a sensitive microphone to record them properly, preferably a condenser with a flat frequency response, as opposed to a dynamic vocal microphone. Aim the microphone somewhere between the sound hole and the end of the neck, but keep your distance, maybe as far as 45 cms.

If you're a singer songwriter you probably prefer to record guitar and vocal together. Tilt the vocal microphone upwards a little and the guitar microphone down, to avoid phase cancelled signals.

To capture the richness of good acoustic guitar, try seating the player in a room with a reflective floor - wood or stone as opposed to carpet. Alternatively, place a large piece of wood under the chair.

Recording brass

Brass instruments produce high sound pressure levels (SPL) so choose your microphone carefully. Condensers with a large diaphragm and flat response are best. Remember to use the pre attenuation switch to cope with the high SPL.

Place the microphone slightly off axis when mic'ing trumpets and trombones because although the higher frequencies are projected in front of the bell, the lower ones are spread over a wider area.

Recording strings

Recording a violin can be tricky. For a start, violinists tend to move about a lot. Ask the player to sit down. This also helps reflections from the ceiling. Use a flat response cardoid microphone like the Shure Performance PG 81 placed over the bridge. The distance depends on the style of music and the type of sound you want. Basically, the closer you go, the scratchier it gets.

Small string ensembles are quite easy to record. Use a crossed pair of microphones (at right angles to each other) above the players.

You can also tape two boundary microphones, one either side of a 1 metre square piece of plywood and suspend that above and in front of the musicians. This should produce a great stereo image.

Recording acoustic bass

A combination of pickup and microphone usually works okay. Experiment with the microphone placement, starting fairly close to the bridge.

Recording grand piano

Place a condenser microphone about 30 cms above the bass strings and another the same distance above the treble strings. AKG C 535 microphones are a good choice here.

Another way - tape a couple of boundary mics to the underside of the lid and close it.

Recording upright piano

Open the lid and place two directional condensers, one at each end, above the treble and bass strings. If that doesn't work, take off the front panel and place the mics in front of the strings.

Another way - use two boundary mics, taped to the wall, behind the piano. You can only do this if it's an overdub because boundary mics pick up other instruments in the room. Alternatively tape them to the front panel, inside, near the hammers.

Monitor inputs

Once you've laid down an initial track (or group of tracks) you'll need to hear the music back as you record any further overdubs. The process is known as 'monitoring' and there are three ways to do it in Cubase. Which one you choose depends on your hardware and your preferred method of working.

If hearing things back with the panning in place along with effects and EQ is important to you then monitoring via Cubase itself is the way to go. Using this method, the input signal is mixed with the audio playback. This is ideal if you like touches of reverb on your voice or you need to hear a certain effect on your guitar while you are recording. However there is a drawback, and that's latency. The signal you hear back will be slightly delayed. It might not be much but even a delay of 20 milliseconds or so can be very off-putting to most musicians. The latency value depends on your audio hardware and drivers and it's usually possible to lower them by reducing the size and number of buffers in the VST Audio System panel (Devices > Device Setup).

If your audio hardware is ASIO 2 compatible you may be able to use direct monitoring. The audio hardware handles the monitoring and sends the input signal directly out again. You can easily check to see if you have this facility by opening the VST Audio System panel and selecting your audio hardware. If the Direct Monitoring check box is greyed out you don't have it. If it isn't, you're up and running with direct monitoring. However you can't use any internal EQ or effects because the signal doesn't actually pass through Cubase. Cubase just 'controls' the monitoring.

A straightforward way to monitor your performance is to use an external mixer. It needn't be expensive. A small desktop mixer will suffice. This way a signal is sent to your main studio monitor speakers and an additional feed is sent from the mixer's auxiliary sends to your sound card. If the mixer has direct outputs use those instead.

Quick tip

If you're using an external mixer for monitoring ensure that 'Manual' mode is selected in preferences (VST page – Auto Monitoring drop-down menu) and leave the Monitor buttons off when recording.

Lane recording

One of the best things about recording with a sequencer is the ability to cycle record. Cubase has a brilliant cycle record mode that allows you to stack multiple takes on a single audio track. With 'Keep History' or 'Cycle History + Replace' selected and activated on the Transport panel, recording takes place as normal with the last recorded take active and shown on top. However, click the 'Show Lanes' button and all the takes are stacked on separate lanes, each with a different number. By chopping them up into smaller events and choosing the best of the bunch you can quickly assemble a perfect take. This process is usually referred to as comping.

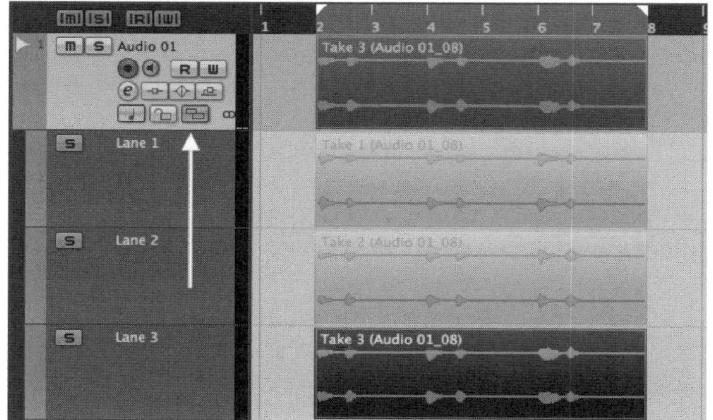

Figure 5.18
Click the Show Lane button to display recorded takes on different lanes

Comping

After recording a few continuous takes and displaying them as lanes it's easy to assemble a perfect take. Simply cut at the appropriate points in the timeline. Cutting one event cuts all the other events at the same time.

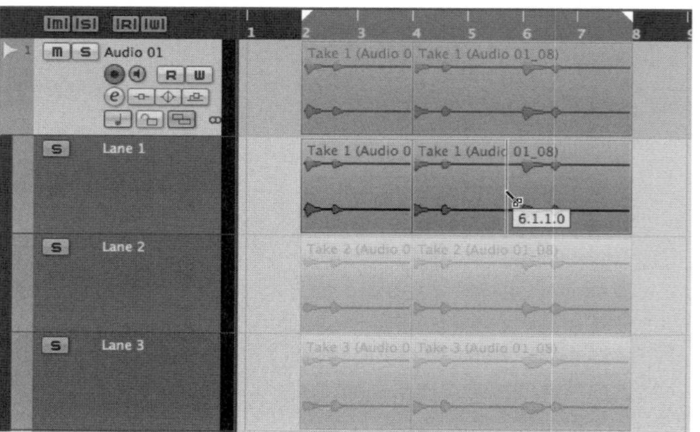

Figure 5.19

Use the arrow cursor (object selector) to select the split events that you wish to hear…

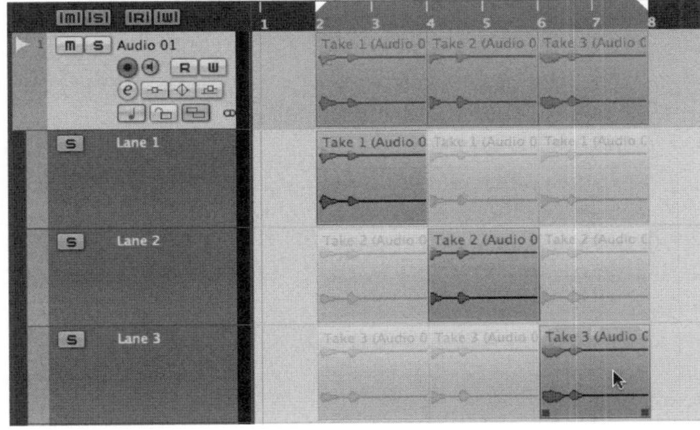

Figure 5.20

… and use Bounce Selection (Audio menu) to assemble a take.

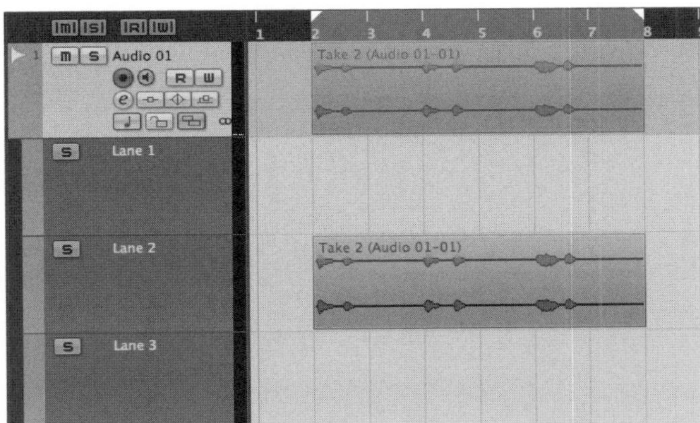

Figure 5.21

Deleted takes

Everybody finds their own way of doing things when recording in Cubase; comping (mentioned above) being just one method. You can also do it the old fashioned way, by recording a 'take', listening back and if you like it, great, you keep it; if you don't, you can delete it and record another one. But here's the clever bit. In Cubase this 'take' - referred to as an audio event - is not actually deleted, but remains on the hard disk, in the Pool's Trash folder, so you can change your mind and recall it later. Just don't empty the trash!

Punch In/Out

Playing an instrument and recording your performance at the same time can be an unwieldy, and potentially dangerous task to say the least (pressing record buttons on and off and so on). Fortunately the whole process can be automated in Cubase.

For example - you need to drop in and repair a guitar solo between bars 17 and 21. Set the locators to encompass those bars and activate the Punch In and Punch Out buttons on the transport panel. Now scroll back to a point

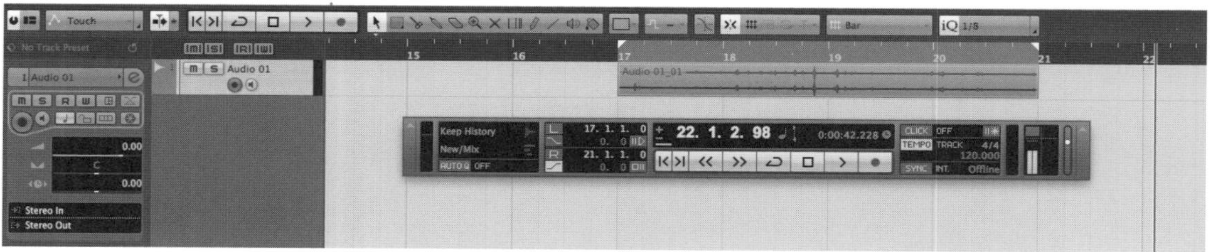

Figure 5.22
Punch In and Out recording

before the drop in - let's say bar 13 - and activate playback (not the record button). When the cursor reaches bar 17 the sequencer begins recording and when it reaches bar 21 it stops (playback continues).

> **Info**
>
> You can only play back one audio event at a time on a single audio track. If you happen to record over part of a previously recorded event and create an overlap, only the visible event will be played back.

Waveform display

Creating waveform images as you actually record is all very well but it's CPU intensive. If you find things are slowing down as a result, turn it off in the preferences (Audio > Record page) and un-tick the 'Create Images During Record' box.

Remaining Record Time Display

The amount of remaining record time can be found in the Info line, if you activate it. However, you can also have it displayed in a resizable floating window (Devices > Remaining Record Time Display).

Figure 5.23
Remaining Record Time Display

> **Quick tip**
>
> Use 'Move to Front' and 'Move to Back' (Edit menu) to get at overlapping events.

Lock Record

It's easy to accidentally hit the Space bar when recording, which usually means having to redo the take. It can be avoided, though, by setting up a Lock Record key command (Transport section). When Lock Record is activated the Record button turns grey until you use Unlock Record, also available as a key command.

MIDI recording

MIDI track setup

In common with other MIDI sequencers, Cubase sometimes plays back the wrong synthesizer or sound module sounds from time to time. To prevent this happening, create a one bar set-up part and manually insert a program number for each MIDI track. This is best done using the List Editor.

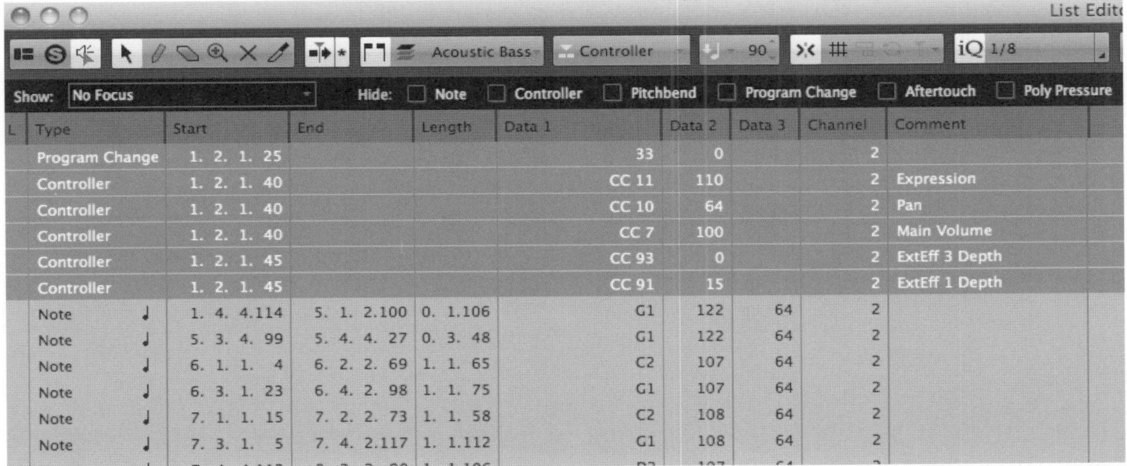

L	Type	Start	End	Length	Data 1	Data 2	Data 3	Channel	Comment
	Program Change	1. 2. 1. 25			33	0		2	
	Controller	1. 2. 1. 40			CC 11	110		2	Expression
	Controller	1. 2. 1. 40			CC 10	64		2	Pan
	Controller	1. 2. 1. 40			CC 7	100		2	Main Volume
	Controller	1. 2. 1. 45			CC 93	0		2	ExtEff 3 Depth
	Controller	1. 2. 1. 45			CC 91	15		2	ExtEff 1 Depth
	Note	1. 4. 4.114	5. 1. 2.100	0. 1.106	G1	122	64	2	
	Note	5. 3. 4. 99	5. 4. 4. 27	0. 3. 48	G1	122	64	2	
	Note	6. 1. 1. 4	6. 2. 2. 69	1. 1. 65	C2	107	64	2	
	Note	6. 3. 1. 23	6. 4. 2. 98	1. 1. 75	G1	107	64	2	
	Note	7. 1. 1. 15	7. 2. 2. 73	1. 1. 58	C2	108	64	2	
	Note	7. 3. 1. 5	7. 4. 2.117	1. 1.112	G1	108	64	2	

Figure 6.1
Set-up bar with Program, Expression, Pan, Volume, Chorus and Reverb controllers inserted

Chase Events Filter

If you have placed program changes on a MIDI track, when you start playback from a point other than the beginning of a project, you may hear the wrong sounds. Use the Chase Events Filter in the preference settings to ensure that Cubase chases the MIDI events (Figure 6.2).

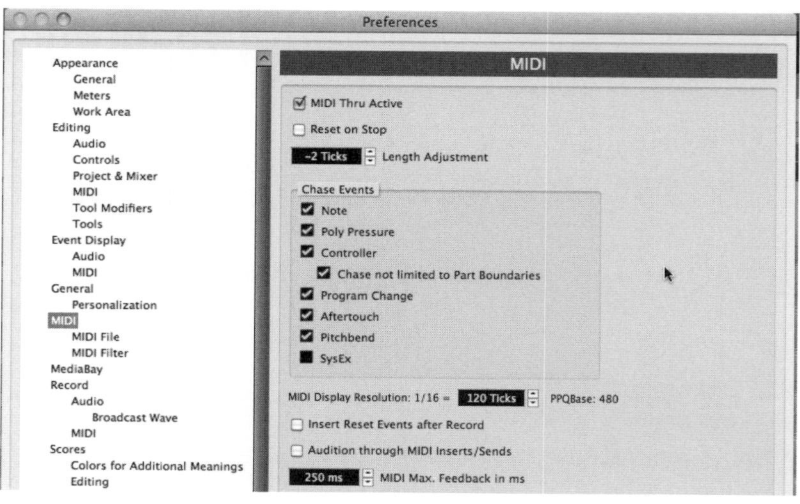

Figure 6.2
The MIDI Chase Events Filter

Cycle recording

One of the most useful things about recording MIDI in Cubase is the option to record in a cycle or loop. You can set up a loop by positioning the left and right locator and activating the Cycle button on the Transport panel.

Handy Key Commands

Cycle: Pad /
Play Loop: Shift G

Delete doubled notes

Watch out when cycle recording and quantize are combined; there's a danger of double notes being recorded. These not only sound strange but can cause problems such as stuck notes on some synthesizers.

They're easily spotted in the Score Editor where they show up as note clusters. Fortunately, you can erase them quickly using MIDI > Functions > Delete Doubles.

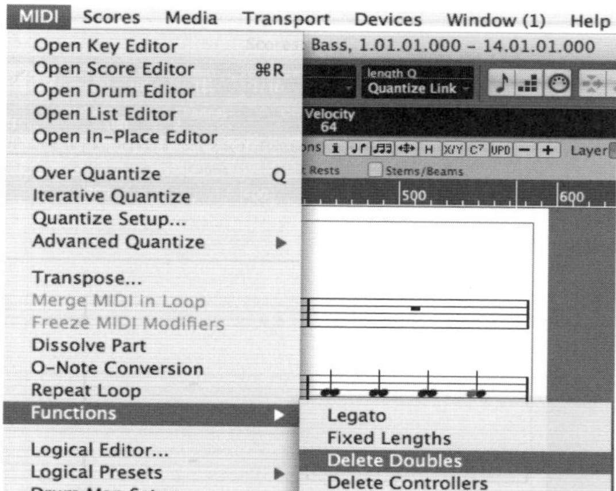

Figure 6.3
Deleting doubled notes

Info

There are various options available when cycle recording. Perhaps the most useful is the combination of Cycle Record Mode set to 'Mix' on the transport panel together with either 'New Parts' or 'Merge.'. Using 'Mix' avoids erasing the music on each pass.

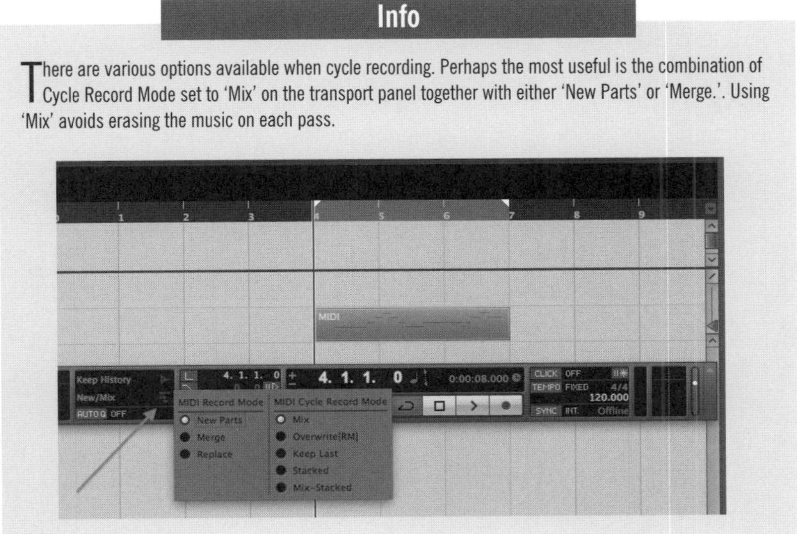

Stacked recording in cycle mode

Stacked recording is available when you cycle record. On each pass a new part is created and given it's own 'lane' in the track. When you've finished recording, you can choose the best bits from each 'take' and join them together using the Merge MIDI in Loop feature.

Catch range

If you're prone to playing a little ahead of the beat when recording, you've probably experienced the annoying habit Cubase sometimes has of not recording your first note. To prevent this from happening raise the MIDI Record Catch Range in the Preferences (Record MIDI page).

Retrospective recording

We lost it in SX1, it appeared again in SX2 and it's still with us in Cubase 6 - the option to record everything into the buffer memory. Check the Retrospective Record option in the Preferences (Record MIDI page). That way, if a MIDI track is record enabled and you happen to be doodling about in stop mode or even during playback, everything you play is recorded in the buffer. To hear it, check 'Retrospective Recording' (Transport menu) and a MIDI part will magically appear,

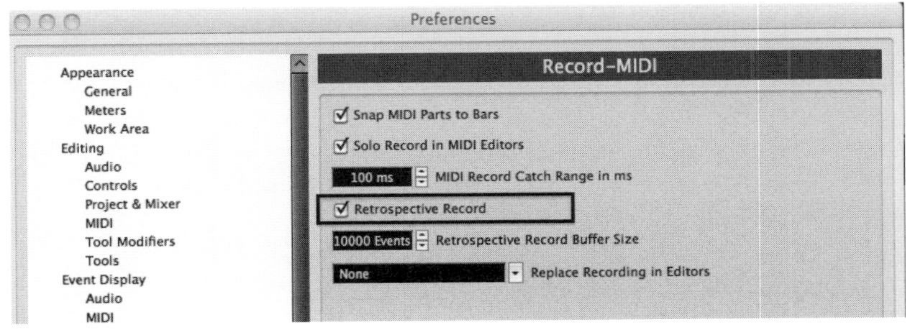

Figure 6.5
RetroRecord

HALionSonic

If you need a virtual GM sound module, perhaps to play an imported MIDI file, you can use HalionSonic SE, a cut down version of Steinberg's flagship sample player. Apart from an extensive range of synth sounds for modern electronic production it also contains a complete General MIDI sound set. To turn it into a virtual General MIDI player, go to the Options page and activate General MIDI Mode in the Global section.

Figure 6.6
HALionSonic can be transformed into a General MIDI file player

Realistic performance

If your music uses acoustic samples and you're after a realistic interpretation of real instruments forget the keyboard and concentrate on the virtual instrument you are recording. For example, if it's a violin, imagine yourself actually playing it. Become that violinist. The same applies to any instrument. Try to get inside the mind of your virtual musician. Before you can do this confidently, you will almost certainly need to spend time listening to real instruments in the hands of expert performers.

Delete overlaps

When emulating monophonic instruments (those that play one note at a time such as woodwind and brass), be careful not to create overlaps when playing from the keyboard. If it happens, clean them up, from within the editor window you are using, with MIDI > Functions > Delete Overlaps mono/poly.

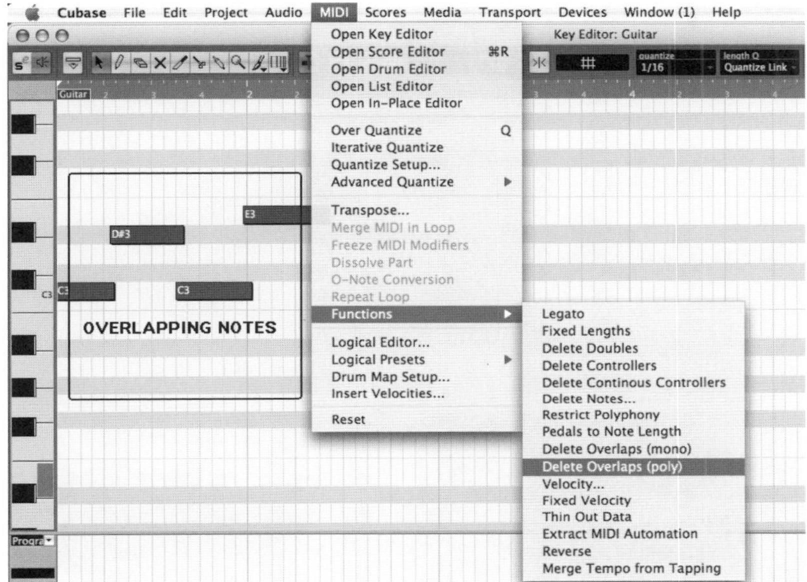

Figure 6.7
Deleting overlapping notes

Note length adjustment

Overlapping notes of the same pitch - sometimes referred to as multiple notes - cause problems on some synths. Avoid them using Length Adjustment in the preferences (MIDI page). You can adjust the length of notes of the same pitch and MIDI channel so that there is always a short time-gap between the end of one note and the start of another. The default setting is -2 ticks.

Pitch bend and modulation

Use controllers such as pitch bend and modulation to help to make sampled sounds more convincing. It's best done whilst playing, using the pitch bend controller on your MIDI keyboard. You can add the pitch bend afterwards but it's hard to beat the spontaneity of playing it live. Vibrato is often used on strings and wind instruments and you can achieve this by adding modulation (CC1). Go easy though, to avoid that 'nanny goat' sound.

Another way to add pitch bend: in the Key Editor, click on the arrow, just below the keyboard, on the lower-left side of the screen. A menu appears. Choose 'Pitch Bend' and a graphic representation appears in the controller display. Pitch bend can be drawn and edited here using the pencil tool. Of course you are not restricted to just pitch bend and modulation here. All the usual MIDI controllers appear on the menu.

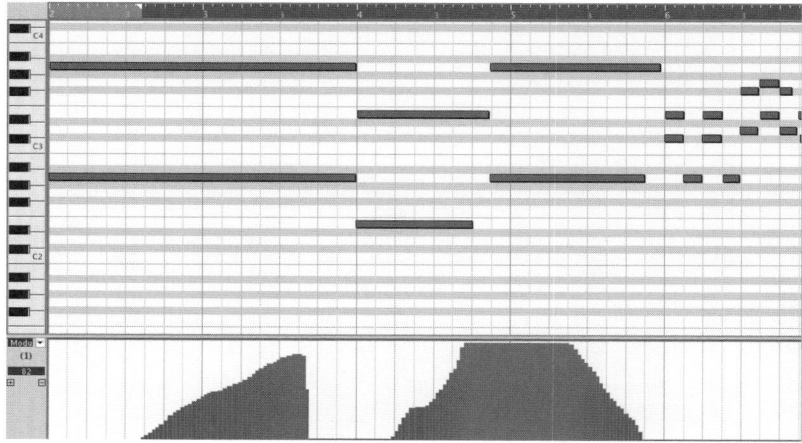

Figure 6.8
You can draw pitch bend, modulation and so on, in the Controller Lane

Applying legato

To smooth things out, after playing a fluid line (strings maybe), select the recorded notes in the Score or Key editors and apply Legato (MIDI > Functions > Legato). Set a suitable legato overlap with Legato Overlap in the Preferences (Editing-MIDI page).

Figure 6.9
Applying legato

Delete unwanted ghost notes

When playing a MIDI keyboard, particularly the mini variety, it's very easy to leave unwanted ghost notes scattered about the track. These are usually very short in duration and weak in velocity value. Although you can't always hear them they can wreak havoc on some synths and sound modules. Weed them out by using MIDI > Functions > Delete Notes. After selecting 'Delete Notes', you set the criteria using this dialogue box (Figure 6.10).

Restricting polyphony

Too many voices sounding at once in a busy MIDI sequence can result in unpredictable dropping out of notes if your instrument has limited polyphony. You can restrict the number of voices used with MIDI > Functions > Restrict Polyphony. Just enter a value (Figure 6.11).

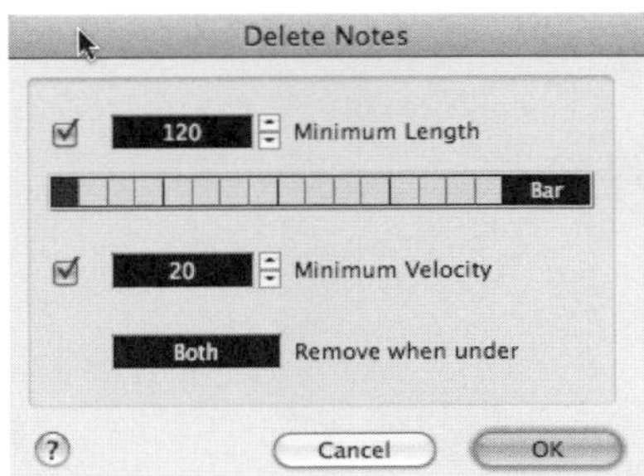

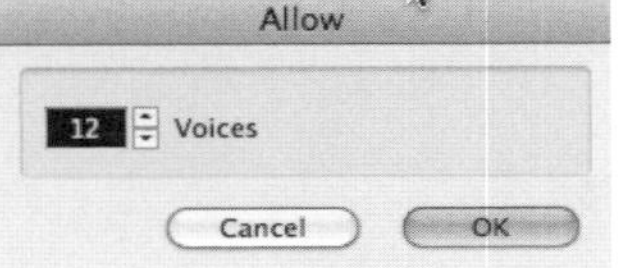

Figure 6.11
Restricting Polyphony

Figure 6.10
After selecting 'Delete Notes', you set the criteria using this box

Adjusting note velocities

There's a very handy box for increasing, reducing, compressing and limiting velocity values under MIDI > Function > Velocity. Use Fixed Velocity, from the same menu, to force all selected events to correspond with the Insert Velocity feature on the Key Editor toolbar. Use it on selected events in the Project window or any of the MIDI editors including the score.

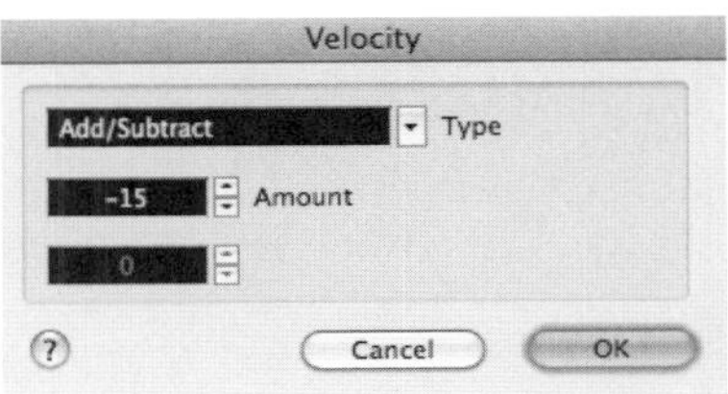

Figure 6.12
Function box for adjusting note velocities

Smoother playing

If you're not too hot on the keyboard your MIDI recordings may sound a bit lumpy due to uneven playing. To avoid this, smooth the velocity data as you play using the Velocity Shift and Velocity Compress MIDI Modifiers. If you want to make the data permanent, select it and apply Freeze MIDI Modifiers (MIDI menu).

Figure 6.13
Compress as you play

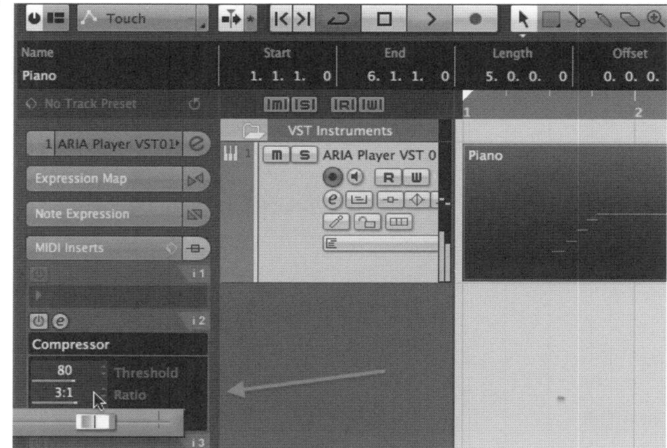

Figure 6.14
Compress - the audio style approach to MIDI compression

If you prefer a more conventional 'audio style' approach to compressing MIDI data try using Compressor, one of the many excellent Cubase MIDI plug-ins. Parameters are threshold, ratio, gain.

Human touch

Again, if you're a technically challenged keyboard player, you might quantize-correct your performance. If so, your recordings will probably sound a little mechanical. To loosen things up a bit use the Random settings in the MIDI Modifiers. Select 'Position' from the pop-up menu then play the track and vary the Min and Max parameters in real time until it sounds loose enough. You can also randomize velocity, note length and pitch from here.

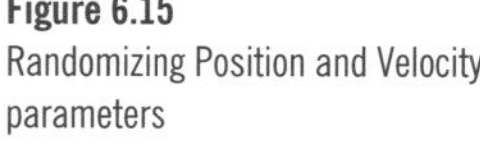

Figure 6.15
Randomizing Position and Velocity parameters

Info

If you use Merge MIDI in Loop or Freeze MIDI Modifiers to make the random parameters permanent, it's likely that there will be overlapping notes of the same pitch. As a precaution use MIDI > Functions > Delete Overlaps (mono).

Plug-in trick

The MIDI plug-ins with Cubase are truly superb and a great way of generating ideas for arrangements and compositions. Try experimenting; there's much fun to be had. If you're not quite sure how to begin, try this trick:

1 Create an instrument track, assign the output to HALion Sonic SE and then choose a piano sound.

Figure 6.16

2 Open the MIDI inserts folder and choose the Chorder MIDI plug-in. This is a MIDI chord processor. Pressing a single key on your MIDI keyboard will play complete chords according to the chosen settings.

Figure 6.17

3 Set Chorder to Global mode and from the preset menu, select a chord type. A straight major chord will serve the purpose to begin with.

4 Set the project tempo to 120 bpm (default) and using single keys or the Pencil tool, record or draw a simple four bar sequence like the one below: one bar of C4, one bar of D4 and two bars of A3.

Figure 6.18

5 Set up a four bar cycle and play it back. You should now be hearing complete major chords wherever a key was pressed. Obviously, that sequence on its own is not going to set the world on fire. To make it more interesting…

6 Open the Inserts folder again. There are still three more insert slots available. In the second one, choose Arpache 5. Arpache 5 is an arpeggiator. Experiment with the presets and quantize settings. The simple up-down preset works well combined with a quantize value of 16T.

Figure 6.19

7 In the third insert slot, select AutoLFO. The 'left and right and…' preset provides an interesting, constantly changing stereo picture.

Save the project as plug-in-trick.cpr. However, we're not finished yet...

Figure 6.20

Step sequencing

If you're into step sequencers there's a perfectly adequate one in the MIDI plug-ins folder. To step sequence a simple bass line, follow these steps:

1 Create another instrument track in plug-in-trick.cpr, assign the output to HALion Sonic SE, and then select a bass synthesizer sound.

Figure 6.21

2 Open the MIDI inserts folder and choose the Step Designer MIDI plug-in. Step Designer is a MIDI pattern sequencer that sends out MIDI notes and controller data.

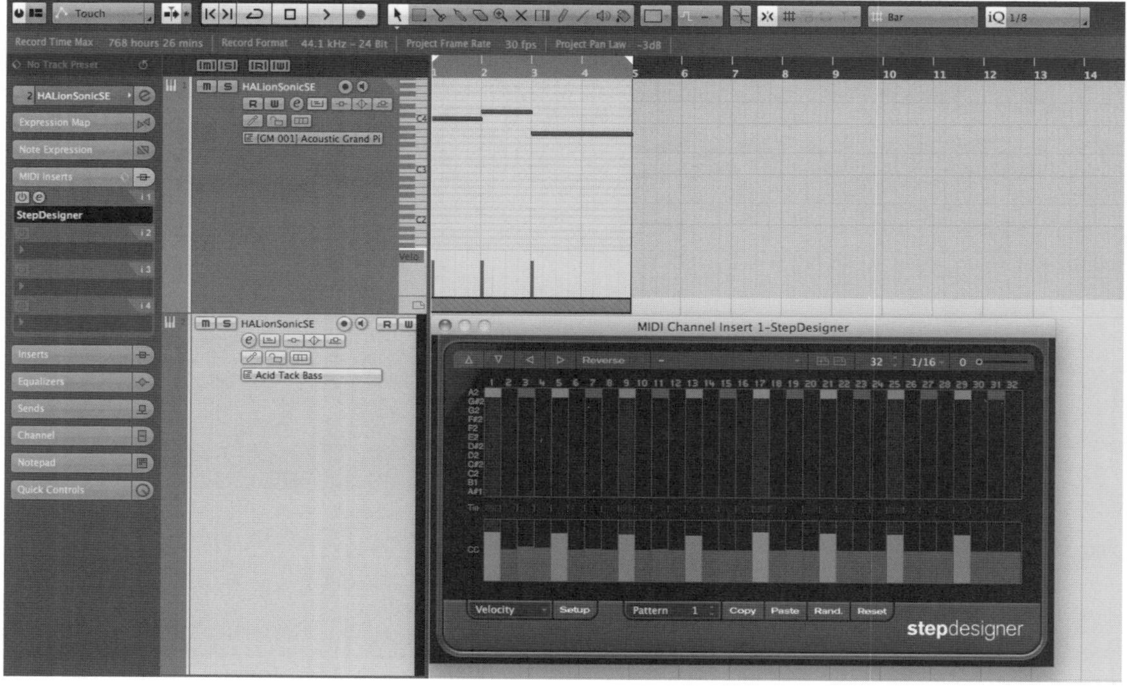

Figure 6.22

3 Change the 'Step size' setting to 1/16 and change the Length setting to 32. This will give us four bars of 1/16-note steps to play with.
4 Fill in the first square on the A2 line and then fill in every other square until you have completed the row. Use the Shift Octave arrows to drop it down an octave if you wish. Play it back. You now have a simple bass line accompanying the arpeggios. Experiment with different settings and bass patterns to discover more.

Info

When using the Step Designer MIDI plug-in to create bass lines, experiment with the velocity settings to accent certain notes.

To make notes shorter in Step Designer, select 'Gate' on the Controllers pop-up menu and lower the bars in the controller display. To make notes longer, you can tie two notes together. Insert two notes and click the Tie button below the second note.

Creating a sequence with Step Designer

You can create up to 200 different patterns in Step Designer and have them play back in the order you require by drawing them in the automation sub track.

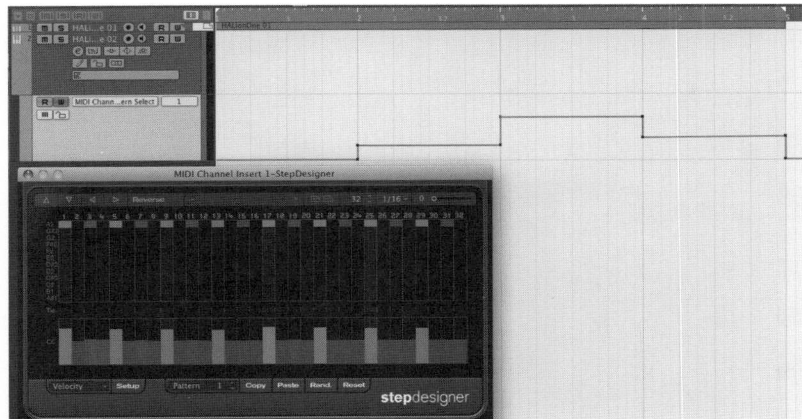

Figure 6.23

If Pattern Select is not on the menu, choose More... to add it to the list.

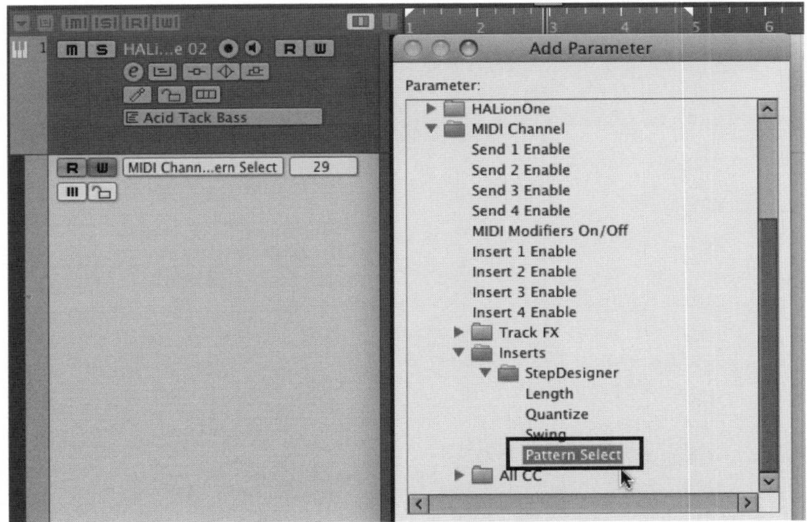

Figure 6.24

Perhaps an easier way to arrange a sequence of Step Designer patterns is to set up Step Designer as an insert on a MIDI track and enter notes in the Key Editor. C1 will trigger pattern 1, C#1 triggers pattern 2, D will trigger pattern 3 and so on. You could, of course, just as easily record enable the track and press the desired keys on a MIDI keyboard to create a sequence.

Figure 6.25

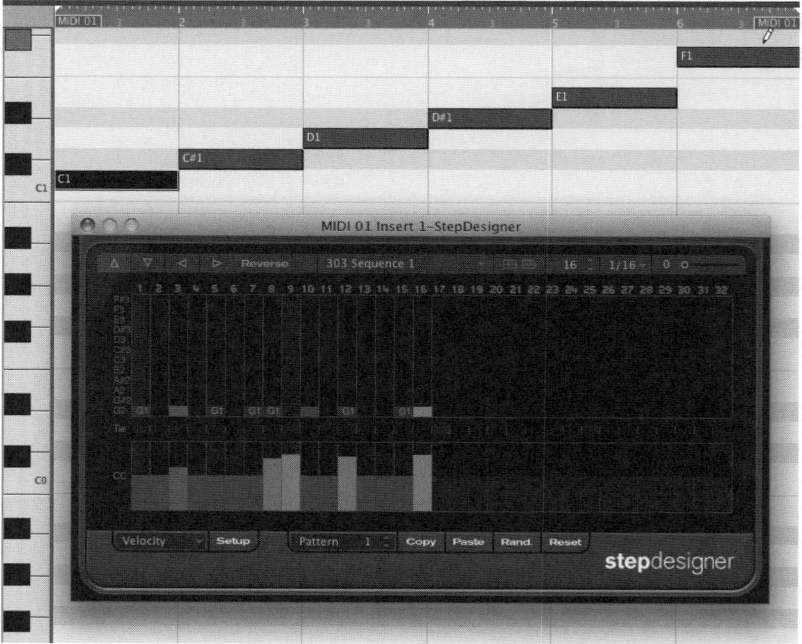

Transposing parts

A common problem: There's a four bar section on a piano track that you would like to transpose. The transpose feature in the track parameters folder transposes the whole track. What do you do?

Solution: With the Scissors tool, make the four bars you need to transpose into an individual part. Now select it and use the Transpose feature (MIDI menu) to alter the pitch of the notes.

Hidden data

A common problem: you've made a really great track using the Chorder and Arpache 5 MIDI plug-ins as Inserts and you want to turn it into MIDI data. But there's nothing showing up in the editors.

Solution: To turn your entire MIDI plug-in data into real events on this track use the Merge MIDI in Loop feature (MIDI menu).

1 In the Project window, mute any tracks you want left out of the operation.
2 Set up the left and right locators around the area you want to convert.
3 Select an empty track and use MIDI > Merge MIDI in Loop.
4 A dialogue box appears - check the 'Include Inserts' and click OK. A new part appears on the destination track.
5 Open the List Editor and you'll find a veritable mass of data!

VST Expressions

Anyone who uses large orchestral sample libraries to realize their compositions will be familiar with the time consuming task of entering articulations into their scores. Most libraries use a 'key switching' system with out-of-range keys assigned specifically to changing the articulation of particular notes. Of course, the articulations can be played and captured in real-time but, quite frankly, only the most accomplished keyboard players can usually manage it. That means, for the rest of us, painstakingly entering them afterwards in either the Key, Score or List editors.

The task of entering articulations, however, was improved a great deal with the inclusion of VST Expression Maps in Cubase. Using a set of Expression tools, you can now draw articulations directly into the Key, Score, List and Drum editors. Here's a rough guide to how VST Expression works:

> **Info**
>
> Articulations refer to the different playing techniques associated with acoustic instruments. This might be pizzicato strings (plucked) as opposed to arco strings (bowed). Or staccato notes (short) instead of a legato passage (flowing notes). Individual notes may be accented. Some sample libraries have performance articulations that include trills, slurs and glissandi.

- An instance of HALion Sonic SE has been assigned to an Instrument track and a Tenor Sax VX track preset has been selected. The notes are displayed in the Key Editor with their corresponding articulations in the Controller Lane, below. The available VST Articulations each have their own sub-lane and are easily entered at the appropriate points with the pencil tool.

Figure 6.26

- The articulations are also displayed in the Score Editor and coloured blue, to distinguish them from other markings in the score. These articulations, too, can be entered manually with the pencil tool by selecting them from the VST Expression panel on the left (Figure 6.27).

Figure 6.27

- Chosen VST Expression Maps can be displayed in the Track Inspector. As the track plays, green arrows, to help you keep track of which ones are being used, indicate the various articulations. With high zoom levels, you can also work with the articulations in the Project window using the In-Place Editor.

Figure 6.28

Articulations can also be added using the Info Line. In Figure 6.29, a saxophone note is being assigned a 'fall'.

Figure 6.29

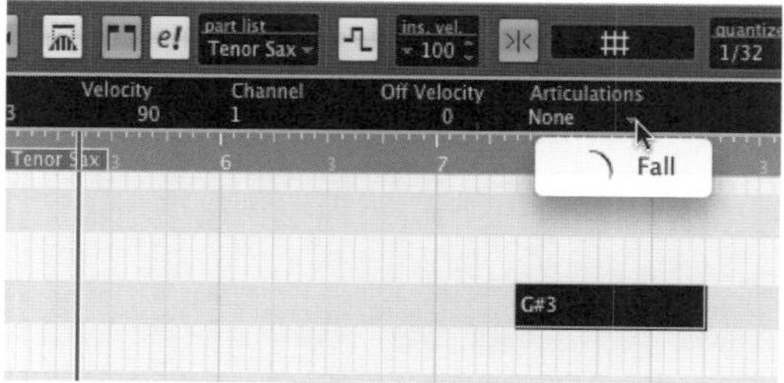

Time and tempo

Creating tempo changes

You have two choices for creating tempo changes in a project:

Add a Tempo Track (Project > Add Track > Tempo), turn it on and draw in the data…

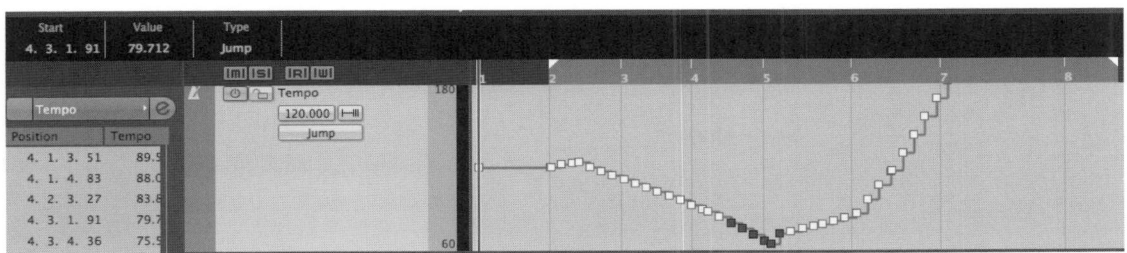

Figure 7.1

Open the Project Browser and double-click the Tempo Track icon (Project Structure column) to access the Tempo Track Editor.

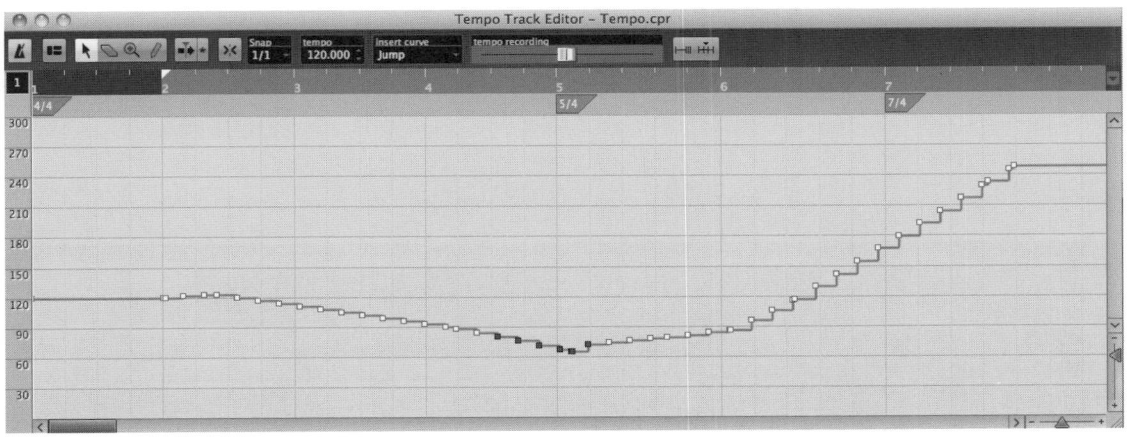

Figure 7.2

For really precise tempo editing you can also use the numerical list found in the Project Browser.

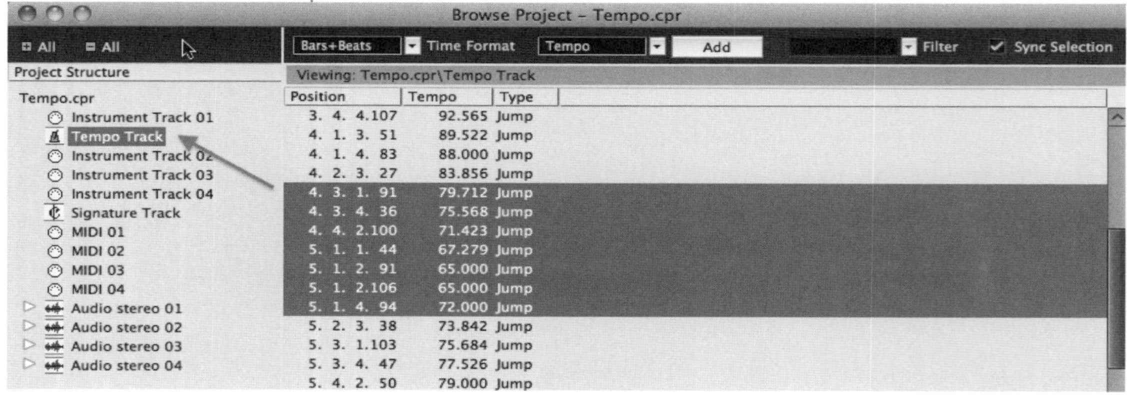

Figure 7.3
Use the numerical list found in the Project Browser

Time signature changes

Here's a quick way to enter a time signature change in the Tempo Track Editor. Hold down the Alt key (on the Mac, Option), and click with the mouse in the signature area (just below the ruler). The new entry will always be 4/4, whatever the time signature at the beginning of the project. However, you can easily edit it afterwards.

> **Info**
>
> Time signature events can only be positioned at the beginning of bars. Think about it.

Tempo changes

If you can't play something at a fast tempo, slow it down. For example, you're recording at 120 bpm and suddenly come up against a passage that you can't play at that speed. On the Transport Panel, turn off the Tempo Track and scroll the tempo to something more comfortable, like 80 bpm. After recording the awkward passage you can turn the Tempo Track back on again, to hear the track at the right speed.

Alternative Metronome click

The default audio click generated by the Metronome can become tiresome after a while but it can be substituted with something much easier on the ear. Here's one way of setting up a four-to-the-bar hi-hat click.

1 Set up an Instrument Track and assign it to HALion Sonic SE.
2 Select the Stereo GM drum preset.

Figure 7.4

3 Select the GM drum map in the track Inspector.
4 Draw a 1-bar part and double-click it, to open the Drum Editor.
5 Enter an open hi-hat hit on beat 1 (A#1) and enter a closed hi-hat beat on beats 2, 3, and 4 (F#1). Increase the velocity of beat 1, to make it more accentuated than the following beats.

Figure 7.5

6 Close the Drum Editor, select the part and then use Repeat Events (Edit > Functions > Repeat...) to enter enough bars to cover the project. Be sure to tick the Shared Copies option.

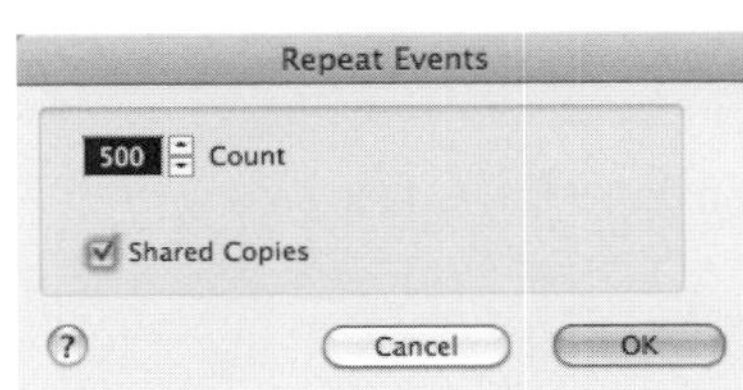

Figure 7.6

7 Turn off the Metronome.

In 4/4 time, HALion Sonic SE will play back an open hi-hat on the first beat of the bar and a closed hi-hat on the second, third and fourth beats. Because the first beat has a higher velocity than the others, it provides a strong down-beat at the beginning of each bar and the open high-hat re-enforces this.

Experiment with other devices and sound combinations until you find something that suits you. For example, high-hats mixed with a low audio click (use the volume slider in the metronome setup to achieve a suitable balance).

Quick tip

To toggle the Metronome on and off press C.

Metronome setup for 6/8 time

In earlier versions of Cubase recording in 6/8 time at any tempo above 90 bpm was a frustrating business due to the 'six beats in a bar' click. Now, as any musician knows, moderate to upbeat 6/8 music has a 'two-to-the-bar' feel - **1** 2 3 **4** 5 6 becomes **1** 2 3 **2** 2 3 - and two beats to the bar is all we want to hear, not six, unless the tempo is very slow.

Fortunately this can now be done in Cubase by ticking the Use Count Base box in the Metronome Setup.

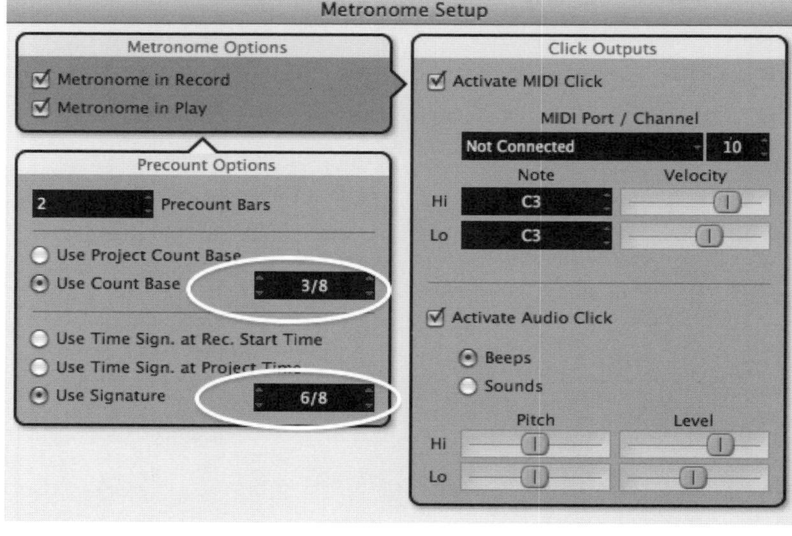

Figure 7.7
The Metronome Setup with a time signature of 6/8 and a count base of 3/8, which sounds two beats to the bar, not six.

Quick tip

You've been working in 4/4 time, your Count Base is set at 1/4 and you switch to a new project in 6/8 time; remember to alter the count base to 1/8 (slow) or 3/8 (fast) otherwise you'll hear three clicks to the bar.

When Count Base is turned on you can define a 'rhythm' for the metronome click. It's usually set to 1/4 (suitable for 2/4, 3/4 and 4/4 time signatures) but with a time signature of 6/8, setting it to 3/8 will result in two clicks to the bar. Likewise, a time signature of 12/8 set to a count base of 3/8 will result in four clicks to the bar.

Musical v Linear time base

You are given the option of Musical and Linear time based tracks to record on in Cubase and you can switch between them by clicking the musical/linear time base button in the Inspector. Which do you use?

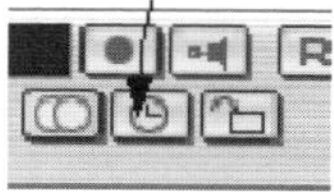

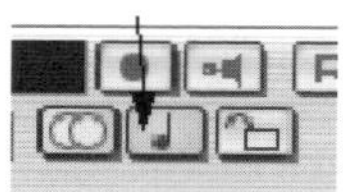

Figure 7.8
Linear (left) and Musical (right) time base buttons

For the majority of conventional music projects you'll be using musical time based tracks where the events and their time positions are shown as bars, beats and divisions of a beat such as 1/8 notes, 1/16 notes and so on, all very familiar to most musicians.

If you change the tempo of a project the events are played back either earlier or later and the length of the project will be adjusted accordingly; a faster tempo resulting in a shorter project and a slower tempo resulting in a longer one. This is all very straightforward stuff but change the tracks to a linear time base and something more difficult to understand happens. The events will be locked to specific time positions and changing the tempo will not alter those positions one jot. How can that be? Well, the fact that MIDI and audio tracks use a musical time base by default and video and marker tracks use a linear one gives us a clue.

Video files are shown as events on a video track with individual frames displayed as thumbnail images.

Figure 7.9
A Video Track has a Linear timebase

This isn't musical material and it can be thought of as seconds or frames per second (fps). A certain group of frames, containing certain visual images will appear so many seconds along the time line. They have a linear time base and cannot be sped up or slowed down (there's no reason to anyway).

Linear time based tracks are useful for freezing speech overdubs and sound effects to a particular point. Suppose you've written some routine background music to accompany a circus video. Besides the music, you have a separate MIDI track set up to record a few cymbal crashes. These crashes will coincide with some clowns falling over. What happens, though, if you decide to increase the tempo of the music slightly? Now you have a problem; the cymbal crashes will play back in the wrong place. The solution is to change the track containing the hits to linear time. Now you can alter the tempo of the music to your hearts content but the cymbal crashes will remain in place.

Of course, that's all very well if the music has been recorded on MIDI tracks, but what happens if there are audio tracks as well? They won't fit. For example, you've increased the tempo of a project but the audio tracks no longer fit the tempo. What do you do?

Determine in advance what the new speed is going to be and open the Time Stretch dialogue (found in the 'Audio > Process' menu). Select the audio parts and enter the original tempo in the input section and the new tempo in the output section. Press 'Process' and the audio will be stretched to fit.

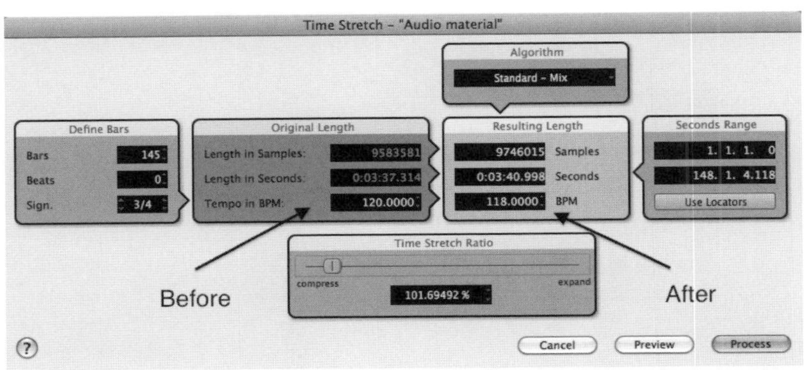

Figure 7.10
Timestretching Audio

Cross-fading music at different tempi

Strange though it may seem, linear time based tracks can be used for recording music to playback at different tempi simultaneously.

For example, you might want to cross fade two pieces of music, each containing a different tempo, along with a video track in the same project. Here's what you do:

1 Finish the first piece of music and change all the tracks to a linear time base.
2 Enter a new tempo event where the second piece of music will be starting (before the first one finishes).
3 Now write the new piece - on new tracks, of course!

Beat calculation

If you need to calculate the tempo of an imported audio file, a drum loop perhaps, the Beat Calculator does a reasonable job of it.

First, you home in on one or two bars of the audio, and use Transport > Loop Selection, to loop and play the selection. Then, with Snap turned off, you drag the start and ends of the selection until you have it just right and the music loops seamlessly (pressing Shift/G will adjust the Locators).

When you're satisfied, open the Beat Calculator (found in the project menu) and enter the number of encompassed beats in the Beats field (this loop is one bar long and contains four beats; the tempo is calculated and displayed as 123.77 bpm). Now insert the loop's tempo into the Tempo Track, by clicking one of the buttons in the lower left corner of the beat calculator window.

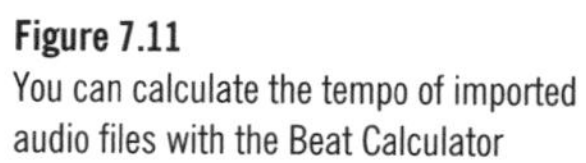

Figure 7.11
You can calculate the tempo of imported audio files with the Beat Calculator

Tap Tempo

A quick way to determine the average tempo of freely recorded music is to use the Tap Tempo option in the Beat Calculator. With playback on, open the Tap Tempo option and tap along, using the computer spacebar or your mouse. The program calculates the average tempo of the music.

Tempo mapping (tap along method)

You've recorded a live session in Cubase but the song changes tempo in several places. You want to add a few MIDI tracks. So how do you create a tempo map that follows the audio?

Play back the audio, tap along on your MIDI keyboard and record the taps to a time based MIDI track. Play the recording back, check the results and edit any stray beats. After selecting the events in the Key Editor, open the 'Merge Tempo From Tapping' dialogue (MIDI > Functions). Enter the beat value that you tapped, 1/2, 1/4 or whatever and click OK. The tempo events are inserted into the Tempo Track.

Tempo mapping with the Time Warp tool

You can create a tempo map from just the drum track of a recording using the Time Warp tool in the Sample Editor. It's slower than using the 'Merge Tempo From Tapping' feature but more accurate.

1 Make sure that the very first beat of the recording is placed at the beginning of a bar; let's say bar 1.
2 Locate bar 2, in the ruler, and if it's not there already, drag it's position, with the Time Warp tool, to line up with the first drum beat of bar 2.
3 Continue working through the track, matching only the beats that drift from the ruler.

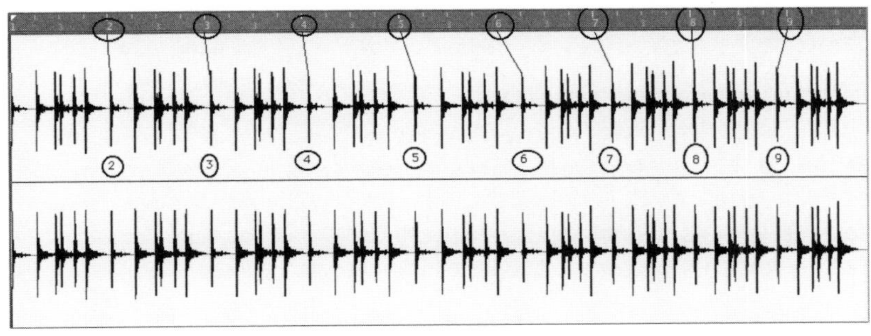

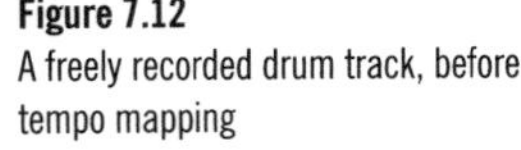

Figure 7.12
A freely recorded drum track, before tempo mapping

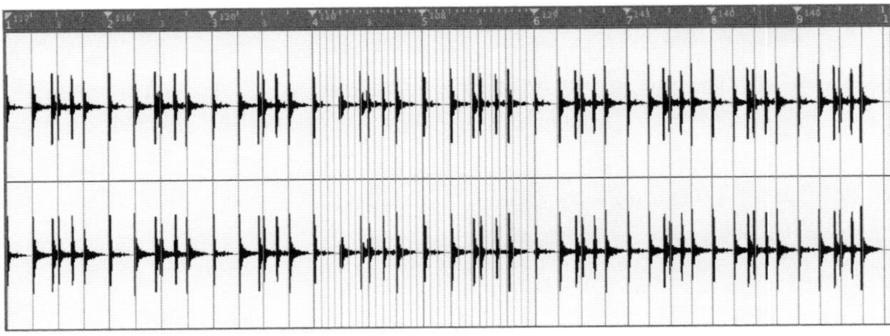

Figure 7.13
The drum track after tempo mapping with the Time Warp tool

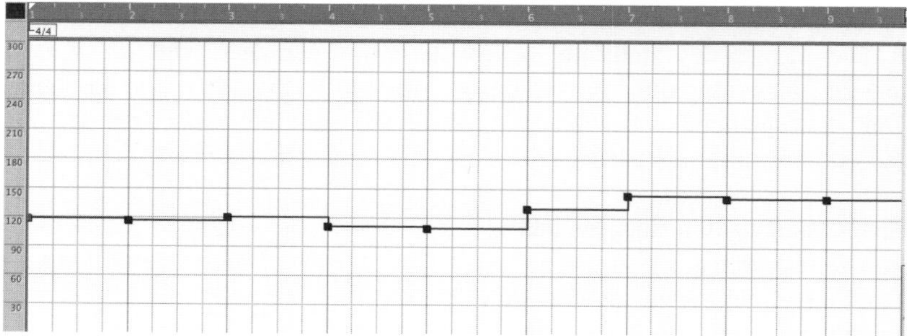

Figure 7.14
The resulting Tempo Track

What if you've recorded a solo piano part on a MIDI track, that drifts in and out of tempo? Again, you can use the Time Warp Tool to create a tempo map, only this time use the Key Editor.

Info

In Cubase SX2 we saw the introduction of the Time Warp tool. You use it to drag a musical position (tempo related) and match it to a position in linear time (clock related). This makes tasks such as matching sound and picture or creating a tempo map from freely recorded audio and MIDI material much easier than it ever was in previous versions of Cubase.

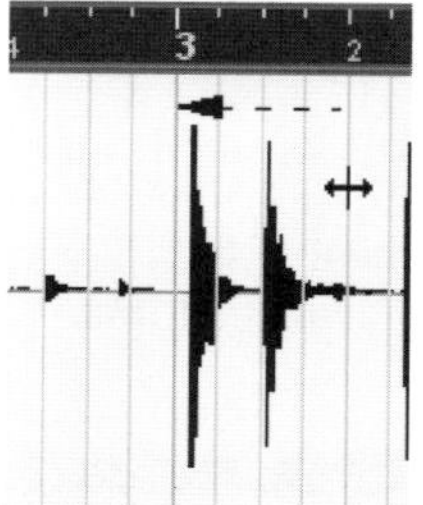

Figure 7.15
The Time Warp Tool

Figure 7.16
You use the Time Warp tool to match musical positions (tempo related) to positions in linear time (clock related).

Quick tip

To speed things up when tempo mapping, try using the Merge Tempo From Tapping feature first. Then, when the tempo map is complete, fine-tune it with the Time Warp tool.

Quick tip

Define a range, with the Range tool, before you use the Time Warp tool and the tempo events outside of that range will remain unaffected.

Importing and exporting tempo maps

The facility for importing and exporting tempo maps, lost in SX 1 was revived in SX2. It remains in Cubase 6 (File menu, Import/Export). If you want to export a Tempo Track for use in another project, perhaps for music to video, you can save its information as a special XML file. You can also import a Tempo Track but of course, it replaces the one you're already using.

Tempo slider

Tools for drawing tempo data have become standard fare in most sequencing packages but not the facility to record tempo changes 'on the fly' by dragging with the mouse. After all, it's much easier to make subtle changes this way. Last seen in Cubase VST, this feature popped up again in Cubase

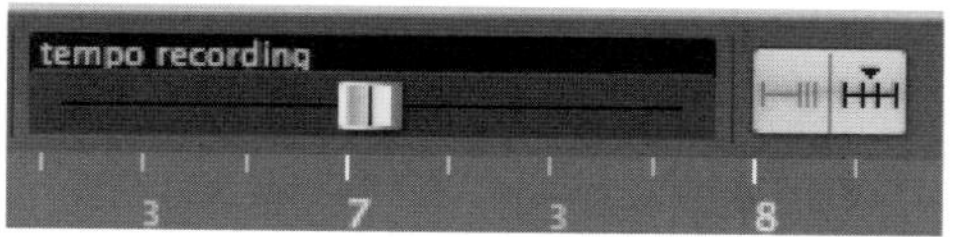

Figure 7.17
You can record 'on the fly' tempo changes using the tempo record slider

SX2. It's still with us in Cubase 6. All you do now is start playback and adjust a slider to record natural sounding tempo changes into the Tempo Track.

Time-stretching

The new time-stretching algorithms from zplane are very impressive and everybody should try this one out for production ideas and inspiration.

1 Open a project containing audio files and, if it doesn't already have one, add a tempo track and switch it on.
2 Select Ramp as a tempo point type.
3 At some point in the project enter a downwards ramp, to slow the tempo.
4 Open the Pool and select all the audio files and tick the Musical Mode boxes.
5 Select the elastique Pro – Time algorithm and play the track.

When the cursor reaches the tempo ramp you will hear the entire project slow down with its timing preserved. The audio quality remains superb. Experiment with the other options. Tape is brilliant if you want to replicate the slowed-down sound of a reel-to-reel tape machine.

Info

You don't necessarily have to match the downbeats when tempo mapping from a drum track with the Time Warp tool. Offbeats are just as good, or any obviously significant hit.

Figure 7.18

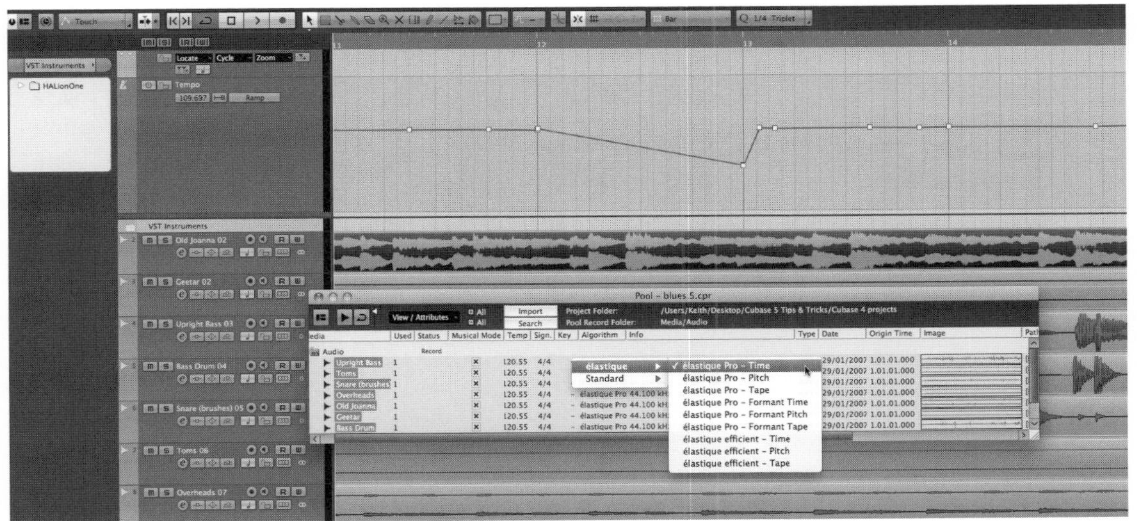

Inspector tips

The Inspector can be confusing to the newcomer. What's displayed varies depending on whether an Audio, Instrument or MIDI or track is selected.

Audio track

The sections displayed by default for an audio track, in descending order, are:

- The main Inspector.
- Inserts - 8 slots.
- Equalizers - hi, hi mid, lo mid, lo.
- Sends - 8 slots.
- Channel - channel strip and fader.
- Notepad.
- Quick Controls.

Figure 8.1
Audio tracks and the Inspector with Equalizers open

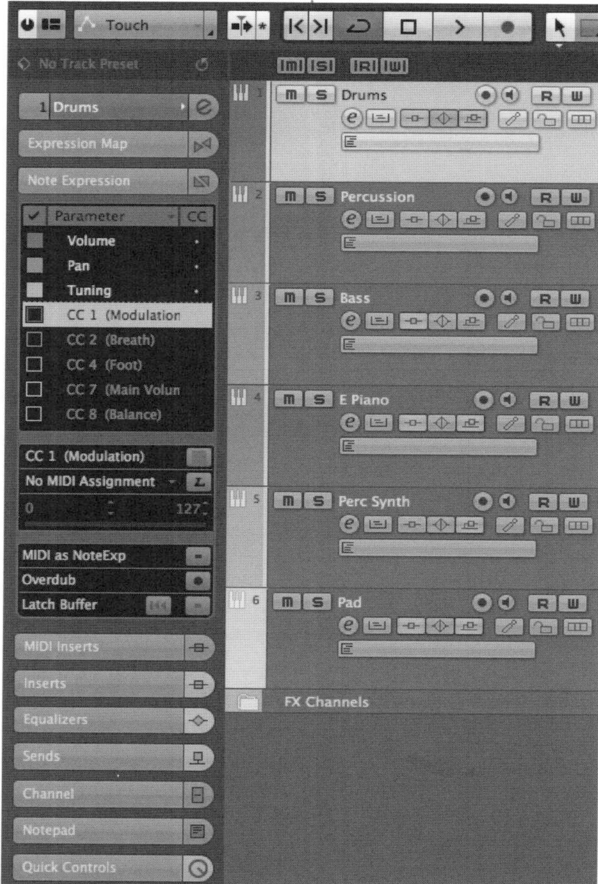

Figure 8.2
Instrument tracks and the Inspector with Note Expression open

Instrument track

The sections for an Instrument track, in descending order are:

- The main Inspector.
- Expression Map.
- Note Expression.
- MIDI Inserts – 4 slots.
- Inserts – 8 slots.
- Equalizers - hi, hi mid, lo mid, lo.
- Sends - 8 slots.
- Channel - channel strip and fader.
- Notepad.
- Quick Controls.

MIDI track

The sections for a MIDI track, in descending order are:

- The main Inspector.
- Expression Map.
- Note Expression.
- MIDI Inserts - 4 slots.
- MIDI Fader.
- Notepad.
- Quick Controls.

To have more than one section of the Inspector open, use Ctrl (on the Mac, Command) as you click on the tabs. Using Alt (on the Mac, Option) as you click will open or close all the sections at once.

Quick tip

Right-click (ctrl-click, on the Mac) on an empty space in the Inspector panel to reveal hidden Inspector sections. What's displayed will depend on the track type selected. For example MIDI Modifiers, missing from the MIDI track Inspector, will now appear in a previously hidden list.

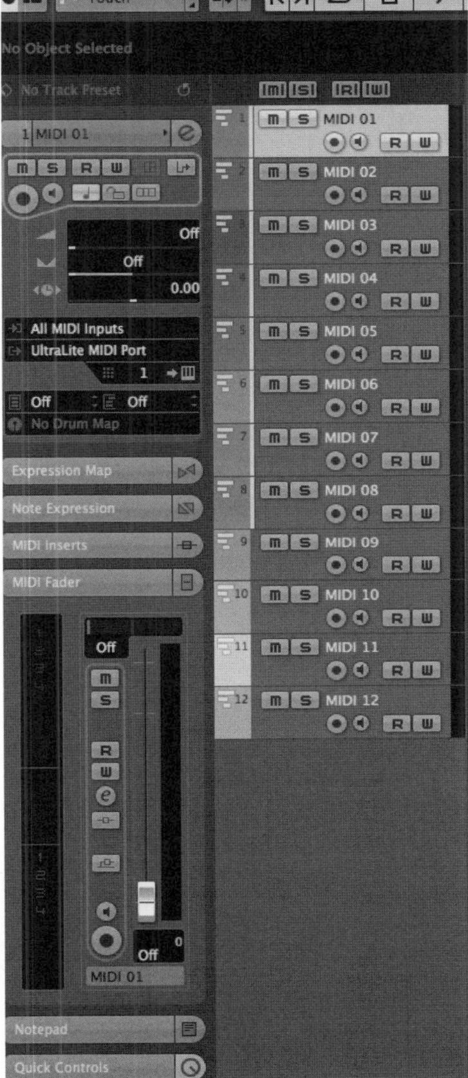

Figure 8.3
MIDI tracks and the Inspector with MIDI Fader open

Show/Hide Inspector

Sometimes having the Inspector displayed is inconvenient. You can show and hide the Inspector using the Set up Window Layout.

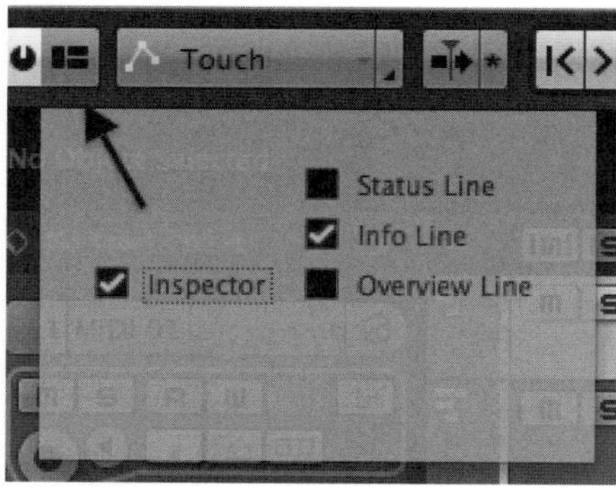

Figure 8.4
Un-tick the box to hide the Inspector

Ctrl click (on the Mac, Command clicking) an Inspector tab to bring a hidden section into view without closing an already open one. Alt click (on the Mac, Option clicking) to either open or close all sections at once.

Alternative mixer

You can mix an entire project without leaving the Project window (except for Stereo Out) by using the Inspector. Use the Edit buttons for quick access to the Channel Settings window and you're off. What you see varies, depending on whether it's an Audio, Instrument, FX or MIDI track.

- Use the Edit button 'e' on a MIDI track to reveal the MIDI Channel Settings – MIDI inserts, MIDI sends, mixer channel and fader.

Figure 8.5
Use the Edit button 'e' on a MIDI track to reveal the MIDI Channel Settings – MIDI inserts, MIDI sends, mixer channel and fader

- Use the 'e' button on an audio track to reveal the VST Audio Channel Settings - inserts, equalizers, sends, mixer channel strip and fader.

Figure 8.6
VST Audio Channel Settings

- Use the 'e' button on a track with a VST Instrument to reveal the VST Instrument Channel Settings – inserts, equalizers, sends, mixer channel strip and fader.

Figure 8.7
VST Instrument Channel Settings

- Use the 'e' button on an FX track to open the VST FX Channel Settings – inserts, equalizers, sends, mixer channel strip and fader.

Figure 8.8
VST FX Channel Settings

Inspecting Marker and Folder Tracks

As well as the usual suspects – audio and MIDI tracks – you can scrutinize Folder tracks in the Inspector too; a list of tracks contained within the folder appear. Click on their icons to reveal an Inspector view with all the usual parameters for that track.

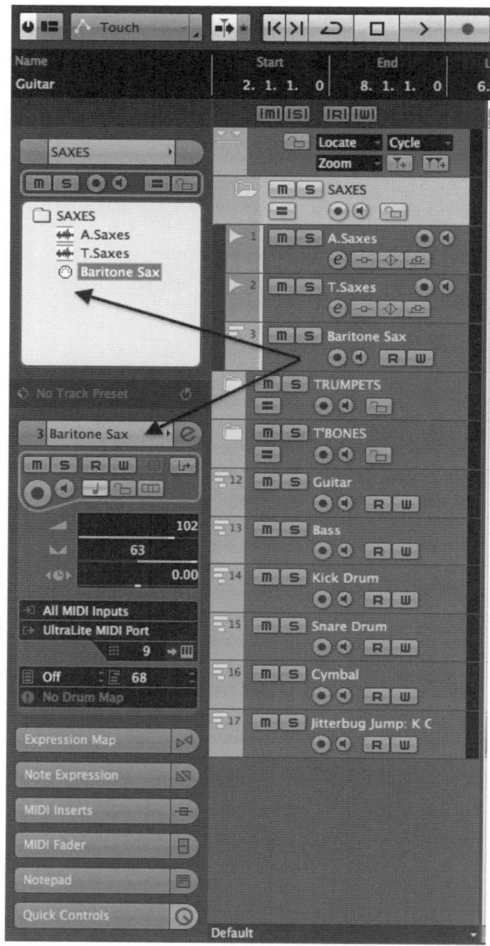

Figure 8.9
The baritone sax track is highlighted within a folder and its parameters are revealed in the Inspector

Marker tracks also show up in the Inspector with a list of Markers and their positions. You can edit this list here too.

Figure 8.10
You can examine Marker tracks in the Inspector

Auditioning sounds

Auditioning sounds on your MIDI tracks is so easy when using the Inspector. Click in the centre of the Program Settings and a menu appears containing the patch names of your instrument. Play a track and you can hear the program change in real time as you flick through the menu.

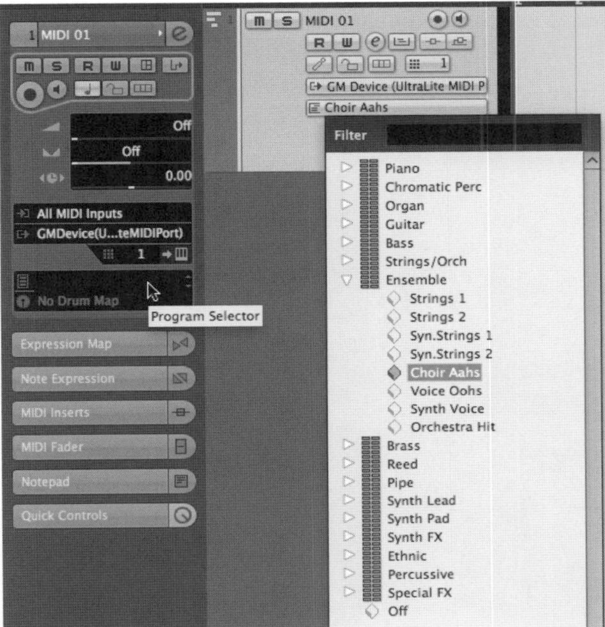

Figure 8.11
Auditioning MIDI patches using the Inspector

Info

Naming and saving Track Presets is not just restricted to instruments. There are four types of Track Presets: Audio, Instrument, MIDI and Multi (any number of the aforementioned preset types in any order).

Track Preset box

If you're uncertain about which instrument to load on a track but you know which kind of sound you want, use the Apply Track Preset box located at the top of the Inspector. Select a sound and the correct instrument will be loaded for you. You can also create and save your own Track Presets there.

Figure 8.12
An Audio track with the '1960s Blues' Track Preset loads with three processors – AmpSimulator, ModMachine and Limiter

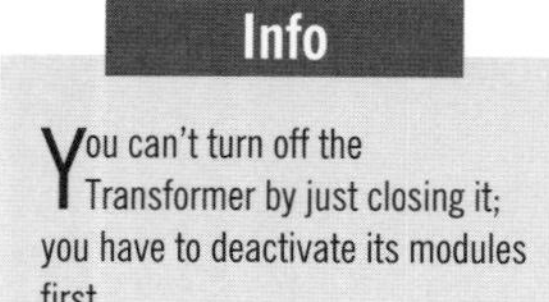

Info

You can't turn off the Transformer by just closing it; you have to deactivate its modules first.

Input Transform

A great Cubase feature is the Input Transformer. It's a real time version of the Logical Editor. It enables you to filter out and alter the incoming MIDI data before it's recorded. In other words, you will hear the changes as you play. What's the point? Well, you could turn a foot pedal controller into a MIDI kick drum for example and play it with your feet, or set up a split keyboard with a different sound for each hand. Open it by using the button in the top right corner of the Inspector.

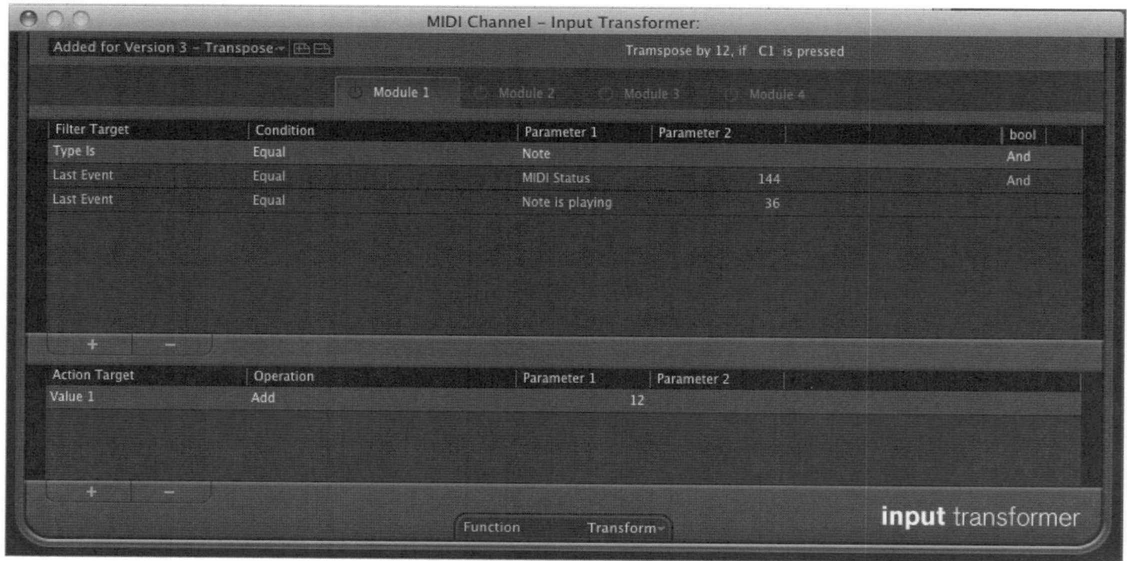

Figure 8.13 (above)
You can alter incoming MIDI data in real time with the Transformer

Figure 8.14
Press the button in the top right corner of the Inspector to access the Transformer

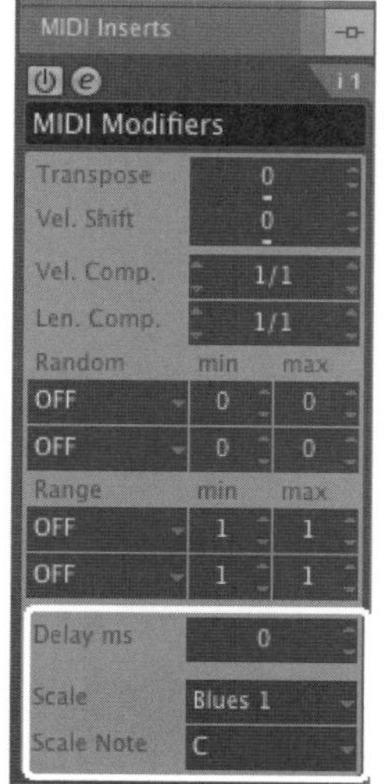

Info

The Transformer is a real time version of the Logical Editor, covered in Chapter 13. Get to grips with the Logical Editor first and you'll find the Transformer easy to understand – see Chapter 13.

Extra track parameters, including Scale Transpose

The MIDI Modifiers section (found in the MIDI Inserts) provides note transposition, velocity shift, compression and a range of randomization settings. However, if you need extra track parameters, open up the MIDI Inserts section and choose MIDI Modifiers from the pop-up menu. Essentially a duplicate of the MIDI Modifiers section, this area also contains another feature that not many people seem to know about, called Scale Transpose.

Figure 8.15
You can choose from 21 scales in Scale Transpose

All MIDI notes passing through Scale Transpose are transposed to fit a selected scale and key. There are 27 to choose from, ranging from straightforward majors and minors to exotic far eastern varieties such as Balinese. Route some of your music through it and listen to the result. Use it experimentally.

Quick tip

If you're stuck for musical ideas try using the Scale Transpose feature. Put a melody line through the Hungarian scale, for example, and your tune could take off in a completely new direction.

Length Compression

Use the Length Compression feature in the MIDI Modifiers (found under MIDI inserts) section of the Inspector to experiment with the length of notes on a particular MIDI track.It works in a similar fashion to compression and is applied to the entire track.

You may, for example, have recorded a bass part with a fretless bass patch using fairly long notes. You then decide that a pick bass would be more suitable. There's no need to record it all again. Apply '1/4' to make all the notes a quarter of their true length. The same thing works in reverse. Enter '4/1' to make the notes play back four times as long.

MIDI Modifiers v MIDI menu

A frequently asked question: When editing MIDI tracks, should I use the Inspector MIDI Modifiers or the MIDI menu functions?

Answer: It depends on whether you need a permanent alteration or a temporary one. If you're experimenting use the MIDI Modifiers because any changes you make there are in real time. Remember, though, that they affect the entire track and will not be reflected in the editors. However, you can make them permanent by using the Freeze Modifiers function (MIDI menu). If you need to make specific changes to parts or events then use the functions. These are permanent (unless you undo them, of course) and will be reflected in the editors.

Key Editor

Coloured Parts

There may be times when you need to work on several parts on different tracks at once in either the Key or List Editors. Finding the notes you want to edit is easy using the Colors pop-up menu on the toolbar. Select 'Part' from the pop-up menu. Click on a note and all the corresponding notes in that part will be highlighted in the part's colour – providing that you've already coloured the parts in the Project window, of course.

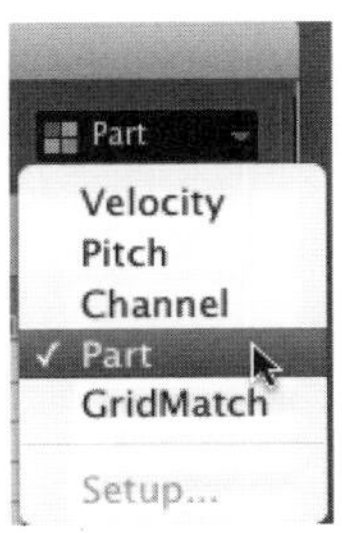

Figure 9.1
Use the Colors pop-up menu on the toolbar to find notes of the same pitch, channel and velocity value as well as notes belonging to selected parts

Velocity values

Make use of the Insert Velocity feature (MIDI menu and Key Editor toolbar) to determine the velocity you require when you're entering notes with the mouse. You can define five different velocity levels.

Even with five different levels to choose from, it's likely that the result will sound a little stiff. However, you can soon fix that using the Random feature, in the MIDI Modifiers section.

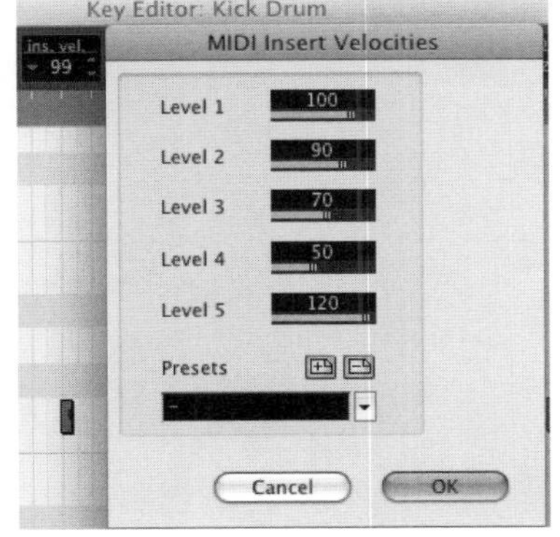

Figure 9.2
You can have five levels of Insert Velocity values

Alternatively go to MIDI > Logical Presets > standard set 1 > random velocity (60 - 100).

If those velocity values are not right for your project, open the Logical Editor itself (MIDI menu) and choose the same preset. Now you can customize the velocity values to suit you.

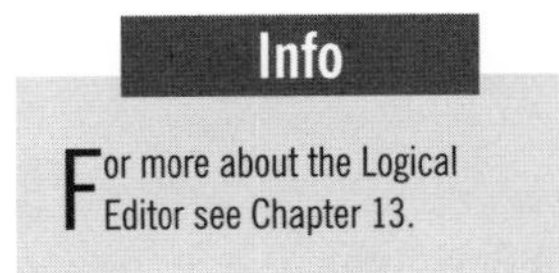

Info

For more about the Logical Editor see Chapter 13.

Selecting notes

Selecting notes is far easier and much quicker when you use the computer keyboard. Here are a few tips:

- Use the right and left cursor keys to move from event to event.
- Hold down the shift key and use the right and left cursor keys to select a group of events.
- Use the Ctrl and Alt keys (on the Mac, Command and Option) in

conjunction with the cursor keys to alter the lengths and move selected notes. Ctrl affects the beginnings of a note and Shift+Ctrl affects the ends. Alt moves the notes.

- Use the up and down cursor keys to transpose selected notes up or down in semitone steps. Holding down shift at the same time will move them in octave steps.
- Hold down Ctrl (on a Mac, Command) whilst clicking a note on the virtual keyboard to select all the notes of the same pitch.

Info

Get into the habit of opening the Key Editor from the project window using Ctrl+E (on the Mac, Command+E). It's much faster than using the menu. Alternatively, double click on the event. This works only when 'Open Key Editor' has been chosen as the Default Edit Action in the preferences (Event Display > MIDI section). Press Enter to close it.

Tonic Sol-Fa note display

If you're a singer not used to reading conventional music notation you can display note events as Tonic Sol-Fa. Go to the Preferences and in the Event Display MIDI section choose 'DoREMi' from the Note Name Style pop-up menu. Now all the note events will show up as Do, Re, Mi and so on. Use the Color pop-up in the Key Editor toolbar for even easier note recognition.

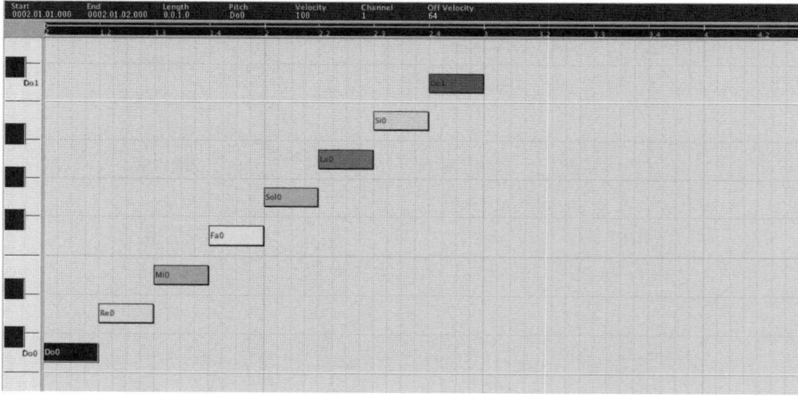

Figure 9.3
Note events can be displayed as Tonic Sol-Fa

Info

Various note name options are available in the Note Name Style pop-up menu (Preferences > Event Display > MIDI) including MIDI and Value, Classic, Classic German and DoREMi.

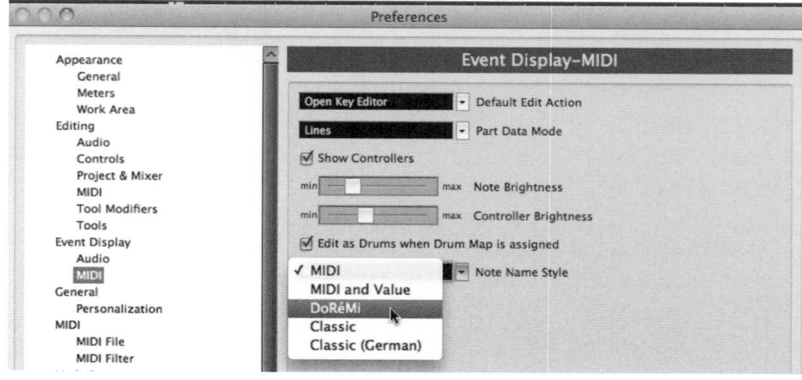

Figure 9.4
Choose your note name display type in the Preferences section

Step Input

If you can't play the piano keyboard very well, enter the notes using Step Input.

If you've ever wondered what the 'staircase' icon on the Toolbar is for, follow these steps:

Figure 9.5
The Step Input buttons

1 In the Project window, turn on Snap and set the locators to encompass a few bars.
2 Between the locators, double click on a MIDI track to create an empty part.
3 Set the track output to play back a piano sound or something else if you prefer.
4 Select the part and use Ctrl+E (on the Mac, Command+E) to open the Key Editor.

(a) Set a Quantize (Q) and Length (L) of 1/4 or Quantize Link.
(b) Click on the Step Input button on the Toolbar (staircase). A blue line appears on the screen If you can't see it, press the right cursor (arrow) key, to bring it into view. This indicates the position where notes are to be entered.

6 Use the right and left cursor keys to scroll the blue line back to the beginning, if it's not there already.
7 Now play these notes, one by one, on your MIDI keyboard: C3, D3, E3, F3. It doesn't matter if you play out of time. The result should look like this.

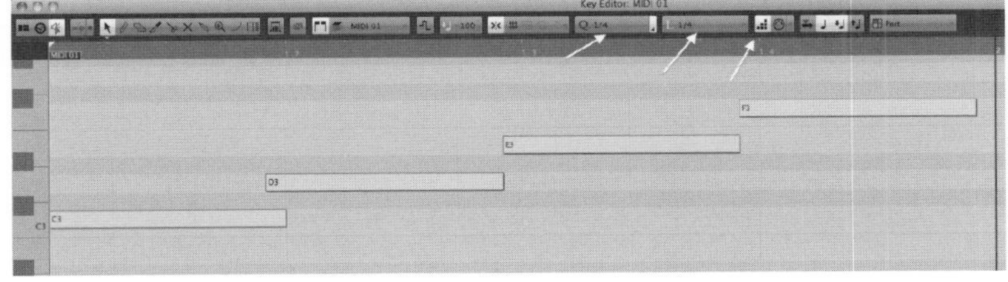

Figure 9.6
Step entered notes

8 Play the notes back.
9 On the Toolbar, select a quantize value of 1/2 Note and ensure that the Length Quantize value displays 'Quantize Link'.
10 Set the blue line to where you left off and play this chord: C3, E3, G3 (C major). The result should look like this.

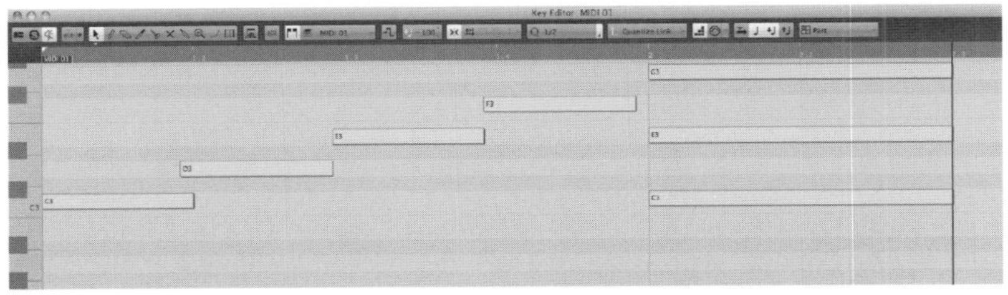

Figure 9.7
Step entered chord

11 Play the chord back.

You can step input entire piano parts this way as well as any other type of instrument. Adjust the Quantize or Length Quantize values as you go along, to change the timing and note lengths. A few more tips:

Figure 9.8

- Turn on Insert mode if you want to move all existing notes to the right, making space for newly inserted notes.
- Press the right cursor key on your computer keyboard to insert rests.
- Clicking on the Key Editor keyboard will also step input notes.

MIDI Input

To the right of the staircase icon is the MIDI Input button (MIDI plug icon). Use it as a fast and intuitive way to edit recorded notes in all the MIDI editors. Here's how it works:

1 Record a few notes on a MIDI track and open the Key Editor.
2 Click on the MIDI Input button on the toolbar – the 'MIDI plug'. Doing that activates the Record Pitch and Record NoteOn Velocity buttons, to its right.
3 Select the first note you played. Now, if you play the same note on the keyboard either harder or softer, the note's velocity will be changed to reflect this. If you play a different note, say a tone higher, the note will be transposed. You'll have noticed that each time a note is edited the cursor moves on to the next note automatically. If you're not happy with the edit, just move the cursor back and redo it.

Info

Step and MIDI Input provide a quick way of entering and editing notes in all the MIDI editors, not just the Key Editor.

The beauty of editing this way is that you can hear the notes making it easy to adjust your keyboard action accordingly.

Splitting notes

It's most likely that you use the Scissors tool to split notes. With a quantize grid value down to 1/64 it's an easy operation with Snap turned on. However, there may be times when you need even more precision. Select the note(s) and position the project cursor at the exact edit point and use Edit > Functions > Split at Cursor. Alternatively press Alt+X (on the Mac, Option+X). This method overrides the Snap value.

Another way. Set up the right and left locators at the split points and use Edit > Functions > Split Loop.

Quick tip

To split chords quickly, select all the notes first before you slice them with the Scissors tool.

Controller Lane uses

Make full use of the Controller Lane at the bottom of the Key Editor window. You can make sweeping changes to this colourful data display with just a single stroke of the Line, Parabola, Sine, Triangle, Square and Paint tools. Here are some of the most useful things you can do here.

- The Line tool can be used to create controller ramps (straight lines). In this example it is used to create a left to right pan sweep (CC 10).

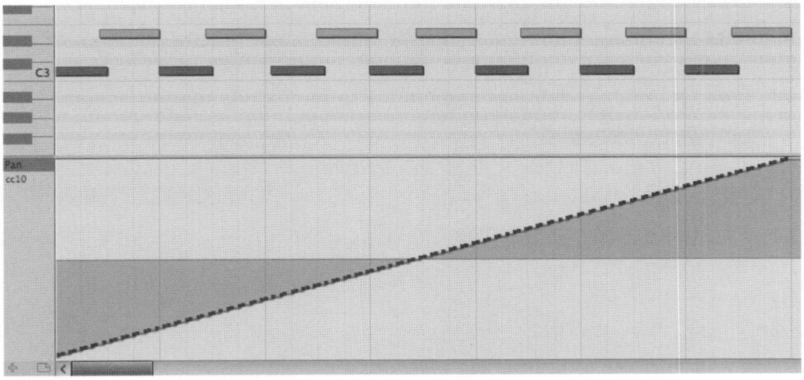

Figure 9.9
Pan sweep

- The Parabola tool can be used to draw natural shaped velocity and controller curves. In this example Breath Control (CC 2) it is employed to create a smooth ending to a long note.

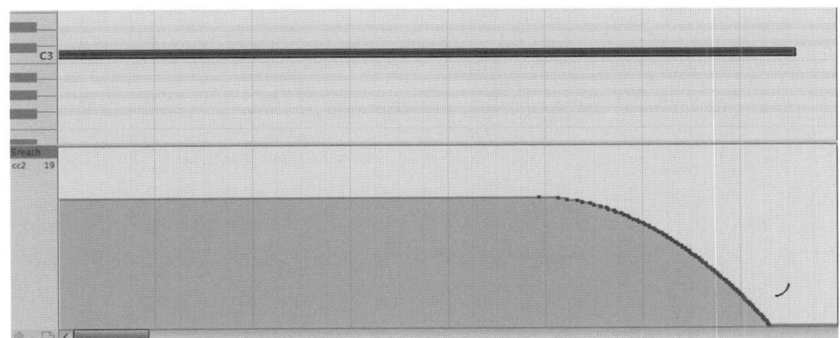

Figure 9.10
Create a smooth ending to a long note

The Sine, Triangle and Square drawing tools can be used to create continuous curves and shapes for special effects. In Figure 9.11 the Square drawing tool has been used to create continuous, alternate left and right panning.

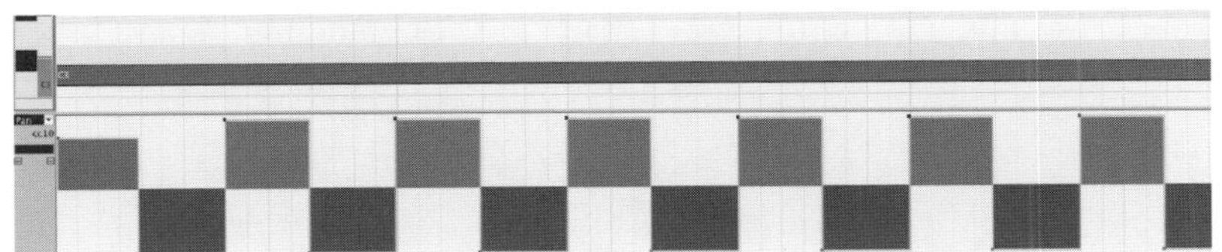

Figure 9.11
The square drawing tool used on panning

You can use the controller lane as an extra mixer. For example: imagine you've sequenced a brass section on a MIDI track. The brass section parts contain sforzando hits, notes that suddenly die and swell very quickly to a climax. That presents a potential nightmare situation when it comes to mixing with many jerky fader movements. Here's a solution?

1 Draw and adjust the individual instrument's dynamic hits and swells using Controller No. 11 - Expression (as opposed to Volume) in the Controller Lane.

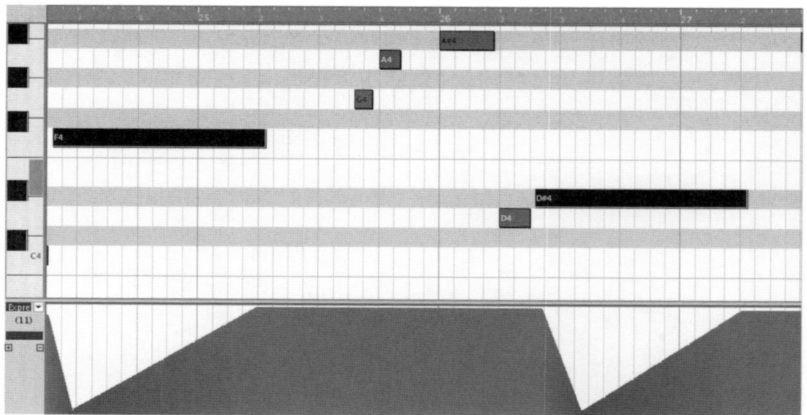
Figure 9.12
Sforzando trumpet hits drawn with MIDI CC #11, Expression.

2 Adjust the overall track volume levels, along with the other instruments, the rhythm section and so on, in the main mixer. You can also do this in the project window using the inspector or automation tracks.

Doing it this way gives you the freedom to raise or lower the brass in the mix, without upsetting the internal dynamic changes. They've all been taken care of with the expression controller. This is particularly useful if you intend to export your mix as a MIDI file, for use on another computer. Professional MIDI file programmers use volume and expression like this all the time.

If you've ever bought a professionally programmed MIDI file (not something for free, that you found on the Internet) dig it out, import it into Cubase and have a look at the data. The chances are that all the volume levels are set at 100 and the dynamic changes have been assigned to expression. This gives the end user the opportunity to alter the mix without ruining the musical content.

MIDI data scaling

To rebalance a section of music, sometimes it's desirable to scale or compress complete ranges of controller data. One way to do this is to make a selection range with the arrow tool and then use the 'smart spots' in the controller lane to manipulate the data.

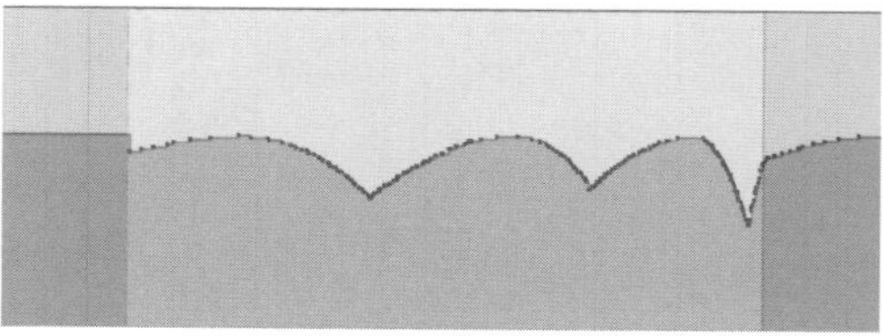
Figure 9.13

You can move data vertically…

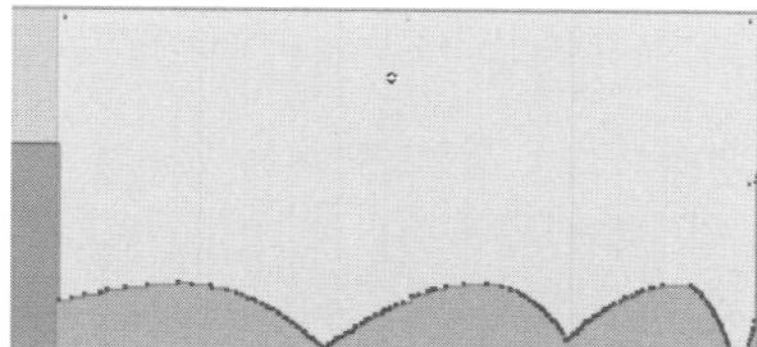
Figure 9.14
Move data vertically

You can scale data vertically...

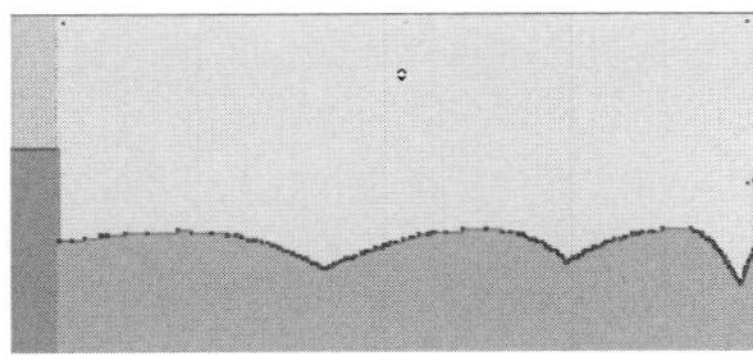

Figure 9.15
Scale data vertically

You can tilt the data right or left...

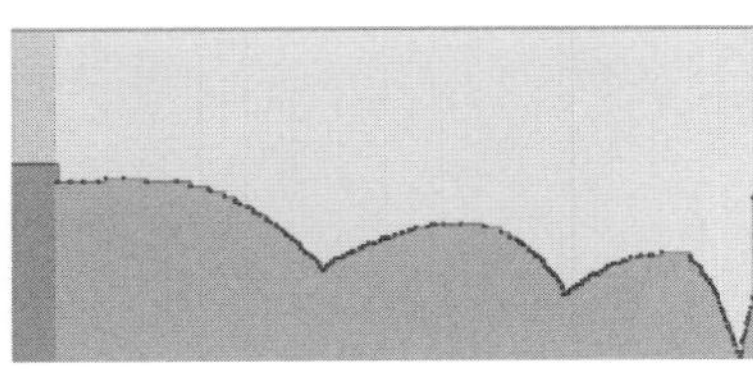

Figure 9.16
Tilt the data right or left

You can compress the data...

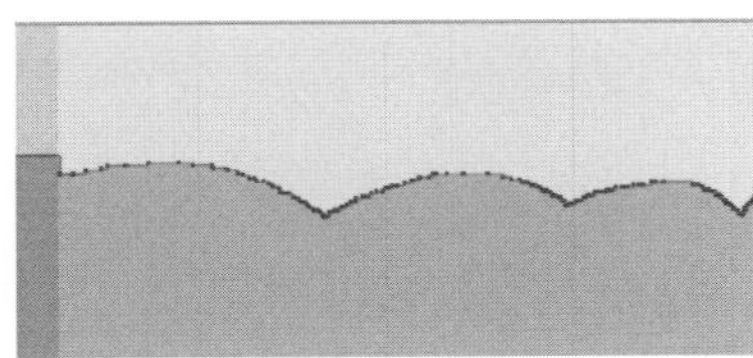

Figure 9.17
Compress the data

You can stretch the data...

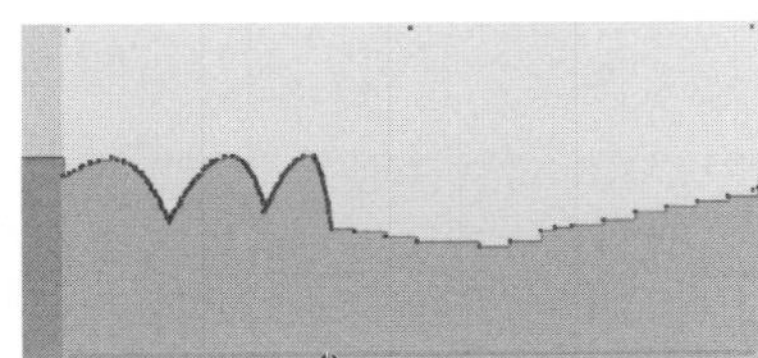

Figure 9.18
Stretch the data

Read page 395 in the Cubase 6 Operation Manual for details on which 'smart tool' to use for the above actions.

Multiple controller lanes

Need to edit more than one controller in either the Key Editor or Drum Editor at the same time? Right-click in the display area (control and click on a Mac) and select 'Create new controller lane' from the Quick menu to add more lanes.

Controller Menu Setup

If the controller you need is not on the Key Editor controller pop-up menu you can add it using the Controller Menu Setup dialogue. Choose 'Setup' from the menu – it's at the bottom. Now you can transfer items from the Hidden list (right) to the menu (left) and vice versa.

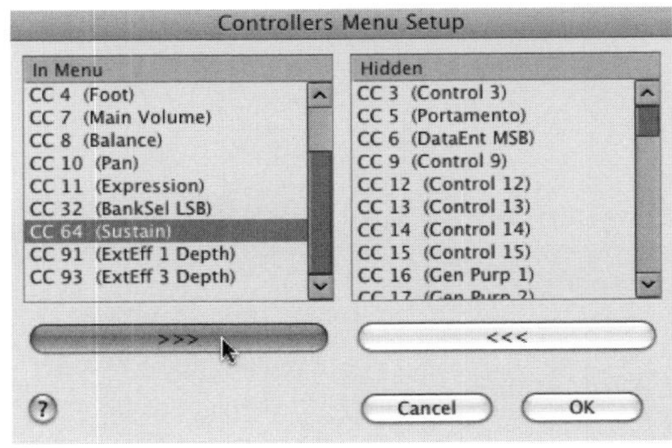

Figure 9.19
Setting up new controllers

Chord recognition

Maybe you're still developing your knowledge of music theory, in which case you'll probably find the chord recognition feature helpful. It works out chord names for you. As the song moves across a group of notes the corresponding chord name is instantly displayed in the status line, a boon for anybody preparing a guitar chord sheet. To show the status line, click the 'Set up Window Layout' button (top left corner) and tick the Status Line box.

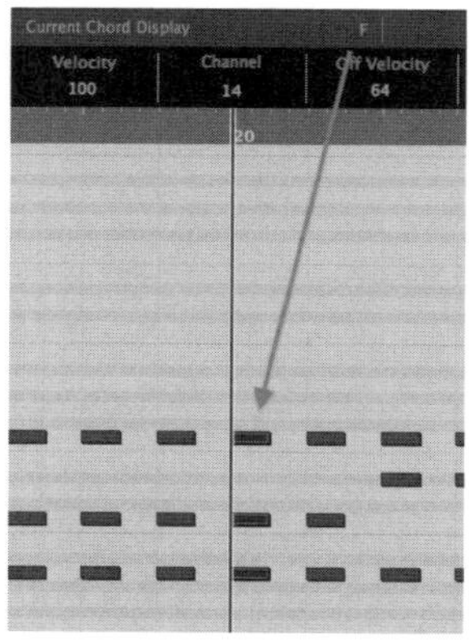

Figure 9.20
The Current Chord Display (Status Line)

Independent track looping

Click on the Independent Track Loop button (on the toolbar) and a defined loop will play independently while the rest of the project continues to play normally, in a linear fashion. Use the Key Editor's locators to define the loop, which shows mauve in the ruler.

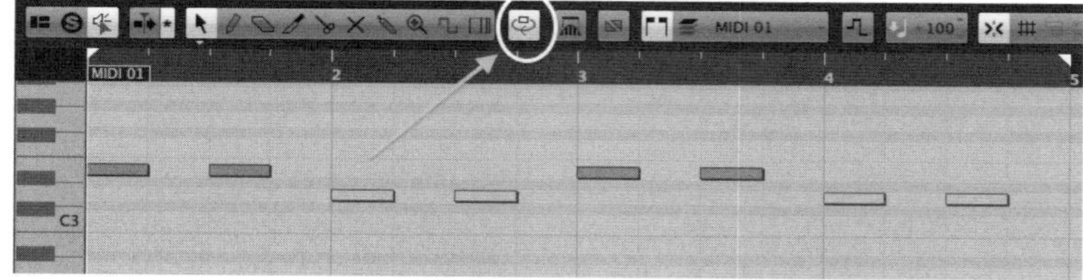

Figure 9.21
You can set up loops with the Independent Track Loop feature

Figure 9.22
The Track Loop button

Multiple Part editing

Another classic Cubase feature is the facility to combine multiple parts and edit them. Of course, you might not be able to fit them all in a single window, in which case you can select the part you want to edit from the Parts List menu (on the toolbar) (Figure 9.23).

You make a part active either by selecting it from the pop-up menu or clicking on a note with the arrow tool. This feature is also available in the List, Drum and audio editors.

Figure 9.23
Multiple parts displayed in the Key Editor. The Guitar part has been selected for editing from the Parts List menu

Part Borders

Another relatively recent feature, the 'Show Part Borders' tool is used to define the borders of an active part. When it's made active, all parts except the active one are greyed out. Two little indicators appear in the ruler, marking its beginning and end. These can be moved about, to alter the size of the actual part itself.

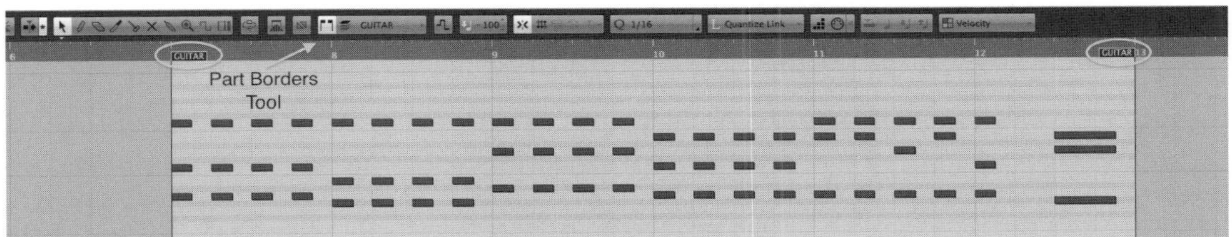

Figure 9.24
Part borders defined using the 'Show Part Borders' tool

Note Expression

MIDI is channel based and each MIDI or virtual instrument track in Cubase has a channel number. Earlier in this chapter we have seen how easy it is to edit monophonic note data such as expression and modulation in the controller lane. If the material is polyphonic, though, and contains chords, then all the notes within those chords will share the same controller data. In some cases this is perfectly okay. A virtual Hammond organ patch, for example, will sound fine because it's emulating a keyboard instrument where the individual notes of a chord, generally, do not vary in pitch or modulation. However, if the same chord is assigned to a solo trumpet sample, the result will sound unnatural because all three virtual players will be playing exactly the same way with identical playing characteristics, each one a musical clone of the other two, apart from their individual note pitches. To make them sound more realistic, you could use the Cubase Note Expression feature.

Here's a chord assigned to a HALion Sonic SE solo trumpet patch. Because all the notes are using the same MIDI channel, any used controller such as pitch bend or expression will affect all them simultaneously.

Figure 9.25

However, using VST Note Expression allows us to add subtle tuning data (VST 3 controller) to the individual notes.

Figure 9.26

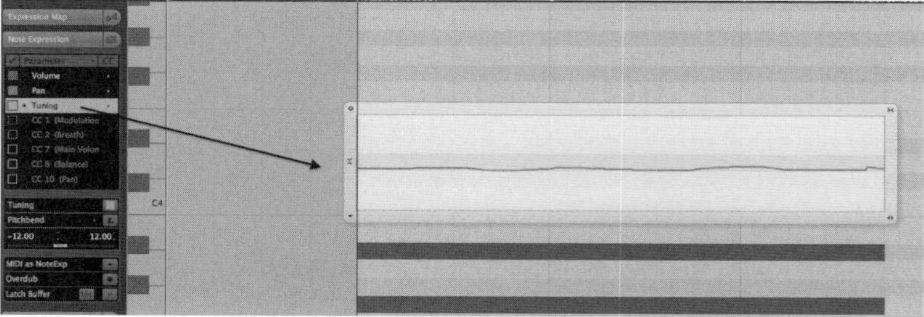

A trumpeter playing a single note over three bars is going to expel a fair amount of breath and towards the end there will be a gradual volume fade. This is also more musically expressive than just an abrupt ending. So we draw or record a fade using expression (MIDI controller cc11).

Figure 9.27

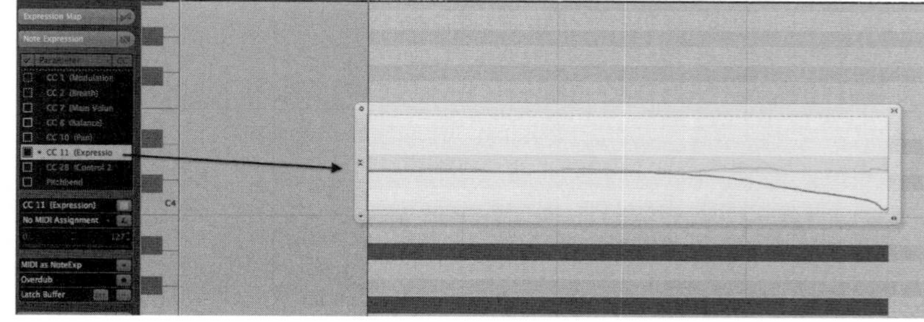

Info

Note Expression works with two types of data – VST 3 controllers and standard MIDI controllers. MIDI controllers are channel specific whereas VST 3 controllers are note specific.

By adding subtly different tuning and expression to each note in the chord the three trumpets now sound much more realistic.

Figure 9.28

Info

VST 3 controllers only work with compatible VST instruments such as HALion Sonic SE and HALion Symphonic Orchestra.

Quick tip

To see note expression data in the key editor, click the Show Note Expression Data button on the toolbar. Click the tiny arrow (to the right) and a slider appears to adjust the display size.

Info

Note Expression will not work without a controller setup in the Note Expression Inspector tab. Top down, VST 3 controllers appear at the top and MIDI controllers appear underneath.

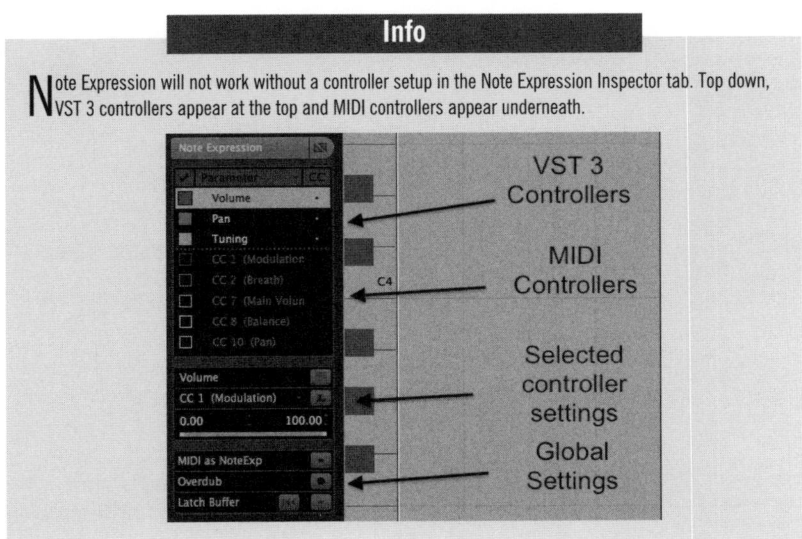

For quick editing of VST instruments in the key editor add the 'Edit VST Instrument' button to the toolbar.

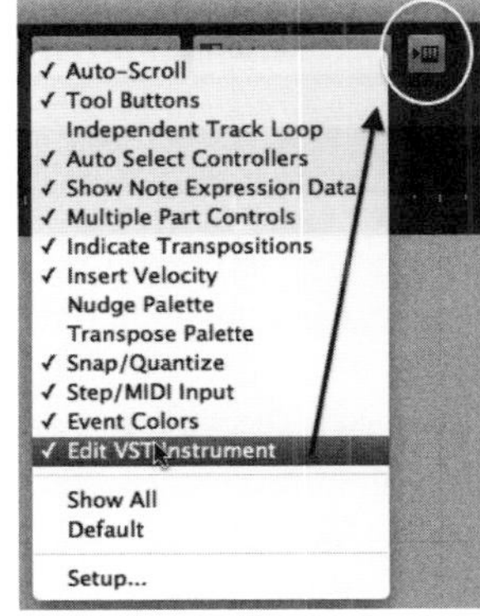

Figure 9.29
Add the 'Edit VST Instrument' button to the toolbar

VST Expression Maps

Most sample-based virtual instruments use keyswitches to change articulations. For example, an orchestral string library might use D-2 for sustained strings (bowed) and F#-2 for pizzicato (plucked). There are many more string articulations, of course, and entering and editing them in the key editor quickly becomes confusing. Cubase 6, however, simplifies the process with the help of VST Expression Maps, which map the keyswitches to named articulations, which can be viewed and edited in the controller lane and the score editor.

In Figure 9.30 the Vienna Symphonic Library strings play arco (bowed) followed by pizzicato (plucked), legato (connected bowed notes), staccato (short) and tremolo (rapid bowing).

Figure 9.30

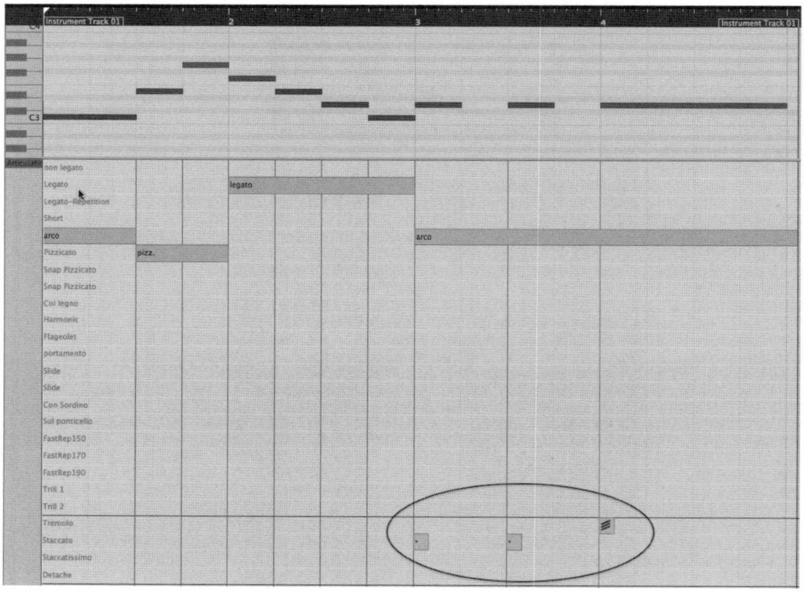

Note how the staccato and tremolo articulations appear beneath the existing arco articulation. That's because there are two distinct types of articulations:

- Directions – applied to a continuous range of notes. For example, a bowed or plucked passage of notes.
- Attributes – applied to single notes. For example, accented pizzicato notes.

This system is preferable in many ways to searching for keyed notes on the grid and has the added advantage of displaying articulations in the score editor as markings, not extra notes that have to be deleted (see VST Expression Maps in Chapter 11, Score Editor).

Info

Predefined VST expression maps are available for many of the included instruments with Cubase 6 but you can also import and convert third-party VST instrument keyswitches as well. Create a track for your instrument, open the Expression Map section in the Inspector and select Import Keyswitches. The Expression Map Setup appears complete with the imported data. You still have to define your own settings, though (page 424 in the Operation Manual), but it's a significant time-saver.

List Editor

The Filter Bar

The List Editor is the best place for detailed MIDI editing in Cubase but first-time users are sometimes put off by its apparent complexity. A lengthy string of data can appear very confusing to musicians who are primarily concerned with notes and not numbers.

To clarify things, click the Set up Window Layout button (top left-hand corner) and tick the Filters box. A filter bar appears with a row of tick boxes, each one representing a data type. Now you can make a complicated list more manageable and hide any unnecessary data from view by ticking the relevant boxes. For example, to hide all the notes in a track just tick the Note box and they will disappear.

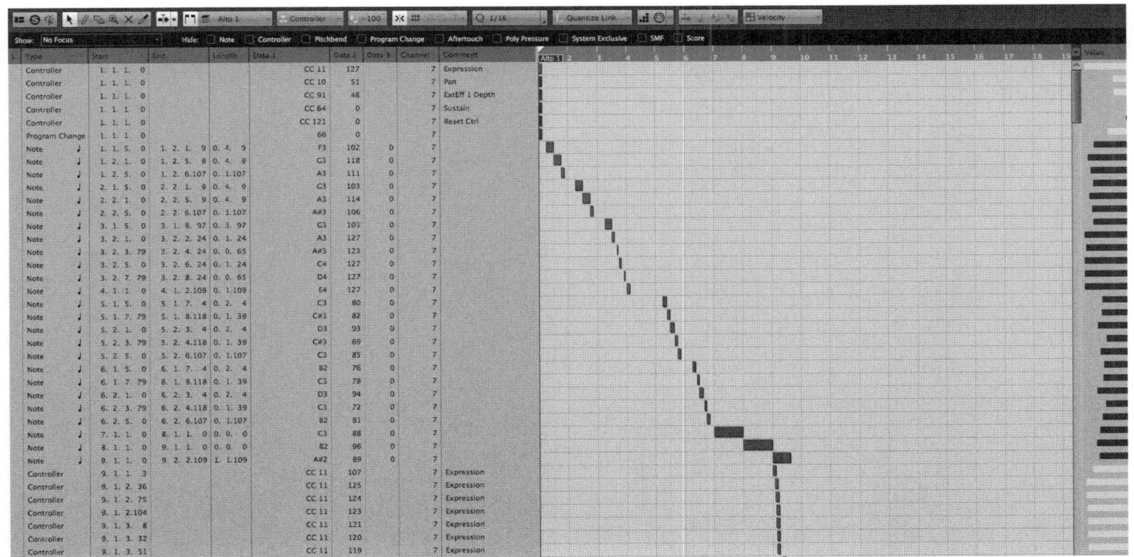

Figure 10.1
List Editor displaying Note, Program Change and Controller information

Type	Start	End	Length	Data 1	Data 2	Data 3	Channel	Comment
Note	1. 1. 5. 0	1. 2. 1. 9	0. 4. 9	F3	102	0	7	
Note	1. 2. 1. 0	1. 2. 5. 9	0. 4. 9	G3	118	0	7	
Note	1. 2. 5. 0	1. 2. 6.107	0. 1.107	A3	111	0	7	
Note	2. 1. 5. 0	2. 2. 1. 9	0. 4. 9	G3	103	0	7	
Note	2. 2. 1. 0	2. 2. 5. 9	0. 4. 9	A3	114	0	7	
Note	2. 2. 5. 0	2. 2. 6.107	0. 1.107	A#3	106	0	7	
Note	3. 1. 5. 0	3. 1. 8. 97	0. 3. 97	G3	103	0	7	
Note	3. 2. 1. 0	3. 2. 2. 24	0. 1. 24	A3	127	0	7	
Note	3. 2. 3. 79	3. 2. 4. 24	0. 0. 65	A#3	123	0	7	
Note	3. 2. 5. 0	3. 2. 6. 24	0. 1. 24	C4	127	0	7	
Note	3. 2. 7. 79	3. 2. 8. 24	0. 0. 65	D4	127	0	7	
Note	4. 1. 1. 0	4. 1. 2.109	0. 1.109	E4	127	0	7	
Note	5. 1. 5. 0	5. 1. 7. 4	0. 2. 4	C3	80	0	7	
Note	5. 1. 7. 79	5. 1. 8.118	0. 1. 39	C#3	82	0	7	
Note	5. 2. 1. 0	5. 2. 3. 4	0. 2. 4	D3	93	0	7	
Note	5. 2. 3. 79	5. 2. 4.118	0. 1. 39	C#3	69	0	7	
Note	5. 2. 5. 0	5. 2. 6.107	0. 1.107	C3	85	0	7	
Note	6. 1. 5. 0	6. 1. 7. 4	0. 2. 4	B2	76	0	7	
Note	6. 1. 7. 79	6. 1. 8.118	0. 1. 39	C3	78	0	7	
Note	6. 2. 1. 0	6. 2. 3. 4	0. 2. 4	D3	94	0	7	
Note	6. 2. 3. 79	6. 2. 4.118	0. 1. 39	C3	72	0	7	
Note	6. 2. 5. 0	6. 2. 6.107	0. 1.107	B2	81	0	7	
Note	7. 1. 1. 0	8. 1. 1. 0	0. 0. 0	C3	88	0	7	
Note	8. 1. 1. 0	9. 1. 1. 0	0. 0. 0	B2	96	0	7	
Note	9. 1. 1. 0	9. 2. 2.109	1. 1.109	A#2	89	0	7	

Figure 10.2
List Editor after Controller and Program Change data has been filtered out

Highlighting specific events

You can highlight specific events using the Show section. For example, let's say that you want to home in on all CC 11 (Expression) events in a list for

Type	Start	End	Length	Data 1	Data 2	Data 3	Channel	Comment
Controller	1. 1. 1. 0			CC 11	127		7	Expression
Controller	1. 1. 1. 0			CC 10	51		7	Pan
Controller	1. 1. 1. 0			CC 91	48		7	ExtEff 1 Depth
Controller	1. 1. 1. 0			CC 64	0		7	Sustain
Controller	1. 1. 1. 0			CC 121	0		7	Reset Ctrl
Program Change	1. 1. 1. 0			66	0		7	
Note	1. 1. 5. 0	1. 2. 1. 9	0. 4. 9	F3	102	0	7	
Note	1. 2. 1. 0	1. 2. 5. 9	0. 4. 9	G3	118	0	7	
Note	1. 2. 5. 0	1. 2. 6.107	0. 1.107	A3	111	0	7	
Note	2. 1. 5. 0	2. 2. 1. 9	0. 4. 9	G3	103	0	7	
Note	2. 2. 1. 0	2. 2. 5. 9	0. 4. 9	A3	114	0	7	
Note	2. 2. 5. 0	2. 2. 6.107	0. 1.107	A#3	106	0	7	
Note	3. 1. 5. 0	3. 1. 8. 97	0. 3. 97	G3	103	0	7	
Note	3. 2. 1. 0	3. 2. 2. 24	0. 1. 24	A3	127	0	7	
Note	3. 2. 3. 79	3. 2. 4. 24	0. 0. 65	A#3	123	0	7	
Note	3. 2. 5. 0	3. 2. 6. 24	0. 1. 24	C4	127	0	7	
Note	3. 2. 7. 79	3. 2. 8. 24	0. 0. 65	D4	127	0	7	
Note	4. 1. 1. 0	4. 1. 2.109	0. 1.109	E4	127	0	7	
Note	5. 1. 5. 0	5. 1. 7. 4	0. 2. 4	C3	80	0	7	
Note	5. 1. 7. 79	5. 1. 8.118	0. 1. 39	C#3	82	0	7	
Note	5. 2. 1. 0	5. 2. 3. 4	0. 2. 4	D3	93	0	7	
Note	5. 2. 3. 79	5. 2. 4.118	0. 1. 39	C#3	69	0	7	
Note	5. 2. 5. 0	5. 2. 6.107	0. 1.107	C3	85	0	7	
Note	6. 1. 5. 0	6. 1. 7. 4	0. 2. 4	B2	76	0	7	
Note	6. 1. 7. 79	6. 1. 8.118	0. 1. 39	C3	78	0	7	
Note	6. 2. 1. 0	6. 2. 3. 4	0. 2. 4	D3	94	0	7	
Note	6. 2. 3. 79	6. 2. 4.118	0. 1. 39	C3	72	0	7	
Note	6. 2. 5. 0	6. 2. 6.107	0. 1.107	B2	81	0	7	
Note	7. 1. 1. 0	8. 1. 1. 0	0. 0. 0	C3	88	0	7	
Note	8. 1. 1. 0	9. 1. 1. 0	0. 0. 0	B2	96	0	7	
Note	9. 1. 1. 0	9. 2. 2.109	1. 1.109	A#2	89	0	7	
Controller	9. 1. 1. 3			CC 11	107		7	Expression
Controller	9. 1. 2. 36			CC 11	125		7	Expression
Controller	9. 1. 2. 75			CC 11	124		7	Expression
Controller	9. 1. 2.104			CC 11	123		7	Expression
Controller	9. 1. 3. 8			CC 11	121		7	Expression
Controller	9. 1. 3. 32			CC 11	120		7	Expression
Controller	9. 1. 3. 51			CC 11	119		7	Expression
Controller	9. 1. 6. 61			CC 11	120		7	Expression
Controller	9. 1. 6.100			CC 11	119		7	Expression
Controller	9. 1. 6.119			CC 11	118		7	Expression
Controller	9. 1. 7. 18			CC 11	117		7	Expression
Controller	9. 1. 7. 28			CC 11	116		7	Expression
Controller	9. 1. 7. 37			CC 11	115		7	Expression
Controller	9. 1. 7. 47			CC 11	114		7	Expression
Controller	9. 1. 7. 61			CC 11	113		7	Expression

Figure 10.3
With No Focus selected in the Show menu, all events in the list

editing. You first select a single CC 11 event in the list and then select 'Event Types and Data1' from the pop-up Show menu. All events except CC 11 are then hidden from view. Various display options are possible and exactly how the Show function behaves is determined in the pop-up menu.

Type	Start	End	Length	Data 1	Data 2	Data 3	Channel	Comment
Controller	1. 1. 1. 0			CC 11	127		7	Expression
Controller	9. 1. 1. 3			CC 11	107		7	Expression
Controller	9. 1. 2. 36			CC 11	125		7	Expression
Controller	9. 1. 2. 75			CC 11	124		7	Expression
Controller	9. 1. 2.104			CC 11	123		7	Expression
Controller	9. 1. 3. 8			CC 11	121		7	Expression
Controller	9. 1. 3. 32			CC 11	120		7	Expression
Controller	9. 1. 3. 51			CC 11	119		7	Expression
Controller	9. 1. 6. 61			CC 11	120		7	Expression
Controller	9. 1. 6.100			CC 11	119		7	Expression
Controller	9. 1. 6.119			CC 11	118		7	Expression
Controller	9. 1. 7. 18			CC 11	117		7	Expression
Controller	9. 1. 7. 28			CC 11	116		7	Expression
Controller	9. 1. 7. 37			CC 11	115		7	Expression
Controller	9. 1. 7. 47			CC 11	114		7	Expression

Figure 10.4
With Event Types and Data1 selected in the Show menu, all events in the list, other than CC 11 controller events, are masked

Display format

The List Editor is a great place for detailed numerical editing and just like in the Project window, you can set the display format by right-clicking in the ruler and making a selection from the pop-up menu. Here the List Editor is displaying timecode as opposed to bars and beats.

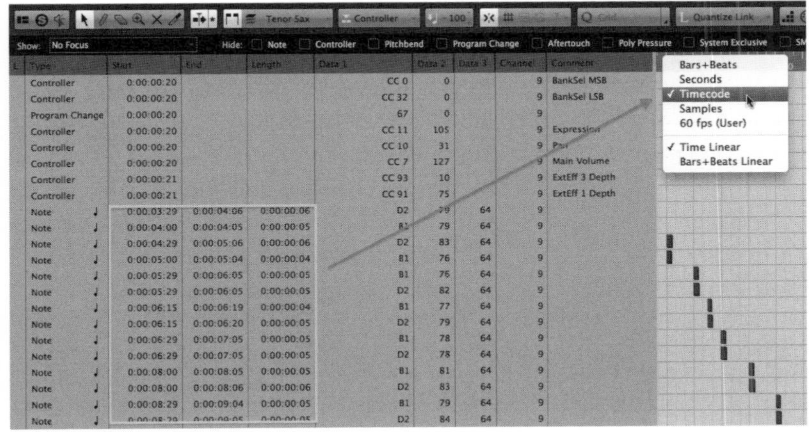

Figure 10.5
Setting the display format

Set-up bars

If you intend exporting your projects as MIDI files or working with an orchestral sample library it's a good idea to create a 'set-up' bar at the beginning of each track containing Program Change, Volume, Expression, Pan and so on. The List Editor is the ideal place to do this. Use the Insert pop-up menu to select a message type and click in the grid area with the pencil tool to insert it. Now scroll the data to the required values. Because some synths and sound modules are slower than others at reading the 'set-up' messages, set them a few ticks apart.

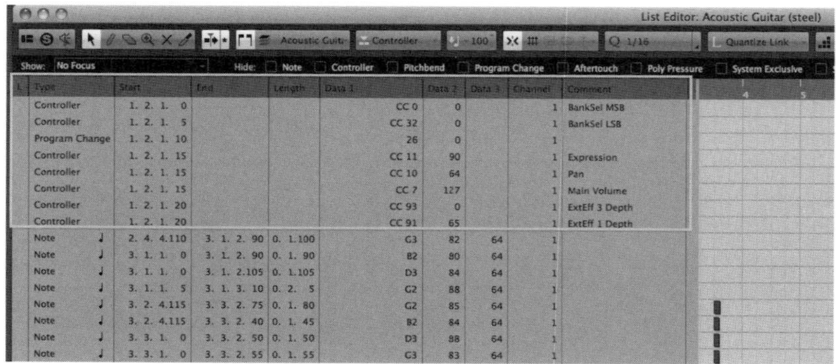

Figure 10.6
A MIDI track set-up bar

Quick tip

Instead of scrolling numerical values for individual events you might like to try altering them in the Value Display.

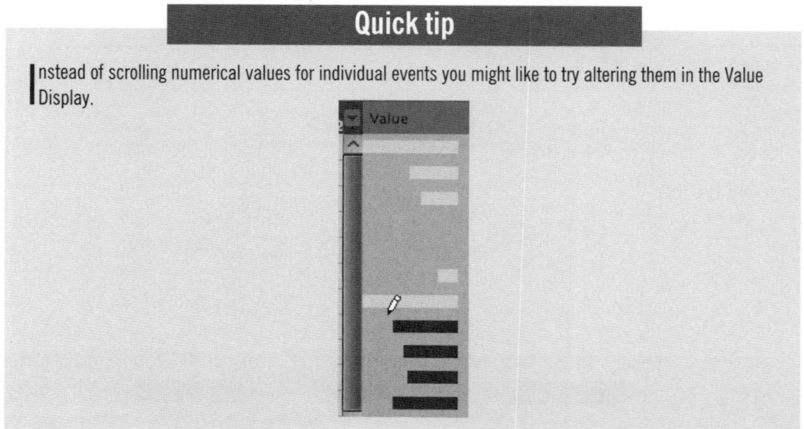

Moving data

If you need to move a whole load of data forward, maybe to make way for a 'set-up' measure, select all the data in the list and scroll only the first event. Everything else will move forward as you do so and remain in place, relative to the first event.

Info

System Exclusive messages are used to transmit information such as patch data and GM reset messages to specific instruments through MIDI. Manufacturers such as Roland and Yamaha each have their own Sys Ex identity code.

The System Exclusive Editor

System Exclusive events are only partly displayed in the list editor and you cannot carry out any editing apart from moving their position. However, you can edit them proper by clicking in the Comments column to reveal the System Exclusive Editor.

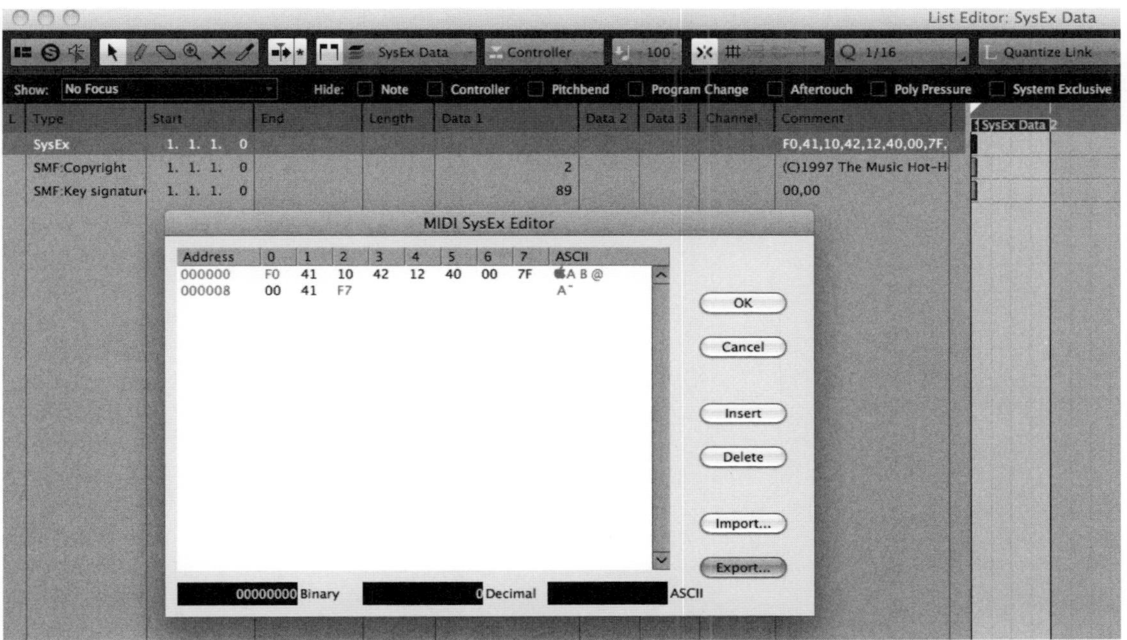

Figure 10.7
Click in the Comments column to open the System Exclusive Editor

Score Editor

Many people give the Score Editor a wide berth, because they don't read music. That's fine, of course, because the entire MIDI editing in a project can be done in the Key, List and Drum Editors, without ever opening the Score Editor. However, if you're a musician who reads the dots you'll very likely feel more comfortable working in the Score Editor. For you, reading notes on the staff will probably be easier than reading events on a piano roll grid.

Even if you don't read music very well, the Score Editor can be very useful. For example: you've recorded a MIDI brass or string part but it doesn't sound very realistic. You may decide to have a friend play the part for real and record their performance on an audio track. How, though, do you tell them what to play? Of course, you can always play the MIDI part over and over and have them learn it by ear. A much quicker way would be to give them the music to read. After all, it's all there in the Score Editor, ready to be printed out. Even so, you can't just open the Score Editor and press the 'print' button for the best results. You might need a few tips.

Page v Edit mode

Once you've opened the Score Editor you can toggle the display between Page and Edit mode (Score > Edit/Page). So which one do you use? If you're editing the MIDI data, as an alternative to the key editor, use the Edit mode. The score scrolls according to the project cursor and the music is more widely spaced and easier to edit.

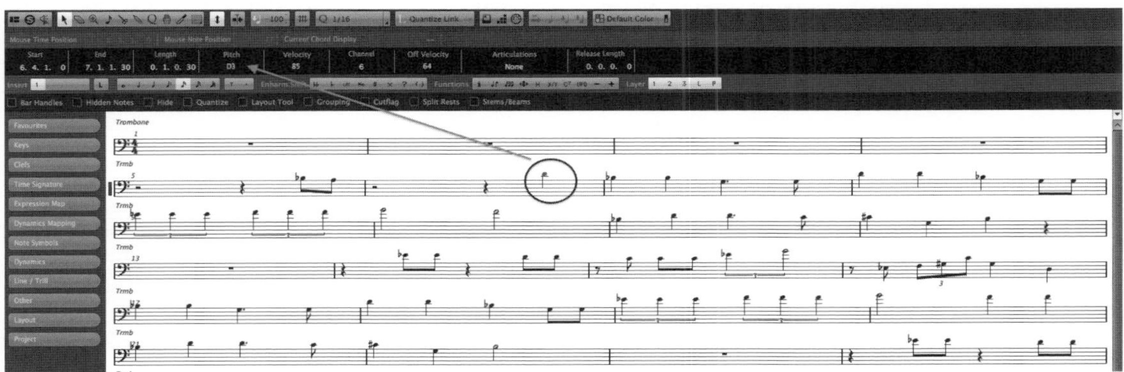

Figure 11.1
Score Editor in Edit mode

If you're preparing a score for printing use the Page mode. You can do everything here that you can do in Edit mode but you also gain access to the special layout tools. Also, the screen now represents a page of manuscript paper, complete with horizontal and vertical rulers, like in a desktop publishing program.

Figure 11.2
Score Editor in Page mode

Info

The Score Editor section of Cubase varies considerably between Cubase 6 and Cubase Artist or Cubase Elements. Both of the latter versions are limited in their layout and printing facilities. For serious layout and printing you'll need the full Cubase 6 version.

Pre edit backup

When you're preparing a score for printing, just altering the display parameters is not always enough to achieve a coherent score. Sometimes you'll have to go a stage further and alter the actual lengths and positions of the notes themselves. Of course, doing this will destroy the playback of your music. To avoid this happening, before you do any layout work in the Score Editor, always make a second copy to work on. That way your original score remains intact and plays back correctly.

Score settings

It's important to understand the relationship between the Score Editor and the rest of the program. You can't display the notes of recorded audio data in the Score Editor, just recorded MIDI data. It's displayed as conventional music notation, according to the settings you make.

Before editing, every note you record as MIDI data is faithfully displayed in the Score Editor exactly as you played it. For example four bars of Jingle Bells recorded in Cubase might look like this.

Figure 11.3
Jingle Bells before Staff Settings applied

As notation the MIDI data looks wrong but if you were to play it through it would probably sound fine. However, to get it to display correctly as well, you would have to change a few settings in the Score Settings (Staff page). The MIDI data itself doesn't change, just the interpretation.

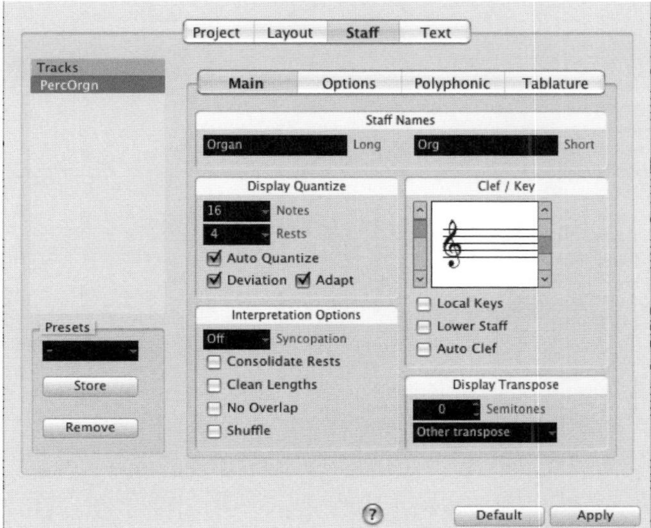

Figure 11.5
The first step to a clean score – the Staff Settings

Figure 11.6
Jingle Bells after Staff Settings applied

Score cleanup

Cubase does a reasonably good job of interpreting MIDI data straight away but in most cases it needs a little help from you. You can clean up your scores quickly by telling Cubase how you want things displayed using the Score Settings (Staff Settings page). Work through each staff in turn, giving each one its own settings.

After selecting a staff, begin the cleanup in the Display Quantize section. If the smallest note recorded on this track was a 1/16-note, choose that value in the Note pop-up field. If the smallest note recorded on this track was a 1/8-note, choose that value in the Note pop-up field. To avoid having unnecessary rests all over the place, the best value to enter in the Rest field is usually 4. A setting that works well with most music is 'Note 1/16 and Rest 4'. Of course, if the music contains triplets use the values with the T appendage, 1/8T, 1/16T and so on.

If the music contains a mixture of triplets and straight note values tick the Auto Quantize box. If not leave it blanked out. Two further boxes, Deviation and Adapt, only appear when the Auto Quantize box is ticked and help further with the cleaning up of freely played notes that are not dead on the beat.

Next, move to the Interpretation Options section. If you played chords they'll probably have different note lengths (it's unlikely that all your fingers left the keyboard at precisely the same time) and ticking the Clean Lengths box will display them properly (Figures 11.7 and 11.8).

Figure 11.7
Chords before Clean Lengths applied

Figure 11.8
Chords after Clean Lengths applied

When you play legato phrases on a keyboard (flowing string lines for example) overlapping notes are inevitable and the result is a messy score display. You can clean these up by ticking the No Overlap box (Figures 11.9 and 11.10).

Figure 11.9
Overlapping notes

Figure 11.10
Overlaps cleaned up with 'No Overlap' ticked in the Staff Settings

If you played something jazzy, with a swing feel, some of the notes will probably lie across the beat. This is called syncopation. Cubase displays syncopated notes logically with ties across the beat unless you tell it to do otherwise. To make them easier to read, turn on the Syncopation box (Full or Relax options).

Figure 11.11
Syncopated notes

Figure 11.12
Syncopated notes after 'Syncopation' is turned on in the Staff Settings

Jazz quavers

Jazz music is written one way – straight, with even eighth notes – and played another – swingy, with a triplet feel. Of course, Cubase is utterly logical in its interpretation and displays triplets until you tell it otherwise. Tick the Shuffle box, in the Staff Settings, to display the triplets as ordinary eighth notes, which are much easier to read. All you have to do now is instruct the player to reinterpret them with a swing feel.

Display Quantize tool

Eventually, you'll probably meet a group of notes that will refuse to cooperate with the display settings you've made. However, you can force the issue by using the Display Quantize tool. Select it and up pops the Display Quantize box. Enter the required settings and with the Quantize tool click on the score at the exact spot that the rogue notes begin. Use the mouse position display for pin-point accuracy.

Sometimes even the Display Quantize tool will fail to deal with a particularly awkward group of notes. In that case you'll have to change the notes themselves. Of course, this will alter the playback so make a backup first.

Figure 11.13
Use the Display Quantize tool to force notes to obey the rules

Quick tip

If you use the Score Editor for most of your editing you might like to make it your default editor. Use the Default Edit Action pop-up menu in the Preferences section (Event Display > MIDI).

Score Event Layers

It sometimes happens: you open the Score Editor and all you can see are the note stems and beams. Everything else is has been greyed out. What do you do? Open the Tool strip and turn on one or all the layers. There are three layers and which score attributes are assigned to which layer can be set using Scores > Event Layer in the Preferences section.

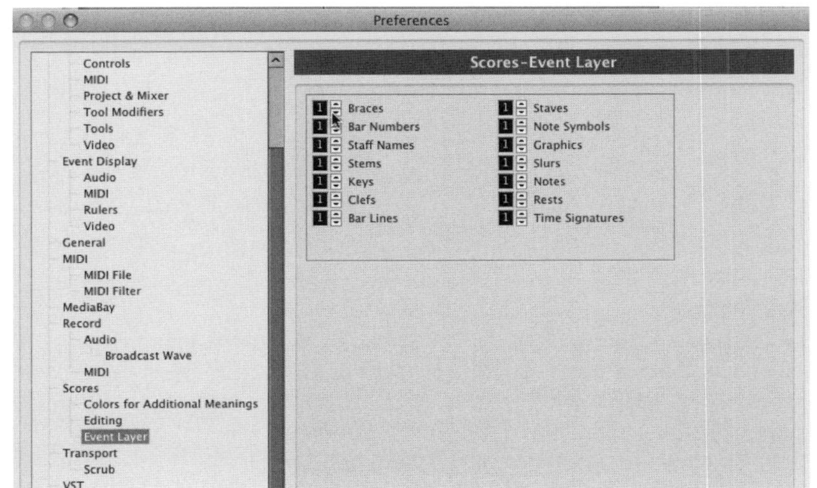

Figure 11.14
Score attributes can be assigned to one of three different layers

Quick tip

It can be very annoying when you're transposing a note and it suddenly jumps on to the staff above or below. To stop this behaviour, turn on the Lock symbol (L). You can also lock layers this way (L–layer buttons).

Selecting staves and notes

If you're working on a score with several instruments you can jump from staff to staff by using the up and down arrow keys on your keypad. The left and right arrows can then be used to scroll to the notes you want to edit.

Selecting chords

You might want to select a group of notes on the same stem (a chord), perhaps to lengthen them all together. Select the bottom note, hold down Shift and use the right arrow key to cursor up. Alternatively, select the top note, hold Shift and use the left arrow key to cursor down. Once selected change their lengths in the info line.

Quick clicks and tips

- You can enter key changes on more than one staff at a time. Hold down the Alt key (on the Mac, Option) while you enter the key change with the pencil tool.
- You can move notes sideways without altering their pitch. Hold down Ctrl (on the Mac, Command) as you do so.
- Double click on a note to open the Set Note Info box. You can use this to change note-heads, set tablature, change stem directions and hide stems. The box floats while you work your way around the score.
- Double click in the white area, to the left of a staff, to open the Staff Settings box.

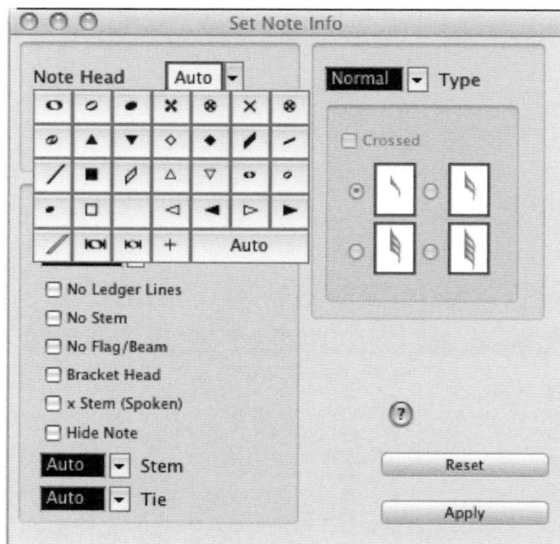

Figure 11.15
You can change note heads and stems using the Set Note Info box

Staff indent

Having the first staff of a music part indented a little to the right looks stylish. Select the first bar line, press Shift, and drag it with the Arrow tool (Figure 11.16). Of course, other measures can also be moved this way. Remember though, it's a layout feature and only works in Page Mode.

Staff split points

If you've recorded a piano part on a single track, all the notes will be displayed on a single staff, which is not what you want when it's printed out. To overcome this problem you need to create a split point. Open the Staff Settings box and select 'Split' in the Staff Mode pop-up (Polyphonic section) and choose a value in the Splitpoint field. The split point is set to a default

Figure 11.16
It's stylish to indent the first staff of a musician's part

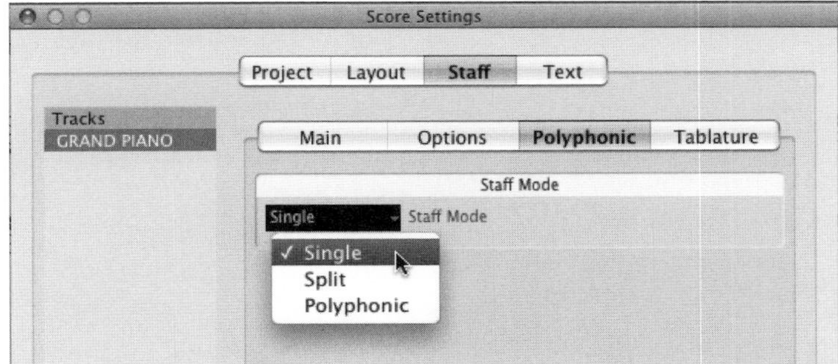

Figure 11.17
Creating a staff split-point

value of C3, (okay in many cases) but you might have to experiment with other values to get things looking correct.

Transposing instruments

For many instruments, just printing out parts in the written key will not do. For example, you sequence a part for the alto saxophone in the key of C, print it out and give it to a real saxophone player to perform. He'll probably take a quick look at it, hand it back and ask for it to be transposed. That's because when you play middle C on the piano an alto saxophone plays the A above middle C. The alto saxophone is a transposing instrument and is pitched in Eb (Eb on the piano is C on the alto saxophone). Now, if this seems too complicated, it's not a problem because Cubase works out the transposition for you.

If you have a part that is to be printed out for a transposing instrument like the trumpet or alto saxophone, open the Staff Settings box and choose the instrument in the Display Transpose pop-up. Press 'Apply' and the score will be instantly transposed, complete with a new key signature. The degree of transposition is shown just above, as semitones.

Speedy note entry

If you enter notes manually onto the score, using a mouse, you'll know that selecting a quantize value helps position the notes correctly on the screen. You'll also know that frequently changing the quantize value is a bit of a pain in the butt. It's faster and easier if you assign a key command to each value. Go to the Key Commands dialogue on the File menu and set them up in the MIDI Quantize folder.

Guitar Tablature display

If you've sequenced a part for guitar but the guitarist doesn't read music, you can convert the staff to guitar tablature. Open the Staff Settings and select Tablature. Select 'Guitar' in the Instrument pop-up and tick the Tablature Mode box and click 'Apply' for instant tablature.

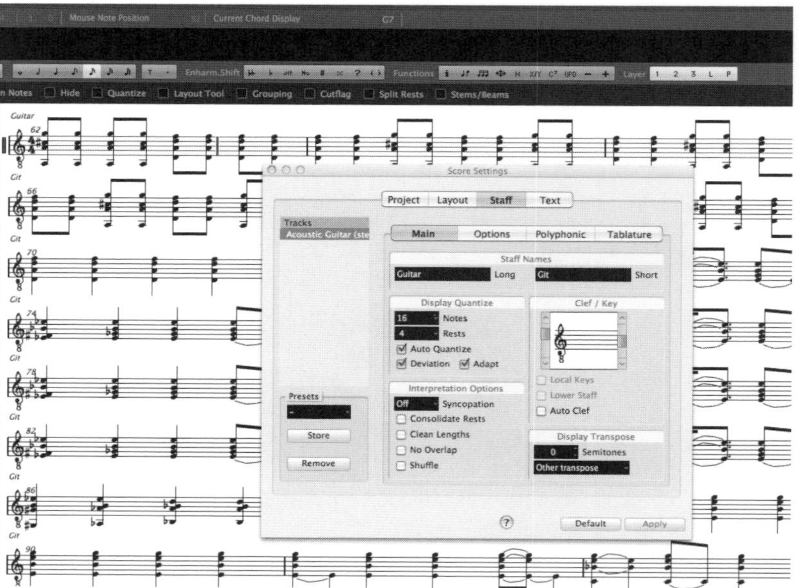

Figure 11.18
Guitar part

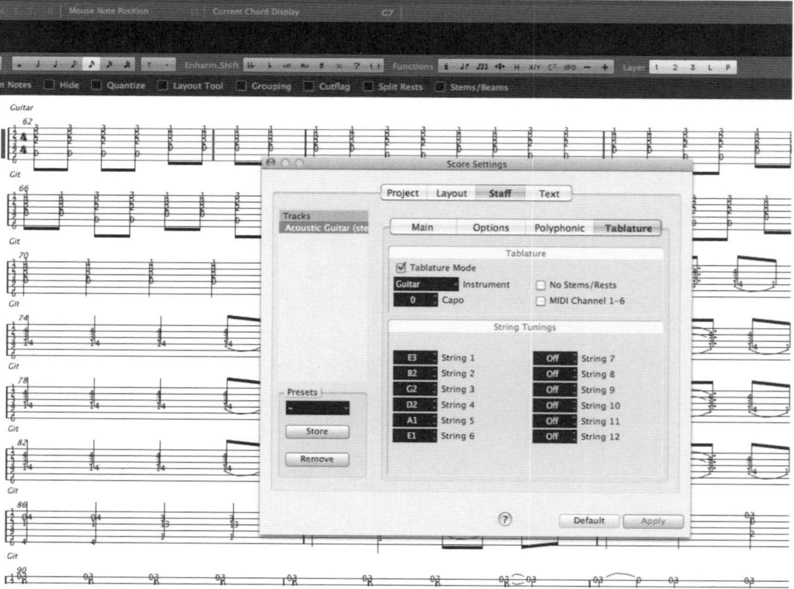

Figure 11.19
Guitar part displayed as tablature

VST Expression Maps

A new feature has been added to the score editor in Cubase 6, the Expression Map tab. As long as you have set up a VST Expression map for a particular virtual instrument, you can enter the articulations directly into your score (page 422 in the Operation Manual). These articulations (separate from regular score articulations and markings) correspond to sample library keyswitches, which previously used to show up as unwanted notes in the score editor. They can also be seen and edited in the key editor control lane (see VST Expression Maps in Chapter 9, Key Editor).

Quick tip

To colour your expression map symbols use the Score–Colors for Additional Meanings in the Preferences dialogue. This way you can easily distinguish them from ordinary score symbols.

Quick tip

For more Score tips and tricks, open page 689 in the Cubase 6 Operation Manual.

Drum tracks

Drum Editor v Key Editor

After recording drums on a MIDI or Instrument track you'll most likely want to edit them. You could use the Key Editor but finding individual drum sounds might prove confusing unless you can remember the exact key mapping. A better way is to use the Drum Editor where all the drums are individually listed in a column and the beats are displayed on a grid. It works in much the same way as the Key Editor but has been optimized for drums. For example, apart from the usual facility to solo the track there's an extra button (Solo Instrument) for soloing individual drum sounds.

Quick tip

When cycle recording drum tracks it's usually best to choose Mix as the MIDI Cycle Record Mode on the Transport panel.

Defining drum tracks

We used to have dedicated drum tracks in previous versions of Cubase and pressing Ctrl+D on the keyboard used to open the Drum Editor. Not anymore. There isn't a keystroke command for accessing the Drum Editor from within the project window at all but if a Drum Map has been selected in the Inspector, pressing Ctrl+E (on the Mac, Command+E) will open it, instead of the usual Key Editor.

Figure 12.1
Drum map selected

Understanding drum mapping

If 'No Drum Map' is selected in the Drum Editor, only three columns are displayed - Pitch, Instrument and Quantize.

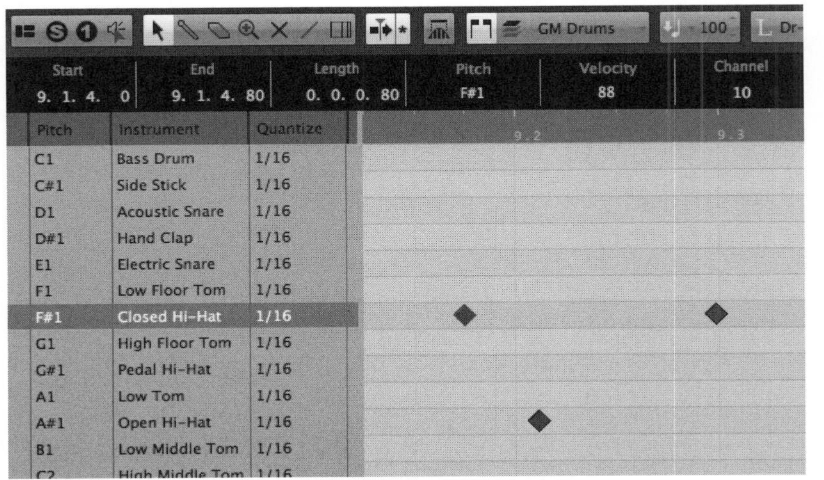

Figure 12.2
Only three columns are shown in the Drum Editor if 'No Drum Map' is selected in the Inspector

Quick tip

You can audition drum sounds by clicking in the far left column of the Drum Editor.

Pitch	Instrument	Quantize	Mute	I-Note	O-Note	Chann	Output
C1	Bass Drum	1/16		C1	C1	10	Track
C#1	Side Stick	1/16		C#1	C#1	10	Track
D1	Acoustic Snare	1/16		D1	D1	10	Track
D#1	Hand Clap	1/16		D#1	D#1	10	Track
E1	Electric Snare	1/16		E1	E1	10	Track
F1	Low Floor Tom	1/16		F1	F1	10	Track
F#1	Closed Hi-Hat	1/16		F#1	F#1	10	Track
G1	High Floor Tom	1/16		G1	G1	10	Track
G#1	Pedal Hi-Hat	1/16		G#1	G#1	10	Track
A1	Low Tom	1/16		A1	A1	10	Track
A#1	Open Hi-Hat	1/16		A#1	A#1	10	Track
B1	Low Middle Tom	1/16		B1	B1	10	Track
C2	High Middle Tom	1/16		C2	C2	10	Track
C#2	Crash Cymbal 1	1/16		C#2	C#2	10	Track

Figure 12.3
Seven columns are displayed in the Drum Editor with a Drum Map selected

These days most drum programming software, such as Cubase's own Groove Agent ONE, includes a GM sound set. The basic GM drum sounds, shown by default in the Instrument column, are all that many people ever need to write and edit drum parts. If on the other hand you are using an older synthesizer or a dedicated drum machine then you'll probably need to get to grips with the Drum Map.

A good way to get started with drum maps is to load a project and view the drums in the Drum Editor using a GM Map. Select the GM map from the pop-up, in the lower left corner of the Drum Editor.

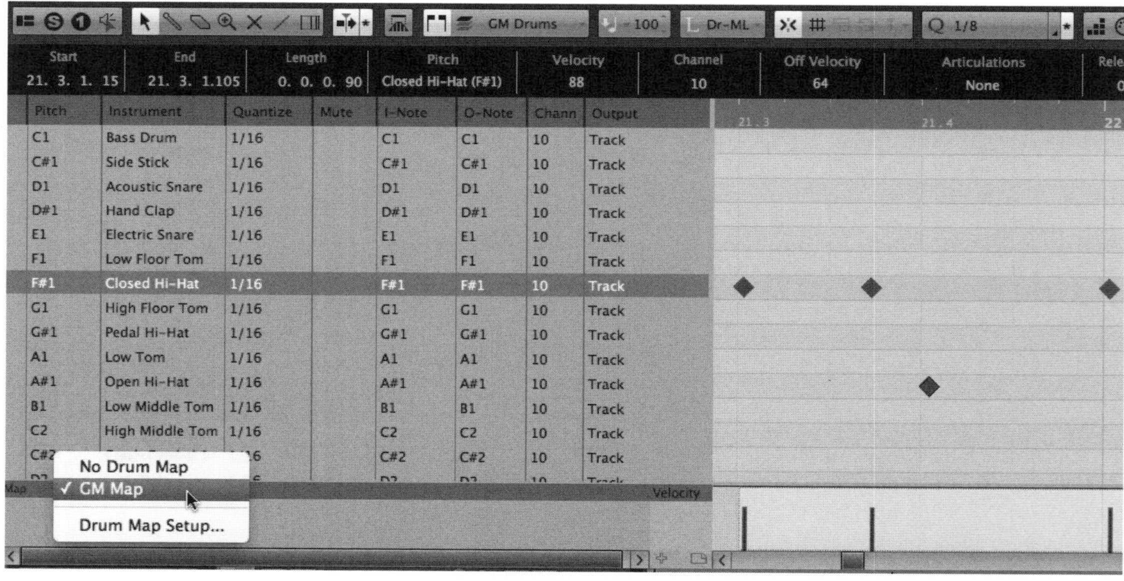

Figure 12.4
GM Drum map selected in the Drum Editor

Here's a quick run down of the column parameters and what they do:

- Pitch - A note number links notes on a MIDI track to drum sounds. In the GM Map C1 is mapped to a Bass Drum, D1 is mapped to an Acoustic Snare and so on).
- Instrument - The name of the drum.
- Quantize - This value is used when entering notes on the grid. You can use different values for different drums.
- Mute - Mutes a drum.
- I-note - The actual note you either play or enter with the Drumstick tool (the input note).
- O-note - The actual note (drum) that's played back after mapping (the output note).
- Channel - The drum is played back on this MIDI channel.
- Output - The drum is played back on this MIDI output.

As far as mapping drums is concerned, the two most important parameters in the list are the I-notes and the O-notes. In the standard GM Drum Map they are all the same – play C1 on a MIDI keyboard (the I-note) and you hear a bass drum, C1 (the O-note). Now suppose you had to play the bass drum (C1), various bongos (C3 - E3) and claves (D#4), on a Latin style track. You would find it a bit of a stretch to say the least, especially if you're no great shakes on the piano keyboard. There is a way round the problem though. Map the Latin instruments close to the bass drum by typing in new I-notes. Now everything will be 'under the fingers' and much easier to play.

Drum maps are also useful if you use a drum machine. Let's say that you've created a drum track for a rock song using GM sounds as a guide and you decide to play them back using your drum machine. To hear the correct sounds, you'll probably need a drum map.

Quick tip

You can change the order of the columns in the Drum Editor by dragging their headings.

Creating drum maps

Creating drum maps is done in the Drum Map Setup (use the MIDI or pop-up menu to open it). It's a replica of the Drum Editor sound list and you can still audition the sounds by clicking in the far left column. All you have to do

Figure 12.5
You can create drum maps in the Drum Map Setup

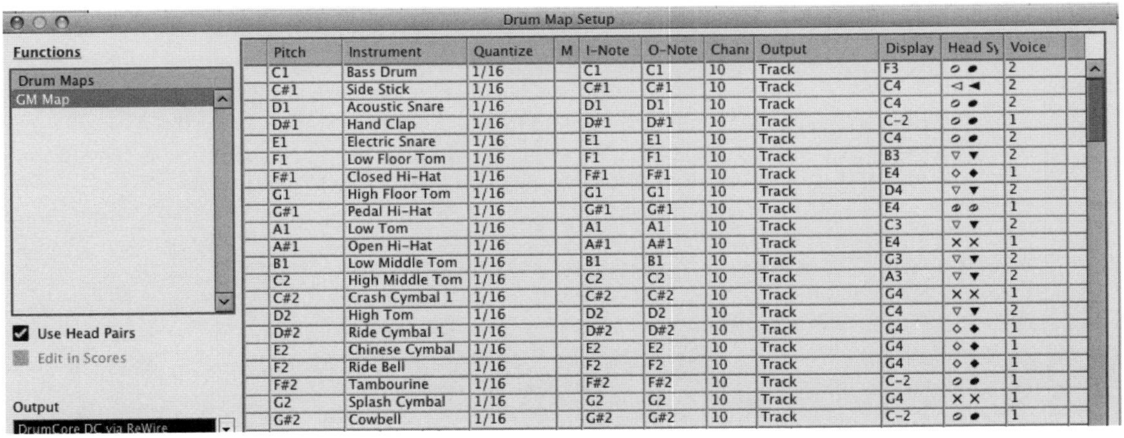

Drum Map Setup

Functions

Drum Maps
GM Map

Use Head Pairs
Edit in Scores

Output
DrumCore DC via ReWire

Pitch	Instrument	Quantize	M	I-Note	O-Note	Chan	Output	Display	Head Sy	Voice
C1	Bass Drum	1/16		C1	C1	10	Track	F3	○ ●	2
C#1	Side Stick	1/16		C#1	C#1	10	Track	C4	◁ ◀	2
D1	Acoustic Snare	1/16		D1	D1	10	Track	C4	○ ●	2
D#1	Hand Clap	1/16		D#1	D#1	10	Track	C-2	○ ●	1
E1	Electric Snare	1/16		E1	E1	10	Track	C4	○ ●	2
F1	Low Floor Tom	1/16		F1	F1	10	Track	B3	▽ ▼	2
F#1	Closed Hi-Hat	1/16		F#1	F#1	10	Track	E4	◇ ◆	1
G1	High Floor Tom	1/16		G1	G1	10	Track	D4	▽ ▼	2
G#1	Pedal Hi-Hat	1/16		G#1	G#1	10	Track	E4	[illegible]	1
A1	Low Tom	1/16		A1	A1	10	Track	C3	▽ ▼	2
A#1	Open Hi-Hat	1/16		A#1	A#1	10	Track	E4	× ×	1
B1	Low Middle Tom	1/16		B1	B1	10	Track	G3	▽ ▼	2
C2	High Middle Tom	1/16		C2	C2	10	Track	A3	▽ ▼	2
C#2	Crash Cymbal 1	1/16		C#2	C#2	10	Track	G4	× ×	1
D2	High Tom	1/16		D2	D2	10	Track	C4	▽ ▼	2
D#2	Ride Cymbal 1	1/16		D#2	D#2	10	Track	G4	◇ ◆	1
E2	Chinese Cymbal	1/16		E2	E2	10	Track	G4	◇ ◆	1
F2	Ride Bell	1/16		F2	F2	10	Track	G4	◇ ◆	1
F#2	Tambourine	1/16		F#2	F#2	10	Track	C-2	○ ●	1
G2	Splash Cymbal	1/16		G2	G2	10	Track	G4	× ×	1
G#2	Cowbell	1/16		G#2	G#2	10	Track	C-2	○ ●	1

is change the I-notes and O-notes to match those of your own instrument, type in suitable names and press the Assign button. You can also save the newly created map here, for future use.

Quick tip

Have a browse about on the Internet - you may find that somebody has already made a drum map for your particular bit of kit.

Exporting MIDI drum tracks

If you have constructed a drum track using a mapped kit and you intend to export it as a MIDI file, for use on another computer or another DAW, use the O-note Conversion function found in the MIDI menu. Cubase scans the selected MIDI part(s) and sets the pitch of all the notes to their O-note settings.

Output mapping

You're not restricted to using just one instrument in a drum map. For example, if you particularly like the sound of a bass drum in a GM kit and the sound of a snare on your favourite drum machine, you can use them both together. Just change the names in the Output column to the names of those instruments.

Quick tip

To select the same MIDI channel or Output for all sounds in a drum map press Ctrl (on a Mac, Command) as you make your selection.

Resorting the drum instrument list

Okay, you've mapped the I-notes and O-notes of your instruments and everything is now easy to play and 'under the fingers' but the editing side of things remains difficult due to the wide spread of instrument sounds in the list. This can be easily rectified – just drag the Instruments up and down to where you want them, as you do the tracks in the project window.

Info

The number of columns displayed in the Drum Editor depends on whether a drum map has been selected or not.

Drumstick tool

A glance at the Drum Editor toolbar shows a slightly different set of tools to those found in the other editors. For a start there's no Pencil tool. It's been replaced with the Drumstick tool, which is used to enter the drumbeats. It also serves as a quick eraser, handy for deleting individual events on the grid; just click on an existing beat and it disappears. If you need to delete several events at once then you'll have to resort to the usual methods, selecting events and either pressing the backspace key on your computer or using the erase tool. There are no Scissors or Glue Tube tools in the Drum Editor either, because we don't need them – think about it...

Cymbal crashes (why you can't alter their note lengths)

Some people are baffled by the diamond symbols, which are used to display the note positions on the grid; they wonder why they can't alter the note lengths, particularly when they represent a cymbal crash. The answer is simple; drum sounds are usually single-hit samples. A snare hit will be short and depending on how it was recorded, may include some reverb. The same goes for bass drum hits. Cymbals, of course, last longer, but they are still represented on the grid as a single hit. Only their starting point, in time, is shown on the grid. The length of the sample itself will determine their decay time.

Selecting beats

Selecting beats is easy and quick when you use the computer keyboard. Here are a few tips:

- Use the right and left cursor keys to move from event to event.
- Hold down the shift key and use the right and left cursor keys to select a group of events.
- Use the up and down cursor keys to transpose selected beats up or down the grid. Hold down shift at the same time and they will move them 12 places on the grid (an octave).
- Press Shift and double click a beat to select all the following beats using the same sound.

Drum Solo Button

If you want to hear the drums in isolation use the Solo button in the usual way. However, you might want to hear an individual drum sound on its own. To do this, select the drum sound and then press the Solo Instrument button on the toolbar (presumably it's meant to be a capital I, but it looks more like a figure 1). All the other drum sounds will be muted.

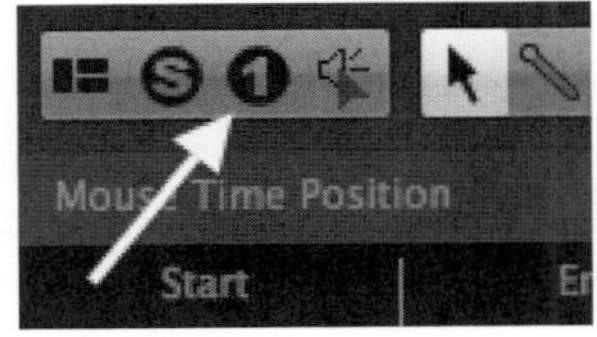

Figure 12.6
Drum solo button

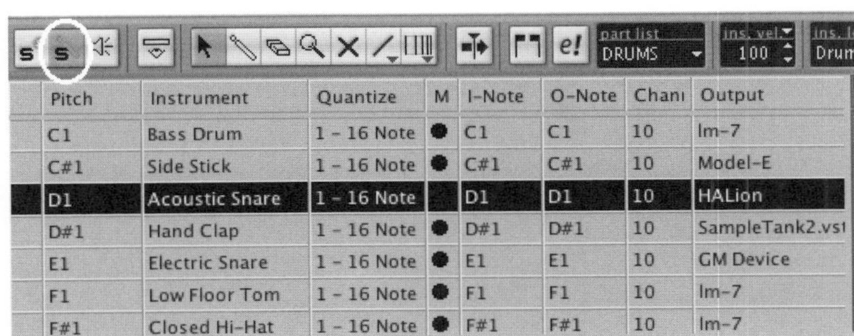

Figure 12.7
Auditioning an individual drum

Speedy beat entry

Forget the mouse, here is a quick way to enter beats on the grid. Let's say you want a bass drum sounding on the first and third beats of the bar (in 4/4 time). If you're using a GM Drum Map:

1. Enter a beat on the top line of the grid (C1 Bass Drum).
2. Set the value in the Quantize column to 1/4.
3. With the beat selected, press Ctrl+D (on the Mac, Command+D) in rapid succession to duplicate it.

Of course, you can select whole groups of beats and duplicate them this way. Another fast way to do the same thing – use Step Input:

1. Set the value in the Global Quantize box to 1/4.
2. Activate the Step Input (Press the 'staircase' icon).
3. Use your MIDI controller to enter the beats.

Recording realistic-sounding drums

Many Cubase users prefer to sequence their drum parts by entering the beats with a mouse in the Drum Editor. This is fine for music that relies heavily on drum loops such as dance music. Others prefer to play a 'virtual kit'. Which way it's done depends mainly on the style of music being recorded. To capture the feel and spontaneity of a real drummer it's probably best to play the part first using a MIDI controller and edit it afterwards in one of the editors. If a repetitive loop is needed, step entry may be the way to go.

Here are a few suggestions for recording 'live style' drums:

- People new to song writing and sequencing often spend hours perfecting a drum track before they even think about recording anything else. Quite often, it has to be scrapped anyway, at a later stage, because it doesn't fit the bass part, which was influenced by the guitar rhythm, which was influenced by the melody and so on. A better bet is to record some melodic material first. Once the melody and bass are down it's much easier to be a 'virtual drummer' and instill some spontaneity and feel into the music.
- If possible record in stretches of eight bars or so at a time. This helps create a natural flow and is preferable to cutting and pasting one or two bar segments.
- Drum rolls are best sequenced by step entry. It's no easy matter to roll two fingers as fast as two drum sticks. Use the Drum Editor.
- Try playing the kick and snare drums first and overdub the hi-hats, cymbals and toms afterwards, on separate tracks. Fills can be left until later too. Having the drums separated like this makes it easier to carry out editing procedures.

Quick tip

Avoid playing three things on the same beat – apart from the kick drum, of course – because drummers don't possess three arms and it may sound unnatural.

Unraveling a MIDI drum track

If all the drum parts in a song are on a single track – you've imported a MIDI file perhaps – and some serious editing is required, use the menu function MIDI > Dissolve Part to unravel them. You'll be presented with a dialogue box asking if you want 'Separate Channels' or 'Separate Pitches'. Choose the latter and each drum sound will be assigned its own track enabling easy cutting and pasting and so on. The original track remains intact, but muted.

Groove Agent ONE

Cubase has its very own drum machine, Groove Agent ONE, a sampling drum machine complete with a range of kits in a variety of styles. Each pad is mapped to a MIDI note so that you can play the kits from your MIDI controller. It's also possible to create your own kits by dragging and dropping sounds from the Media Bay directly onto any of the 16 MPC-style pads. You can even import MPC exchange format files (.pgm). Another handy feature is the provision to drag and drop pre-sliced loops from anywhere in Cubase and have them automatically mapped across the pads. Groove Agent ONE then creates a MIDI file, which can be dragged to a MIDI track for playback.

Figure 12.8
Cubase has its very own drum machine, Groove Agent ONE

Beat Designer

While the Drum Editor is the ideal place to program and construct long detailed drum tracks in a project, Beat Designer is probably a better bet for creating short pattern-based drum parts. Everything you need for constructing short loops and patterns is provided including full control over parameters such as velocity and swing. Once constructed, patterns can be dragged to a MIDI track or triggered with a MIDI controller.

Figure 12.9
Beat Designer is a MIDI plug-in and step sequencer for creating beats

Beat making with Groove Agent ONE and Beat Designer

Groove Agent ONE is a great sample-based drum machine and Beat Designer is a simple but powerful step sequencer. Use them together and you have the perfect combination for creating complete drum tracks. Follow these steps:

Info

You can make changes to the Groove Agent ONE kits by clicking on the pads and using the Edit buttons – Play, Voice, Filter and Amplifier.

1 Create an Instrument track and assign it to Groove Agent ONE.
2 Load one of the many preset drum kits that come with Cubase. I chose the Hard Rock Kit. Tap the pads to audition the individual samples.

Figure 12.10

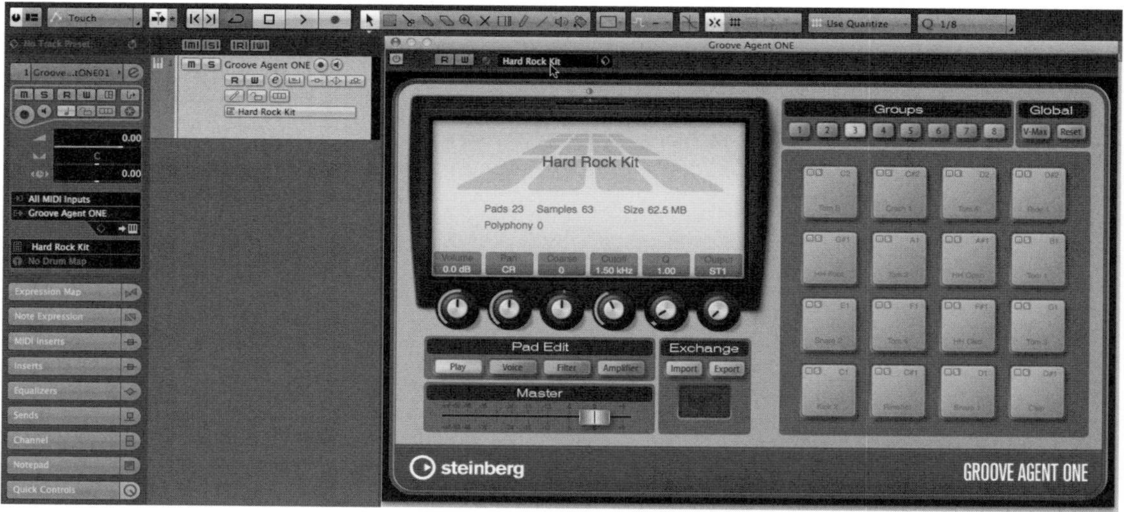

3 Open the track's Insert panel and call up Beat Designer. By drawing notes on the grid you will now be able to trigger Groove Agent ONE's pads.

Figure 12.11

Info

To alter the drum sound for any particular Beat Designer MIDI channel slot click on the tiny white triangle next to the solo and mute icons (it's invisible until you hover your mouse cursor in the area). A menu appears with a list of drum sounds.

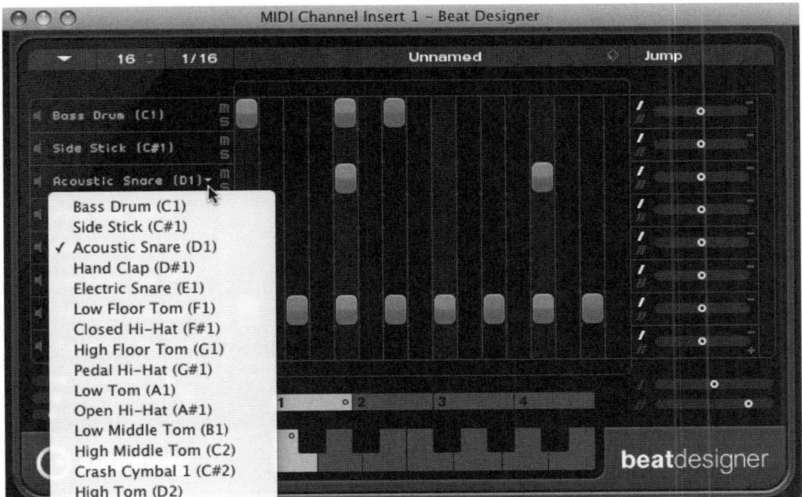

Figure 12.12
Selecting instrument sounds in Beat Designer

Tip

To alter the velocity of notes entered into Beat Designer, click on them and drag your mouse up or down.

Tip

Beat Designer has sliders to the right of each track, which are used to introduce a degree of swing. Using these will make your step-entered beats sound less mechanical and more human.

Logical Editor

At first sight the Logical Editor and Transformer are probably the most forbidding aspects of Cubase, which otherwise is a very user-friendly piece of software. However, any misgivings you may have about them are largely unjustified because they're incredibly useful, powerful features and not at all difficult to understand once you get to know them better. The Logical Editor, in particular, becomes easier to understand and simpler to use with each successive version of Cubase that appears. Most MIDI editing is done within the key and list editors on individual and small groups of events but there are probably times when you wish that you could change a large chunk of data in one fell swoop.

Suppose you need to find all the notes on a track that are between C1 and C3 in pitch, that are 30 ticks long, with a velocity value of between 80 and 100 and then alter all of them to 90 ticks in length with a velocity value of 120; a tall order, that could take hours in the Key Editor but only minutes using the Logical Editor (Figure 13.1).

Filter, functions, actions

This is how the Logical Editor works: you set up 'filter conditions' to find certain events, select 'functions' to perform on those events, followed by the 'actions'. The best way to get to grips with it is to examine the factory presets. An easy one to start with is 'Fixed Velocity 100', from 'standard set 1'. What you see is:

- Type Is - Equal - Note (the Filter Condition).
- Transform (the Function).
- Value 2 - Set to fixed value - 100 (the Action).

In other words, 'Transform all selected notes to a fixed velocity value of 100'.

These presets not only serve as an excellent way to understand how the Logical Editor works but also as templates for use in your own projects. For example, a commonly needed function when polishing a MIDI sequence is randomization. This can be achieved by modifying the 'random velocity (60 - 100)' preset. All you have to do is substitute the preset velocity values with those of your own. This method has an advantage over the MIDI Modifier 'Random' feature because you can select a group of notes rather than the whole track and it's quicker than the Merge MIDI in Loop function.

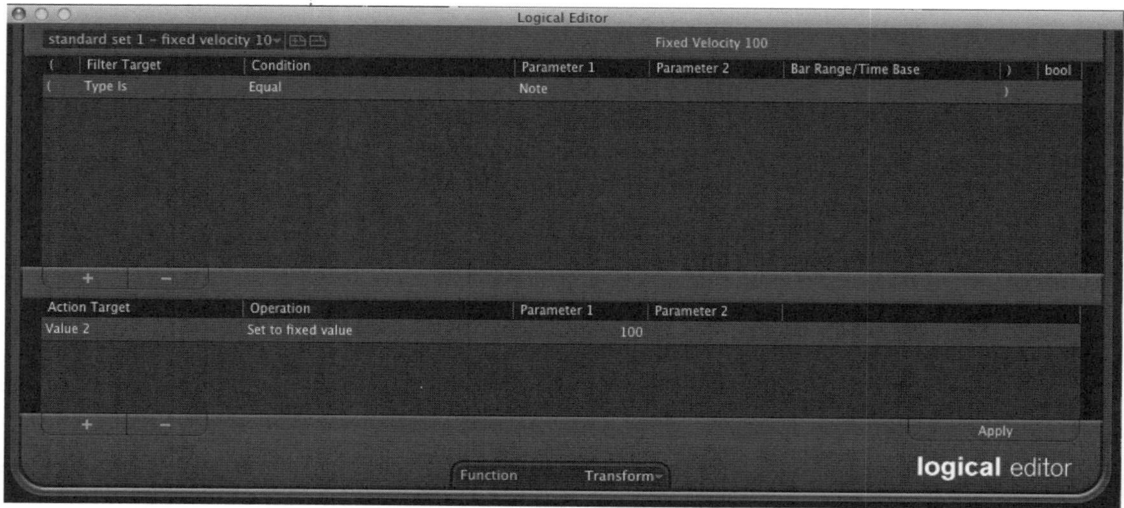

Figure 13.1
The Logical Editor

Logical Editor factory presets

Here's a run-down on many of the Logical Editor factory presets and a few tips on using them.

Standard set 1

- Delete muted - Deletes all muted notes in a selected group. However if no particular notes are selected the muted one are deleted one at a time, in reverse order. A useful function for removing muted notes that would otherwise remain displayed when printing a score.
- Delete short notes - Deletes all notes shorter than the specified length. A default setting of 20 can be modified. This is useful if you need to delete short, mistakenly played notes.
- Fixed velocity 100 - Sets all the velocities to 100. Modify the value to suit.

Figure 13.2
Use the Logical Editor presets as templates

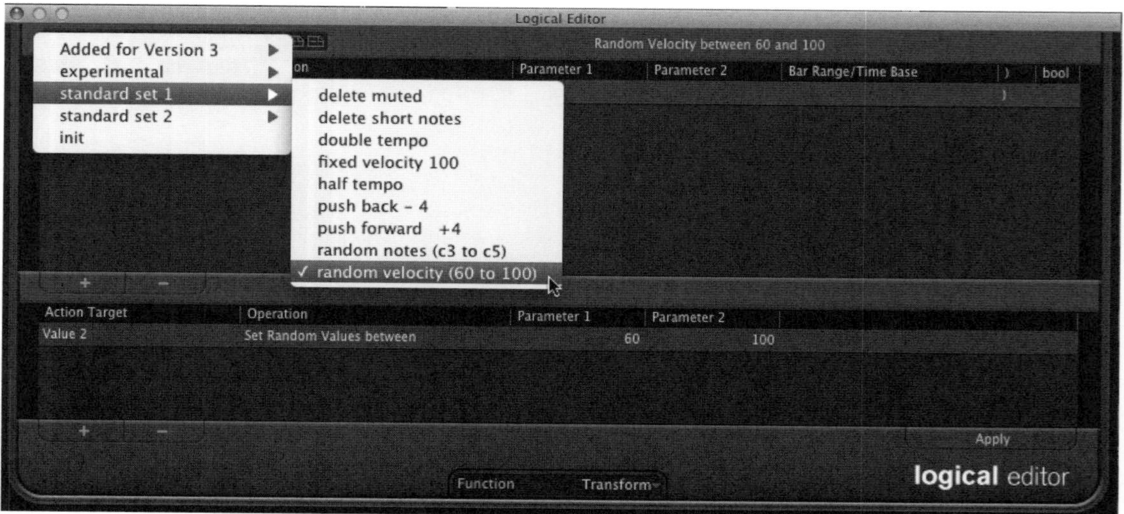

- Double tempo - Repositions events to mimic a double tempo. Do it repeatedly for quadrupled time and so on. Useful as an alternative to modifying the Tempo Track or having different tracks playback in different tempos.
- Half tempo - Repositions events to mimic a half tempo. Useful as an alternative to modifying the Tempo Track or having different tracks playback in different tempos.
- Push back - 4 - Moves all events 4 ticks later in the project. Do it repeatedly to move them further. Handy when tracks have been duplicated to playback different sounds and you don't want their events (particularly the notes) having exactly the same starting points.
- Push forward +4 - Moves all the events 4 ticks later in the project.
- Random notes (C3 - C5) - Randomizes all notes to positions between C3 and C5. This feature is useful for turning perfectly good tunes into unintelligible rubbish.
- Random velocity (60 - 100) - Randomizes note velocity values between 60 and 100. Of course, you can modify this to suit your project. Useful for 'humanizing' fixed velocity notes that were 'painted' in the Key Editor or inserted with Step Input.

Standard set 2

- Del patch changes - Deletes Program changes and Bankselect messages. Useful if you change your mind, I suppose.
- Del velocity below 30, 35, 40 and 45 - Four separate presets that delete notes with velocity values below the set threshold. Useful for deleting accidentally played notes with low velocity values.
- Del.aftertouch - Deletes all Aftertouch/Channel Pressure messages. Useful when exporting MIDI files for use on older synthesizers that do not recognize Aftertouch messages.
- Extract note (C3 60) - Extracts the notes C3 and moves them to a new part on a new MIDI track. Modify it to extract notes of your choice. Useful when you need to extract something like a snare from a drum track, for editing or effects treatment.
- High notes to channel 1 - The default setting transforms notes above C3 to channel 1. For example - a note such as E3 on channel 2 will be transformed into E3 on channel 1. Useful for outputting certain notes to different channels, to play back different instruments within one part. To this ensure that the channel output in the Inspector is set to ANY. Of course, you can modify these settings to whatever suits you.
- Low notes to channel 2 - Works on the same principle as above, only this time the default setting transforms notes below C3 to channel 2.
- Set notes to fixed pitch C3 - Does what it says.
- Transpose +12 – Transposes notes an octave higher
- Transpose -12 – Transposes notes an octave lower

Experimental

- Add volume 0 to end of note - Inserts a Controller value (default is No.11, Volume) at the end of a note(s).
- Delete black keys - Does exactly that.
- Downbeat accent (4 - 4) - The default setting adds a velocity value of 30 to all four down beats in a bar of 4/4. This is useful for stressing certain beats in music that has been entered manually with a mouse or via Step Input. Modify the settings to suit your own music.
- Extract volume and pan - Controllers No.11, Volume and No. 10 Pan, are extracted from the track and inserted in a new part on another track. If you replace 'Extract' with 'Copy' as the function, the data will be pasted to a new part on a new track. The duplicated volume and pan data can now be shared with other tracks by copying and pasting.
- Filter offbeats - Deletes any note not on the beat.
- Insert midi volume for velocity – Inserts a CC7 (Main Volume) event that corresponds to a selected notes velocity value.

Added for Version 3

- Notes after a Mod Wheel event (CC 1) that have a value above 64 are duplicated one octave higher
- Delete SMF Events – Strips out events such as copyright, text and time signature events from commercial Standard MIDI files.
- Delete all Controller in Cycle Range – strips out all the controller events within a cycle range, for example, between bars 1 – 5. Notes remain intact.
- Delete each 5th Note – self-explanatory.
- Scale down Velocity in Sustain Range – Notes situated between CC64 events (on and off, 127 and 0 respectively) have their velocities progressively scaled each time you apply this command.
- Select all Events beyond Cursor – Selects all the events within a Part beyond the cursor position.
- Select all Events in Cycle Range – Selects all the events within a cycle range, for example, between bars 1 – 5.
- Transpose Events In Sustain Range - Notes situated between CC64 events (on and off, 127 and 0 respectively) are transposed one octave higher each time this command is applied.

Quick tip

To get at the Presets > Logical Edit sub folder in Cubase (or any other folder) on a Mac, select the Cubase program icon and press the Control key. Now choose 'Show Package Contents' from the menu.

Store and share Logical Editor presets

You can store Logical Editor presets as individual files within the Cubase program folder. Go to the Presets > Logical Edit sub folder. You can't edit the files here but you can reorganize them into sub folders and so on. Doing this makes it easier to share your presets with other Cubase users. Just copy the files and pass them on.

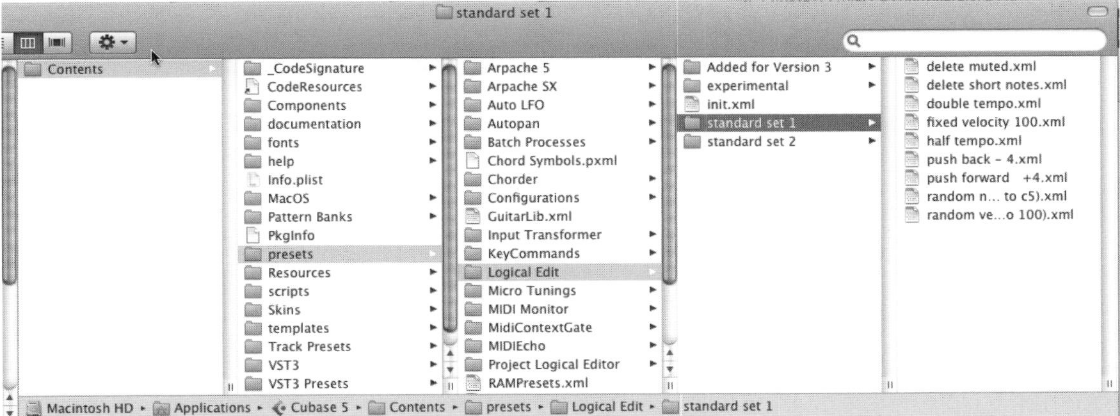

Figure 13.3
The Logical Edit Folder lives within Cubase itself

Bass notes trigger a kick drum

Here's a neat time saving trick. You've recorded a simple bass part and you want a kick drum to shadow it, a beat for every note. This is what you do:

1 Select the bass part in the Project window and use the MIDI menu to open the Logical Editor.
2 Choose 'Copy' as the function.
3 If necessary, change the line in the 'filter' section to read: Type Is (Filter Target) Equal (Condition) Note (Parameter).
4 Change the line in the 'actions' section to read: Value 1 (Action Target) Set to fixed value (Operation) C-1 (Parameter 1)
5 Press 'Apply'.

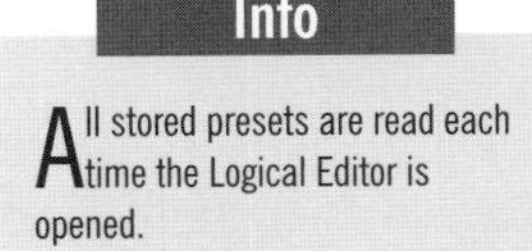
Info

All stored presets are read each time the Logical Editor is opened.

A new part will be created on a new track containing a string of kick drum notes (in this case C1) that follow the bass part note for note. All the velocity values are copied too. We can sum up the whole operation as Copy all notes and fix their value to C1 (the kick drum).

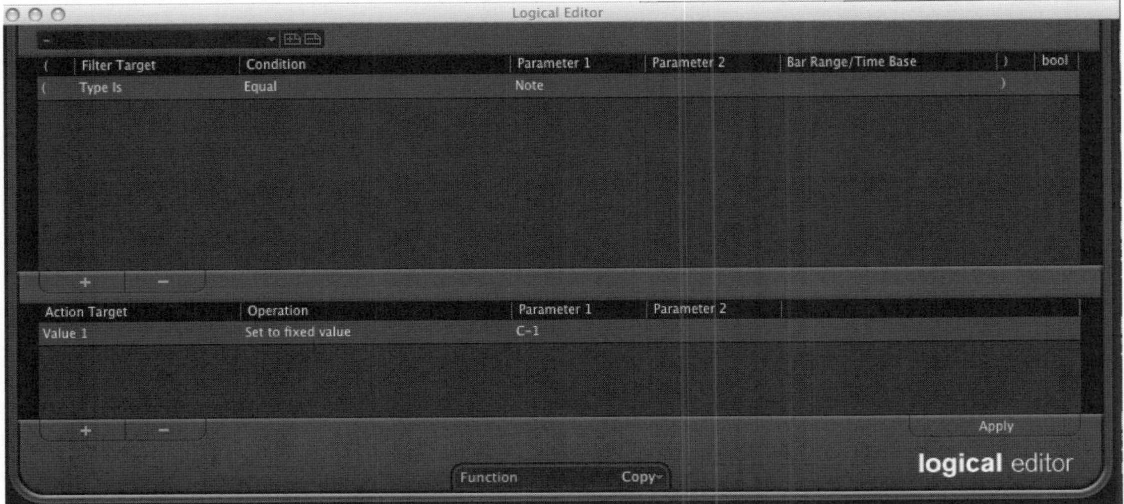

Figure 13.4
'Copy all notes and fix their value to C1' – a new preset

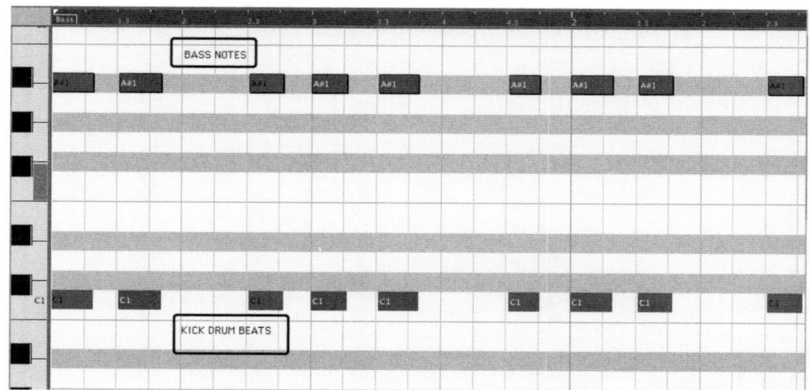

Figure 13.5
Bass notes duplicated as kick drum beats

Audio editing

Time stretching

When you import an audio file it doesn't always fit exactly to bar lengths and using the Repeat function to create loops will often leave small, audible gaps between the parts. Time stretching them first, with the arrow tool, will make them easier to repeat seamlessly.

First, make sure that Sizing Applies Time Stretch is selected for the Arrow tool and that Snap is turned on and set to Grid/Bar. All you have to do is select the audio event, grab the handles and stretch it as far as the next bar. Once stretched, you can use the repeat function to loop the audio.

Figure 14.1
You can stretch audio quickly with the Time Stretch tool

Regions

Regions are very useful. You can create regions easily by selecting audio with the Range Selection tool in the Sample Editor and clicking on the Add Region button. Once a region is created you can:

- Name it
- Drag it into the Project window using the mouse, to create a new event
- Select it in the list and apply processing
- Select it in the list and audition it, using the Play Region button
- Select it in the pool and use 'Bounce Selection' to create a new audio file.

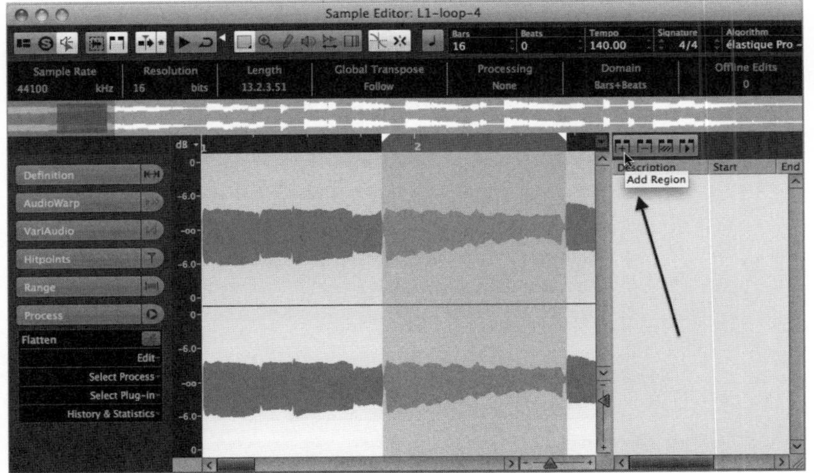

Figure 14.2
Creating regions

Info

As well as using the Time Stretch Tool, you can use the Time Stretch dialogue for more control over the process (Audio > Process > Time Stretch).

Quick tip

By repeatedly pressing the figure 1 you can toggle between the sizing options related to the Arrow tool.

VariAudio

VariAudio, is Cubase 6's pitch and time correction system. Most aspects of using VariAudio can be found in the Operation manual. However, you may prefer to learn on the job and skip the tutorials. Here's a short guide explaining how VariAudio can be used to fine-tune a single vocal line or monophonic instrument track.

- A solo vocal part is opened in the Sample Editor. A click on the Pitch & Warp tool (found in the VariAudio tab) starts the pitch analysis process and the resulting notes are displayed on a piano-roll style grid, in a similar fashion to the way that MIDI notes are viewed in the Key Editor.

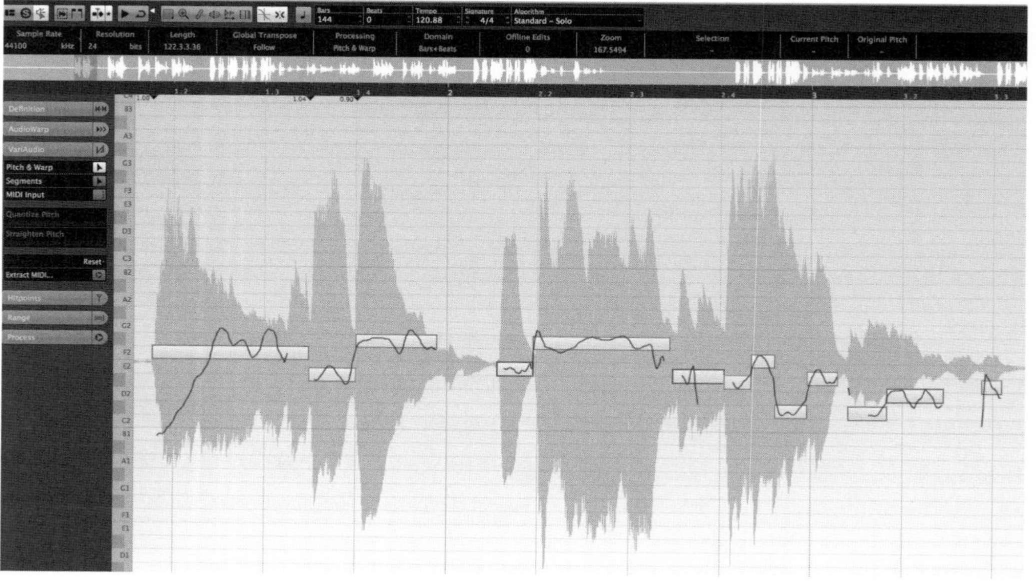

Figure 14.3

- Individual notes (or selections) can be pitch-shifted up or down by holding down the Shift key and moving them with the mouse.

Figure 14.4

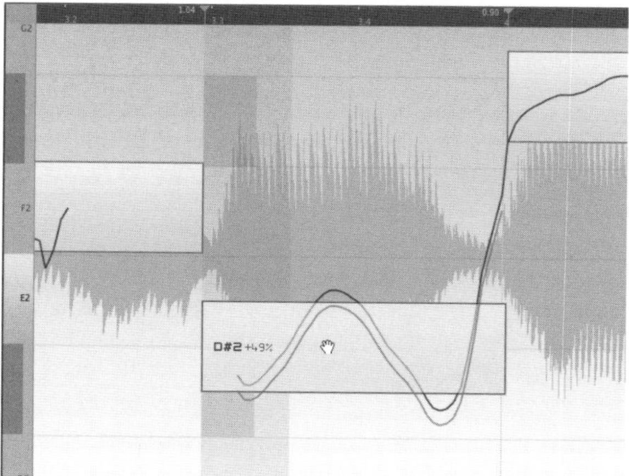

- By selecting a note (or notes) and using the Straighten Pitch slider you can modify a singer's vibrato. It's wise to go easy with this otherwise you may destroy the character of the voice (for demonstration's sake the screenshot here goes all the way and completely flattens the vibrato)

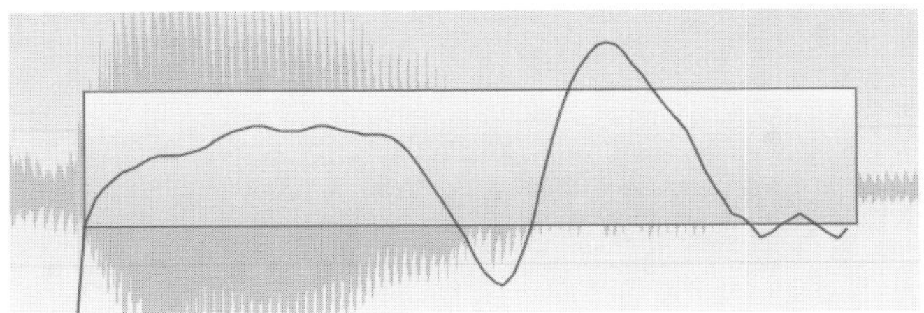

Figure 14.5
Before Straight Pitch and Pitch Quantize

- The Pitch Quantize slider will gradually pull any selected notes closer to the grid. This might be used to correct entire sections that have been sung slightly out of tune.

Figure 14.6
After Straight Pitch and Pitch Quantize

- Using the Functions menu, a MIDI part can be extracted from the vocal line and placed on a MIDI track. This can be used to create a 'shadow voice' by having it trigger a VST Instrument.

Figure 14.7
Extracting a MIDI part from a vocal recording

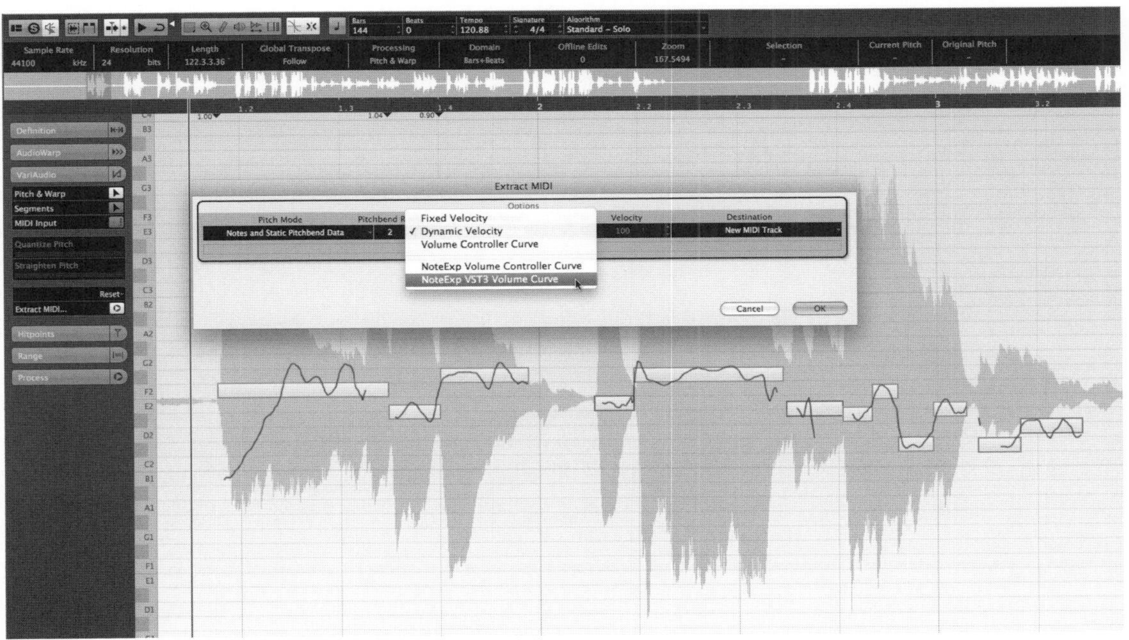

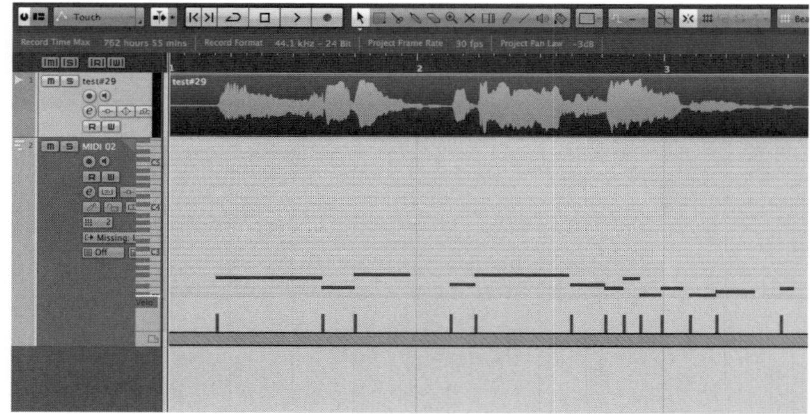

Figure 14.8
A MIDI part is extracted from a vocal line and used to create a second voice

Instant harmonies

Here's a trick for creating quick harmonies on vocals and monophonic instrument lines. Try this example:

1 Record a few bars of singing, single note guitar or another instrument. Select the recorded audio event and drag a copy to the track above. Open the Pitch Shift dialogue (Audio > Process > Pitch Shift). Transpose the event up a fourth (5 semitones).
2 Return to the original event and drag another copy to the track below, open the Pitch Shift dialogue and this time transpose the new event down a fifth (7 semitones).
3 Now play all three tracks together for instant harmonies. The trick works well with instruments like saxophone. For instance, an alto sax line can be used to create a soprano sax line above and a tenor sax or baritone sax line below. Of course it works best over a fairly static chord sequence.

Pitch Correct

As good as VariAudio is, you can only use it in the Sample Editor, to modify an already existing audio file. The new Pitch Correct plug-in, though, works in real-time and you can use it both correctively and creatively. For correcting slightly out-of-tune vocal performances, a range of presets is available. These work fine but it's as a creative tool that Pitch Correct really shines. For example, it can be used to create backing vocals or instrumental harmony lines when used in conjunction with a MIDI keyboard controller.

- Pitch Correct is used as an insert on vocal or mono instrumental audio tracks. A range of presets is available for correcting a slightly out-of-tune vocal performance. However, for creating a backing vocal, a more extreme preset can be used as a starting point such as 'Correction Male 3 Serious'.

Figure 14.9

- By adding a MIDI track with its output assigned to an audio track a MIDI keyboard controller can be used to play a harmony line in real time. For this to work, the 'External – MIDI Note' preset must be selected from the Scale Source pop-up menu.

Figure 14.10

- In a live jamming context, the above points are all that's needed to create on-the-fly alternative versions of the vocal or instrumental material. However, by recording a MIDI part and setting up an Audio Mixdown (File menu) a harmony part can be bounced to a mono audio track.

Figure 14.11

Normalizing

If you've accidentally recorded some audio at too low a level and it's impossible to re-record it, the Normalizing feature (Audio > Process > Normalize) will probably get you out of trouble.

After selecting the event, you set a maximum level for the audio. Cubase will analyze the audio and determine its highest level, subtract it from the

Figure 14.12
Audio before using Normalize

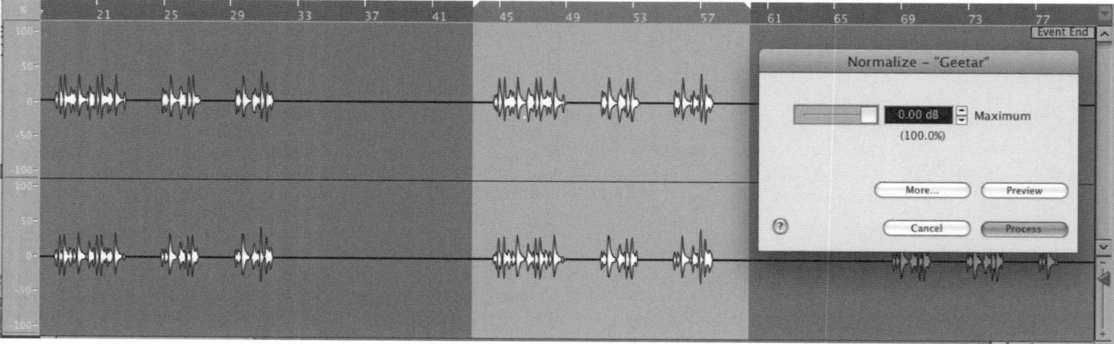

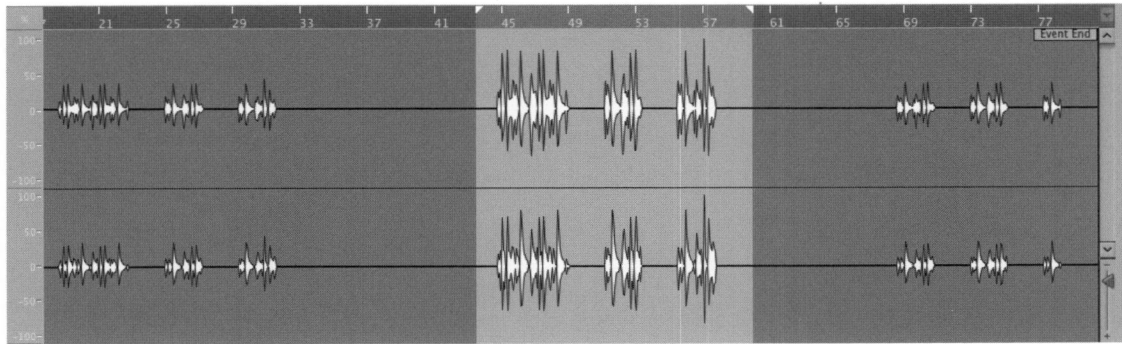

Figure 14.13
Audio after using Normalize

level you have set and then raise everything by that amount. If you want it to be very loud just leave it at 0.00 (100%). Use the Preview button and listen carefully because normalizing an audio signal will raise the noise level, particularly in the quiet sections.

Inserting silence with Noise Gate

As mentioned above, background noise on a recording can be a problem, particularly on material with many gaps in-between notes such as vocals or instrumental solos. The problem can usually be solved with Noise Gate, found on the Audio Processing menu. You set a specified threshold level and Noise Gate scans the audio for sections with weaker levels and replaces them with silence. It works well but on long clips it can be time consuming checking the results with the Preview function.

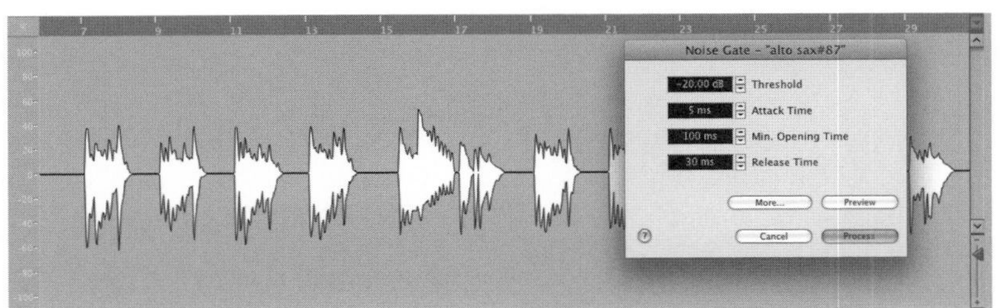

Figure 14.14
Noise Gate looks for weaker audio levels and replaces them with silence

Detecting silence

One way of dealing with background noise is to use the Detect Silence feature (Audio > Advanced >). Because you can see the waveform changes taking place, you have more control.

Unlike Noise Gate, which processes the audio, Detect Silence searches for silent sections in an event and does one of two things – splits the event, removing the silent parts altogether, or creates regions related to the non-silent sections. This way, background noise can be eliminated without altering the audio signal itself. As a rule of thumb, low threshold settings will yield good results on material with frequent gaps – vocals and so on.

Quick tip

To reduce CPU load when using VST3 plug-in processing, turn on the 'Suspend VST3 plug-in processing when no audio signals are received' option in the Preferences dialogue (VST-Plug-ins page).

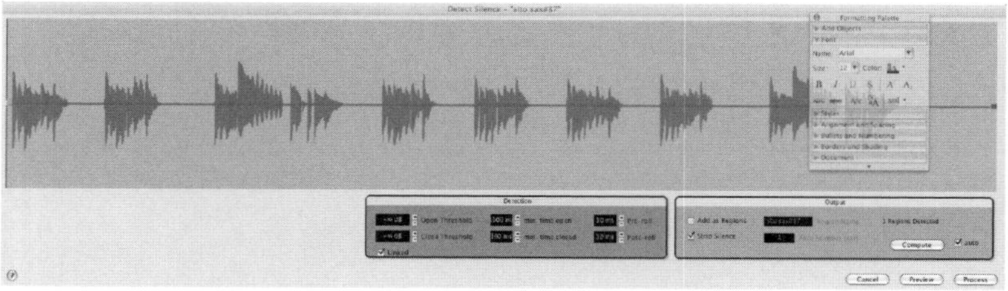

Figure 14.15
Audio file before using computing with Detect Silence

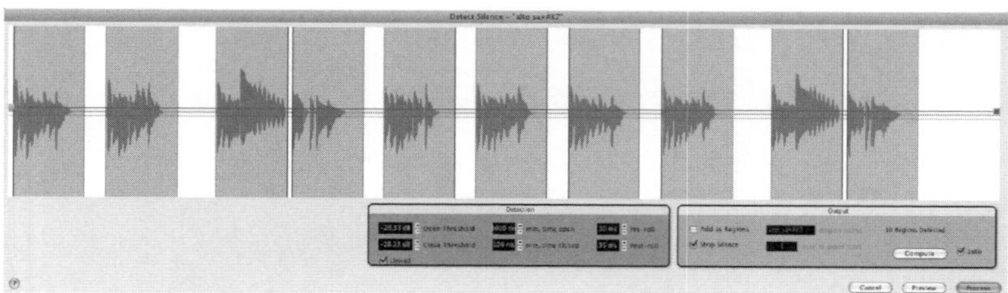

Figure 14.16
Audio file after computing with Detect Silence

As mentioned above, regions can be incredibly useful. Here are a few of the things you can do when you create regions in conjunction with the Detect Silence feature:

- Manipulating speech – You've recorded a section of speech, perhaps as part of a jingle but you need to rearrange some of the words or sentences. After creating the regions you can shuffle the speech segments around to your heart's content.
- Optimizing synchronization – If you're using time code to link with an external recording device you may experience a slight drift between MIDI and audio material, particularly if it's a long sequence. One way round the problem is to create several shorter audio sequences – the more the merrier. You'll get more trigger points between MIDI and audio events.
- ReCycle style drum loops – You can use Detect Silence as an alternative to Hitpoints for slicing up drum loops into small segments. They can subsequently be treated in the same way as MIDI events – sped up and slowed down, just like REX files.

Offline Process History

If you apply processing to an audio clip and later decide that you don't like it you can use the Offline Process History dialogue to remove it, even if it's in the

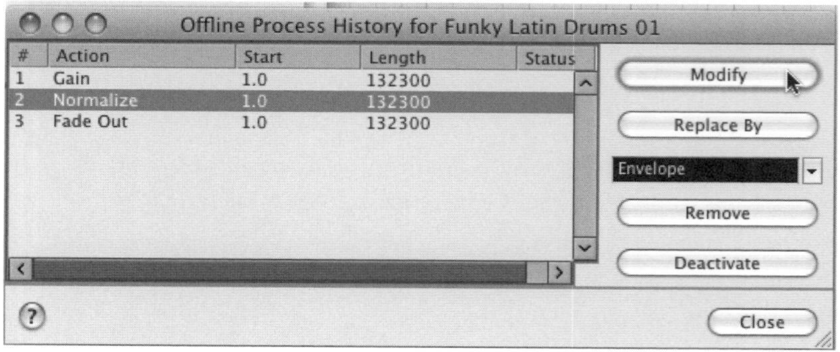

Figure 14.17
You can remove and modify previously processed audio with Offline Process History

middle of the history. Not only can you remove processing, you can also modify it. For example: you have used the Distortion plug-in on an audio clip but the settings are not quite right. Select the clip and find the Distortion processing in the history and use the 'Modify' function to get it just how you want it.

Using the Merge Clipboard function

If you make your own loops it's quite likely that you will want to mix bits from one audio file with another. You can do this by cutting and pasting audio from one file to another, using the Merge Clipboard function, found in the Audio Processing menu.

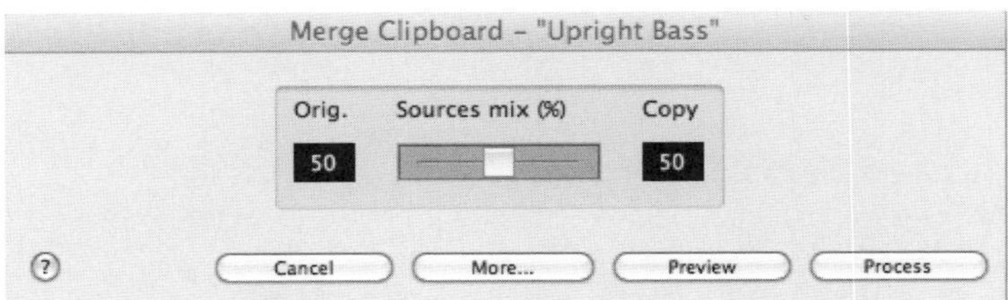

Figure 14.18
You can cut and paste audio from one file to another, using the Merge Clipboard function

First select all or part of audio file 'A' in the Sample Editor and save it to the clipboard using Ctrl+C (on the Mac, Command +C). Close the Sample Editor and in the Project window, select audio file 'B' and use Merge Clipboard (Audio > Process) to paste 'A' across. The audio is pasted at the beginning of the selection. Before you complete the process, use the Preview button to listen to the mix and adjust the balance between 'A' and 'B' using the 'Sources mix' slider. Pressing 'More' will give you crossfade options.

Quick tip

You can create a classic reversed cymbal effect very quickly by selecting the audio and using Audio > Process > Reverse.

Info

You can decide what to display in the Sample Editor - Audio Events, Regions, Info line, Level Scale, Zero Axis and Half Level Axis - using the Quick menu.

Sample Editor Overview

Like the Project window the Sample Editor has an Overview display. Drag it around to work on specific sections of an audio clip. Stretch it to the left or right to resize it and encompass more audio. You can also use it to zoom in on a specific area by shrinking it.

Zero Crossings

If you do any cutting and pasting of audio in the Sample Editor it's advisable to turn on the Snap to Zero Crossing button to avoid nasty pops and clicks. They happen as a result of two juxtaposed signals, each with different volume levels. To avoid the problem when editing in the Project window you'll need to tick the Snap to Zero Crossing box in the Preferences (Editing > Audio page).

Quick tip

Hold down Shift to select more than one clip at a time as you select them.

Inserting audio clips into a Project

You can insert audio clips directly into a project from the Pool.

1 Scroll the Project cursor to the position you want the clip to go.
2 Select the clip and use Media > Insert into Project > At Cursor to insert it.

A quicker way to do it:

1 Alter the clip's position in the Origin Time column.
2 Use Pool > Insert into Project > At Origin. This method eliminates the need to go into the Project window and alter the Project cursor manually.

Pool folders

Large projects usually result in a crowded Pool. Tidy things up by putting different types of audio clips into different folders using Create Folder found on the Pool menu (right-click on the main Audio folder). However you can't place audio clips in a video folder and vice versa.

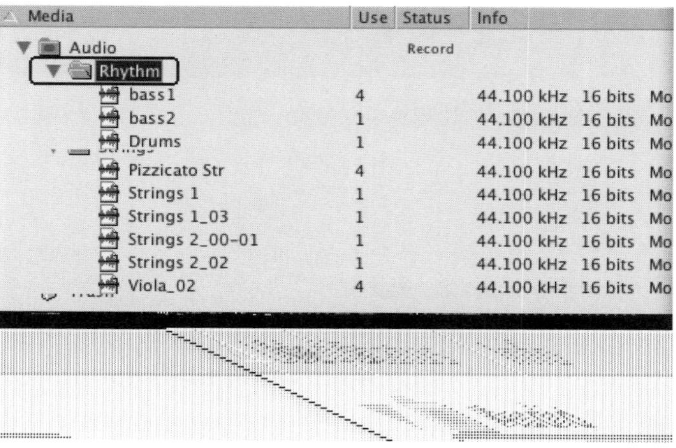

Figure 14.19
Get organized and create folders in the Pool

Quick tip

To sort clips in the Pool by name or date, click on the arrow, in the selected column heading. Click again to switch between ascending and descending order.

Pool cleaning

If the Pool becomes cluttered with unused files you can remove them using Pool > Remove Unused Media. You'll be asked whether you want to remove them from the hard disk altogether or put them in the Pool Trash folder. Unless you're sure that you'll never need them again, either later in the project or for a different project altogether, put them in the Trash folder to be on the safe side.

Missing files

It's not a good idea to rename or move audio files outside of Cubase. Cubase will consider them missing. When you next open the project Cubase will ask you whether you want to locate them yourself or let Cubase try to find them for you. Ignore the dialogue if you wish and choose 'Close'. The project will still open, but without the missing files, which will be indicated by question marks in the Status column.

If you've just moved the files you can probably locate them using Find Missing Files... found on the Media menu. If you've renamed them it might not be quite so easy, particularly if you can't remember their new names. If you do remember their names, use the Search function to find them (opened by clicking on the Search button, on the Toolbar).

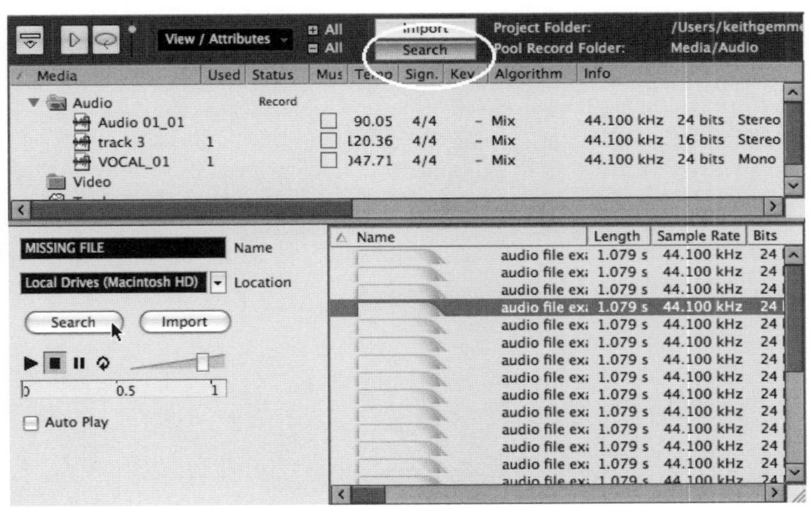

Figure 14.20
Searching for missing audio files

Reconstructing deleted files

Normally, if you delete a file from the hard disk, you can't get it back. However, if you accidentally deleted a file that you've processed at some point in the project you may be able to bring it back from beyond the grave. Open the Pool and with any luck the file will be marked 'Reconstructible'. Select the clip and use Reconstruct (Pool menu) to rebuild it.

Quantizing

Quantize values

Cubase provides plenty of scope for quantizing. Use the Quantize Selector, in either the Project window or any of the MIDI editors, to select a quantize option. However, the various options, what they do and when to use them can be confusing. There are two main types:

- Over Quantize – use this type of quantizing to move all the notes played to the nearest division of the beat. For example, select 1/8 Note to move everything to the nearest eighth note, 1/16 to the nearest sixteenth note and so on. The musical result of course will be dead straight. Use it to correct inaccurate playing and when you need a straight feel, electro or classical music perhaps.
- Iterative Quantize – use this type of quantizing to move the notes towards the closest quantize value. Define how far the notes are moved, and what is considered already close to the Quantize value using the 'Iterative Strength' and 'Non Quantize' values in the Quantize Setup dialogue. An Iterative Strength of 60% is the default setting, and works well as an all rounder. The musical result of this type of quantizing is less rigid than Over Quantize and you can apply it progressively, as needed. In other words, if you record a passage, and after applying Iterative Quantize it's still not tight enough, just apply it again. Of course, you can only do this so many times before everything ends up dead straight, which completely defeats the purpose. Use it to correct your playing without loosing too much feel.

Figure 15.1
Quantize settings are made in the Quantize Panel (Edit menu) and are reflected in the pop-up menus

Quick tip

Press Q on the computer keyboard to apply Over Quantize.

Groove Quantize

Over and Iterative quantization are fine for many uses but if you want to make your own grooves you can further adjust the values in the Quantize Panel. Here's a quick run-down of the main functions:

- Grid value – where you select basic note values for quantizing. Using these menus amounts to the same thing as using the Quantize Selector on the Toolbar, in the Project window.
- Swing factor – scroll the percentage values to create a swing or shuffle feel by offsetting every second note on the Grid.
- Catch Range – where only specified notes, within a certain distance from the grid, are affected. Scroll the percentage values to define the area.
- Non Quantize – allows you set a distance in ticks from the quantize grid that events will not be quantized.

The beauty of the Quantize Panel is that you can hear the results very quickly using the Apply button. The box remains open ready for further changes. Even better, if you tick the Auto box the changes are heard in real time, as you adjust the values, all very intuitive. When you've found the exact setting for the job, save it as a preset ready for further use. It will then show up on the Quantize Selector pop-up menu whenever you need it.

Advanced Quantize

There are a five more quantize features to be found in the MIDI menu under Advanced Quantize. Here's what they do:

- Quantize MIDI Event Lengths – use this function to quantize a note's length without moving it. Set the quantize value in the Length Quantize pop-up menu in any MIDI Editor's toolbar. Why would you need this? Well, it has its uses. For example, you may have played a series of organ chords, one chord per bar for several bars. The notes in each chord are unlikely to be all the same length. After initially quantizing their start positions you could then quantize their lengths to make them sound even.
- Quantize MIDI Event Ends – this is rather like Over Quantize in reverse. Only the ends of the notes are quantized, according to the value that you select in the pop-up menu.
- Freeze Quantize – use this to make the quantizing permanent. You can then re-quantize the notes again if you wish. This function cannot be undone.
- Create Groove Quantize to Preset – use this function to extract the groove from a selected MIDI part and turn it into a Quantize preset.

The fifth function on the Advanced Quantize menu, Create Groove Quantize to Preset, is a great feature. You can use this to extract grooves from MIDI material. Just select a MIDI part and apply. The resulting groove will be added to the existing Quantize menu, ready for further use. You can also do this with a sliced audio part or an audio event containing hitpoints. On the Hitpoints tab in the Sample Editor you will find a 'Create Groove' button (see Creating hitpoints, Chapter 16).

Quantizer - the plug-in

There's usually more than one way to carry out a task in Cubase and quantizing is no exception. If you want to try out different grooves on a track and don't yet want to commit, use the Quantizer plug-in as a MIDI Insert. It does much the same as the normal quantize functions but there's one big difference; you can experiment as much as you need whilst listening to the results as you apply them. Although some of the more advanced features are missing it does contain a couple of unique features of its own, Delay and Realtime quantize.

Delay, unlike the delay setting in the Track Parameters, can be automated. Realtime quantizing can be used in a similar fashion to the Automatic Quantize feature on the Transport Panel. Notes are quantized as you play. However, the display is unquantized. Use Freeze Modifiers to quantize the notes permanently.

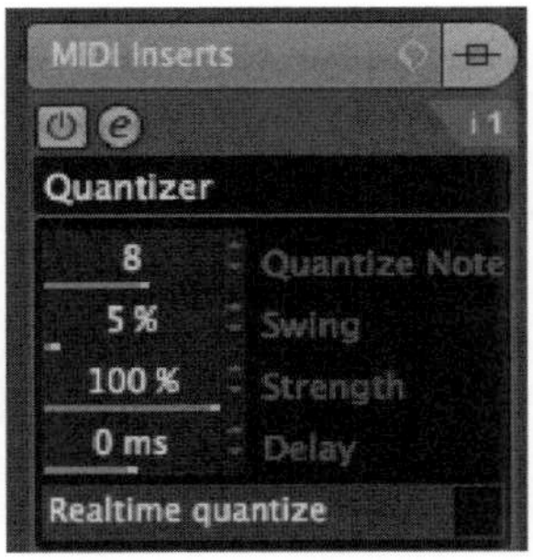

Figure 15.2
The Quantizer effect allows you to apply quantizing 'on the fly', changing the timing of the notes in real time.

Automating the Quantizer

You can apply a whole string of quantize values to a single track by using the Quantizer plug-in as an Insert and using track automation. Here's an example:

1 In the Project window, select a Quantize value of 1/8 Note, turn on Snap and set the locators to encompass a single bar.
2 Between the locators, double click on a MIDI or Instrument track to create an empty part and set the track output to play back a bass sound of some kind.
3 Select the part and use Ctrl+E (on the Mac, Command+E) to open the Key Editor and with the Pencil tool, enter this simple bass pattern (or something similar). Use a Length Quantize value of 1/16 Note.

Figure 15.3
A simple bass pattern

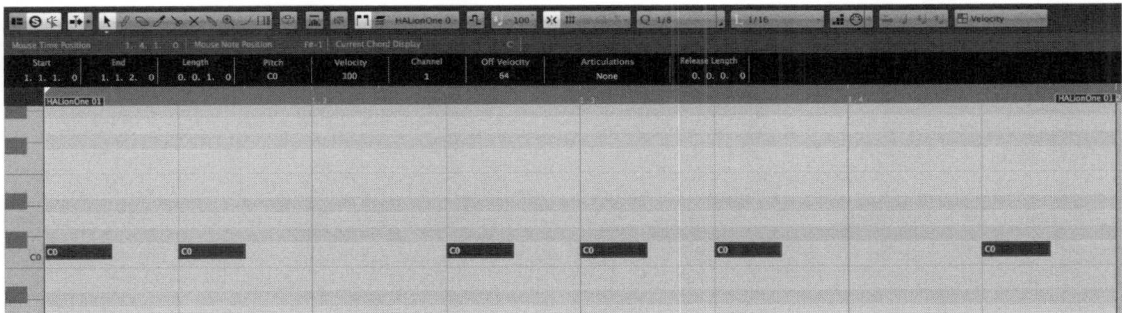

4 Play it back. If necessary, turn Snap off and lengthen the notes slightly.
5 Return to the Project window and use the Repeat function to copy the part 15 times.

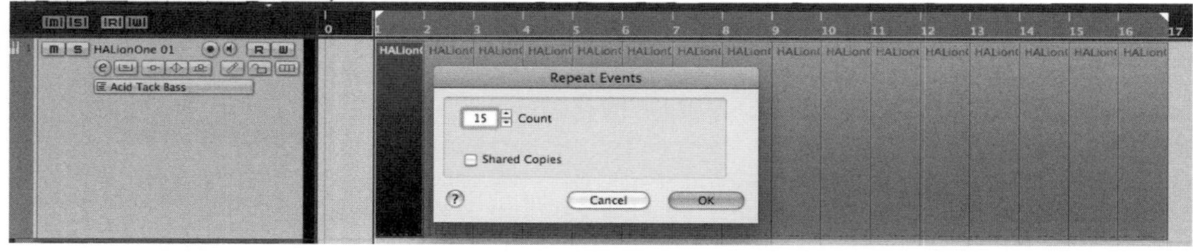

Figure 15.4
Use the Repeat function for multiple repeats

6 Set up the Quantizer plug-in as an Insert on the track. Set a value of '8' as the Quantize Note parameter.

7 Open the automation track and find the 'Swing Ins 1' parameter in the pop-up menu. If it's not there take this route: More... > Inserts > Quantizer > Swing Ins 1.

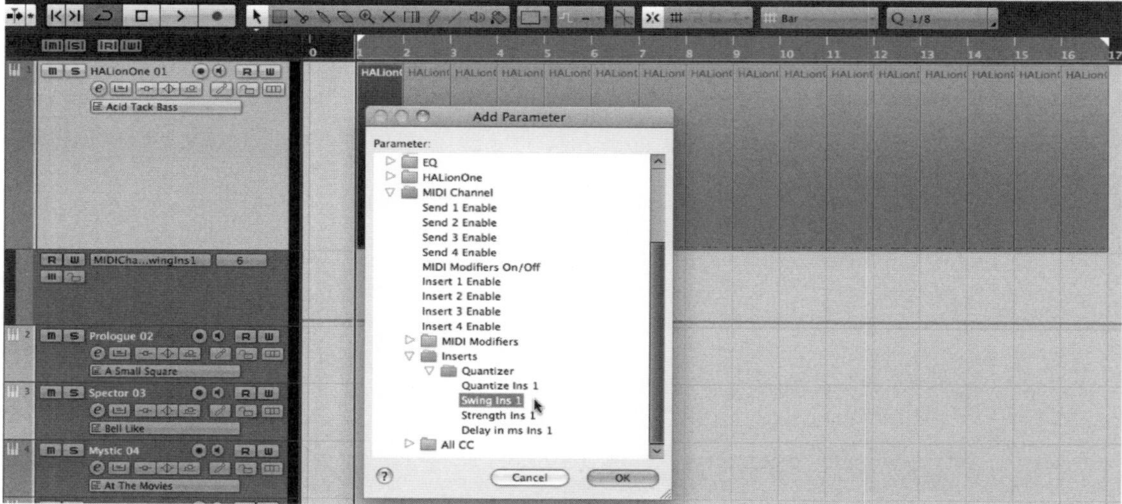

Figure 15.5
Quantizer inserted on a MIDI track with 'Swing Ins 1' selected as the Parameter

8 Turn on Read (R), and enter nodes with the Pencil tool, every few bars or so. Or draw a ramp. This will progressively raise and lower the swing value. Play the track to hear the changes.

Figure 15.6
Automating the Quantizer swing values

Experiment further by automating the other Quantize parameters on automation sub tracks.

Automatic Quantize

Not to be confused with automation. You can use this handy function to automatically quantize events as you play them. Switch on the 'Auto Q' button on the Transport panel before you record a part. This is useful if you know in advance that a certain quantize setting is going to work.

To automatically quantize existing parts or events, select them, set up a loop, tick the Auto Apply box on the Quantize Panel and adjust the settings until you get the desired result.

Quick tip

If Move MIDI CC is ticked on the Quantize Panel, any related controllers, such as pitch bend and so on, will be moved along with the notes as they are quantized.

Loops and hitpoints

As a direct result of programs like Cubase much of the music we hear today includes audio loops. Hip-hop, house and trance music producers use loops extensively and even rock bands are now incorporating them into their tracks. Film composers, too, are using loops alongside conventional orchestras.

To use loops effectively with Cubase you need to know how to work with Hitpoints, a special feature of the Sample Editor. It works best on drums and other rhythmic material and detects attack transients (rhythmic hits) in an audio file and marks them as 'hitpoints'. Once you've created the hitpoints, you can perform all kinds of wizardry on audio files such as making them fit the tempo of a song or even change a song's tempo whilst retaining the timing of a drum loop. In other words, you can work with audio material in the same way as you do with MIDI material.

Quick tip

To filter out hitpoints based on their peaks in dB, use the Threshold slider. The threshold is indicated by a horizontal line. This can be used to eliminate quieter, unwanted hitpoints by keeping the louder hits and ignoring the quieter ones.

Slicing a loop using hitpoints

Open a drum loop in the Sample Editor and select the Hitpoints tab. You need to choose an option from the Beats menu. For example, if your loop contains mainly sixteenth-notes, you would select 1/16. What happens, in this case, is that only hitpoints close to exact sixteenth-note positions will be created. If you choose 1/8, then only hitpoints close to exact eighth-note positions will be created. If you're not sure which one to select, choose 'All.' Cubase analyses the audio and displays the hitpoints as vertical lines.

Next, slice them for real using Create Slices. The Sample Editor closes and the loop is sliced at each hitpoint.

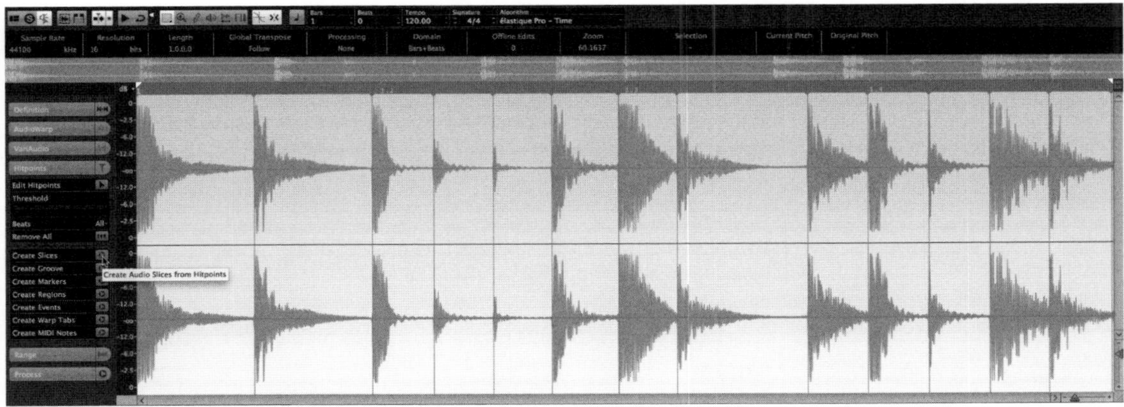

Figure 16.1
Hitpoints calculated in the Sample Editor

The event in the Project window is replaced by an audio part containing the slices and the loop is automatically set to the Cubase tempo. The clever bit, though, is that your loop will now play back at any tempo you choose, within reason.

Figure 16.2
After hitpoints are calculated the sliced audio is converted to an audio part (click on the part to open the Audio Part Editor)

Quick tip

To hide unwanted 'double-hits', zoom in on a segment and use the Pencil tool to divide them further.

Quick tip

Before you slice a loop using hitpoints check that the correct values are displayed in the Tempo, Bars and Beats fields in the toolbar, otherwise you may get some unusual results. For example, if your loop is one bar long and the Bars field displays two bars, the loop will be doubled in tempo and large gaps will appear between the slices in the resulting audio part.

Info

When playing back sliced audio at a tempo lower than the loop's original tempo, there might be audible gaps between the slices. If so, select the slices in the Audio Part Editor and use 'Close Gaps' from the Audio menu (Advanced sub menu) to stretch them to size.

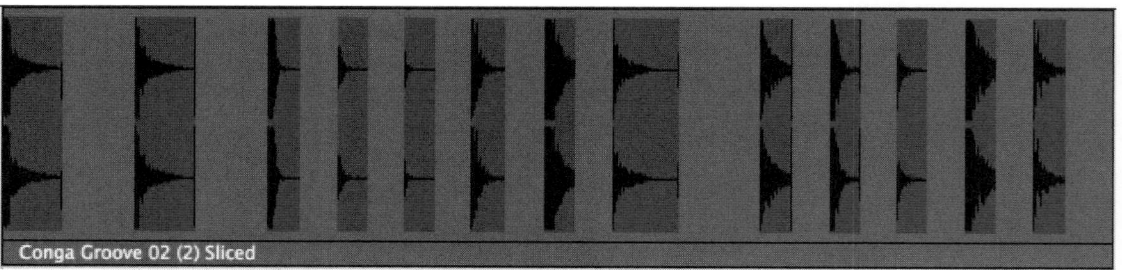

Figure 16.3
Gaps appear between audio slices when they are played at slower tempos

Seven ways to edit hitpoints

- Setting hitpoints according to note values – use the Beats menu. Note values are selected and only hitpoints close to the selected value are used. The correct length of the loop must be set in the Bars and Beats field in the toolbar along with the time signature.
- Locking hitpoints – move the mouse pointer over the grey triangle at the top of the hitpoint and the Lock Hitpoint tooltip will appear. Click on the triangle (it turns blue when locked).
- Disabling hitpoints – press 'Shift' and the mouse cursor changes to a cross and the 'Disable Hitpoint' tooltip appears. Click to disable the hitpoint.

- Disabling locked hitpoints – point the mouse at the blue triangle and the 'Disable Hitpoint' tooltip appears. Click on the triangle.
- Moving hitpoints – press Alt (on the Mac, Option), point the mouse at the vertical hitpoint line and the 'Move Hitpoint' tooltip appears. Drag the hitpoint to a new position.
- Resetting hitpoints – press Ctrl/Command (on the Mac, Alt/Option) and the 'Enable/Unlock Hitpoints' tooltip appears. Drag a rectangle over the hitpoints you want reset.
- Inserting hitpoints manually – zoom in on the waveform at the point you want to edit. Press Alt (on the Mac, Option). The mouse pointer changes to a pencil tool, which is used to add a new hitpoint.

Info

Manually created hitpoints are locked by default.

Creating effects with a sliced loop

Once you've created audio slices you can create all kinds of unusual effects by experimenting with the individual segments. Try muting slices or changing their order, to create a completely new drum pattern. You might want to treat them with effects and EQ. High-hats sound great when treated with the Metalizer plug-in. Reverb could be applied to individual snare hits. You might need to raise the volume of a quiet hi-hat with the Gain processor (Audio menu).

Figure 16.4
High-hats sound great when treated with the Metalizer plug-in

Quantizing loops

You can quantize audio loops after they've been sliced in Cubase in the same way that you quantize MIDI material. In the Project window, double-click the loop to open the Audio Part Editor and open the Quantize Setup box, from the MIDI menu.

Groove quantize

You've found a drum loop that was played with a particularly great feel. You're using it as the basis for a new project and you want to project that feel onto the MIDI tracks. It can be done but you'll have to create a groove quantize map first.

Create hitpoints for the loop in the Sample Editor first (no need to slice them). Then extract the groove by clicking on the Create Groove Quantize button in the Hitpoints tab (Sample Editor Inspector) or select Create Grove Quantize from the Hitpoints submenu (Audio menu). Pull down the Quantize pop-up, in the Project window, and you'll find an additional item at the bottom of the list with the same name as the file from which you extracted the groove. Now you can apply that drummer's feel onto other MIDI and audio drum loops.

Multitrack audio quantization

Rhythmic audio material can be quantized just like MIDI material, which is particularly useful for fixing the timing and changing the grooves of live-recorded drums. However, to avoid phasing problems, all the tracks have to sliced at the same start and end positions. There are four stages to the process:

1 Gather your drum tracks (or other audio material) together into folder tracks (see page 79 in the Operations Manual for detailed information on folder tracks) and click the Group Editing button (=). Selecting any event now will select all the other events in the group (see About Group Editing in the Operations Manual, page 80).

Figure 16.5

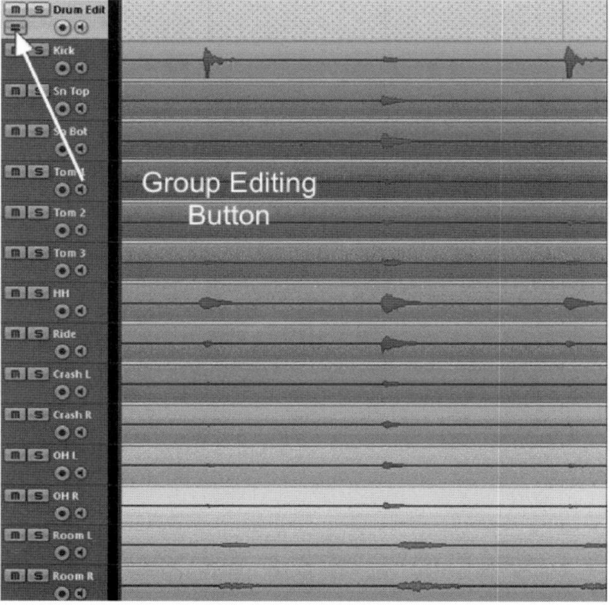

2 Calculate hitpoints in the Sample Editor (as described earlier in this chapter) for the track or tracks that provide the main groove, probably either the kick, snare or hi-hat. When finished, close the sample editor, select all the events and open the Quantize Panel. Because this is an edit group, the Slice Rules section also appears in the quantize panel. There are two columns here – Hitpoint tracks and Priority. Prioritize the tracks by dragging more or fewer stars with the mouse. The track with the highest priority will define where the audio is sliced on all the tracks. Range and Offset parameters can also be set (see 115 in the Operations Manual for details). Press slice and all the audio events in the edit group are sliced according to your settings (Figure 16.6).

3 Set up your quantize settings and click the Quantize button (Figure 16.7).

4 You will have noticed that a further Crossfade section appeared after the audio was sliced. Clicking the Crossfade button cuts the end of the first event at the start position of the following event (in case of overlaps), and stretches the second event until it starts at the end of the previous event (in case of gaps).

Info

If you open the Quantize Panel for an edit group and at least one of the tracks has hitpoints, the 'Slice Rules' section appears. A further Crossfade Panel appears after slicing.

Figure 16.6

Figure 16.7

LoopMash

If you're working on a hip hop or dance music style project and your loops sound a little tired and repetitive, try using LoopMash to inject some variety into them. A brand new interactive synthesizer developed in conjunction with Yamaha, LoopMash creates entirely new variations from existing loops. What follows is a short tutorial that demonstrates how to add variety and interest to a rhythm track using just three loops. To follow this tutorial you will need to install the VST Sound Collection that came with your copy of Cubase 6.

Follow these steps:

1 Open an empty project and add three stereo Audio Tracks. Set the tempo at 120bpm.
2 Open the Loop Browser and locate the file named '120bpm-NDA 013'. The easiest way to find it is to do a text search. Just typing NDA will locate it quickly.

Figure 16.8

3 Drag the '120bpm-NDA 013' file to an empty audio track.
4 Locate these two files – '13 bass 02' and 'strings' – and drag them to the remaining two audio tracks.
5 Set the Locators to encompass four bars (1 – 5). You are going to make a four-bar loop. The string loop is already four bars long but the one-bar drum loop needs to be repeated three times, to match. The two-bar bass loop needs to be repeated once.

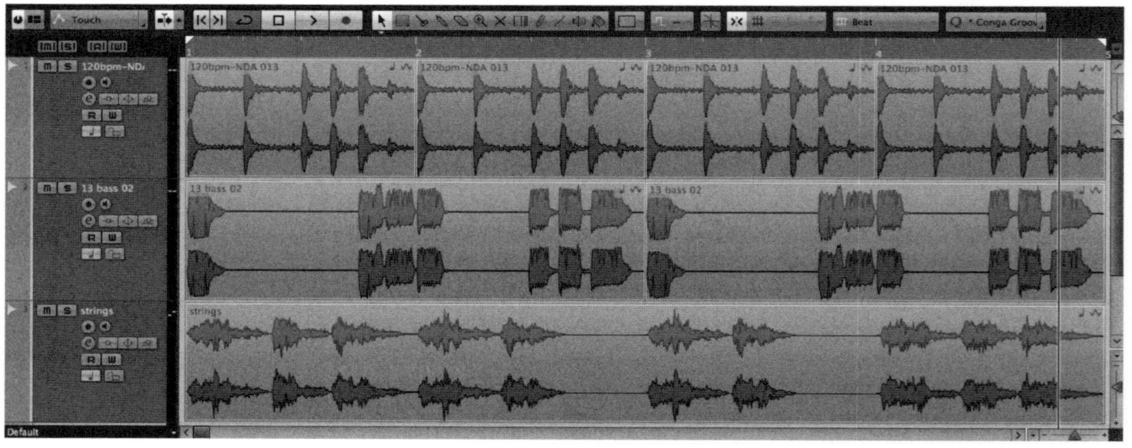

Figure 16.9

6 Create an Instrument Track and assign it to LoopMash.
7 Open LoopMash and drag the '120bpm-NDA 013' file from the Project window to the first channel. LoopMash analyses the loop and arranges them as 1/8-note segments on the track.

8 Again using the Loop Browser, locate the file named '24_hit-vibraslap' and drag it to the second channel. Now locate '02 flute 02' and drag that file to the third channel.
9 Press 'play' and a new pattern will be generated on-the-fly using a mix of sounds from each channel, drums, vibraslap and flute.

Info

Clicking on the button next to the channel slider designates that track as the master track and LoopMash will, then, designate more of its slices to the overall pattern.

From here on, what exactly you hear will depend on how you set the controls and parameters:

- Use the channel sliders to hear more or fewer slices on each track (right for more, left for less).
- Set the transpose interval to match the project.

Tip

You can audition individual slices on a track by clicking on them. The brighter the colour the louder it sounds.

Here's what I did:

- Set the channel-1 slider at the centre position.
- Clicked on the button to the right of the slider to make that channel the master track, so that LoopMash will allocate more of its slices to the pattern.
- Starting from the zero position, moved the channel-2 slider to the right, just far enough for the vibraslap to be heard.
- On channel-3, moved the slider a little to the right of centre.
- On channel-3, set the transposition to +3, so that the flute and bass are playing in the same key.
- Set the Number of Voices heard to three (Slice Selection).
- Set the Number of Voices per Track to one.
- Starting from the left, moved the Slice Selection Offset slider one notch to the right (Audio Parameters).
- Moved the Staccato Amount slider slightly right of centre.
- Adjusted the Dry/Wet Mix slider to achieve a nice balance between the master track (channel-1) and the other two tracks.

Figure 16.10

Info

More information about LoopMash can be found in the Plug-in Reference found in the Cubase Help menu.

Tip

For real-time performance, use notes C–B (any octave) on your MIDI keyboard to trigger the 24 pads.

At this point you can mute the Cubase drum track, press the 'sync' button and use Cubase's transport controls to hear the new patterns along with the bass and strings.

Info

You can save and store setups as scenes using the 24 pads displayed on the Slice Selection and Audio Parameters pages. These scenes can be played back on-the-fly by clicking on the pads.

Automation

Automation panel

When it is time for a project mix-down you will most likely be using automation on some of your tracks. With three different punch-out modes, read/write buttons and performance utilities to manage, automating tracks can be quite tricky. The whole process, though, is much easier if the Automation panel is open as a floating window (Project menu). It provides a visual summary and instant access to all the Cubase automation options.

- Click on the automation icon (toolbar) to open the Automation panel. Alternatively, use the Project menu.

Figure 17.1

- Switching modes is a simple matter of clicking on the Global Automation Mode icon and making a selection.

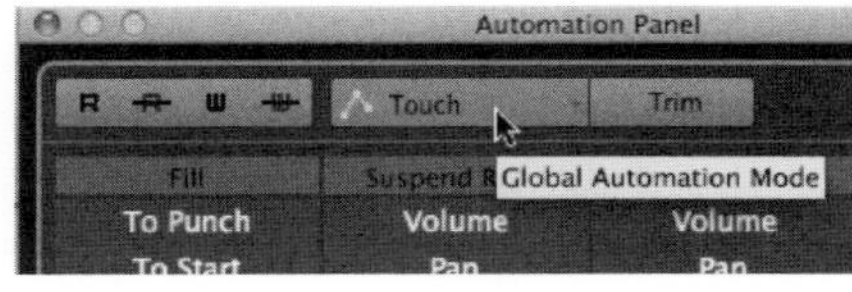

Figure 17.2

- The three automation modes can also be accessed on the toolbar but it's slower than using the Automation panel

How the Automation modes work is described in detail in the Operation Manual but here's a brief summary of the two modes you are likely to use the most:

- This is a volume curve written using Auto-Latch.

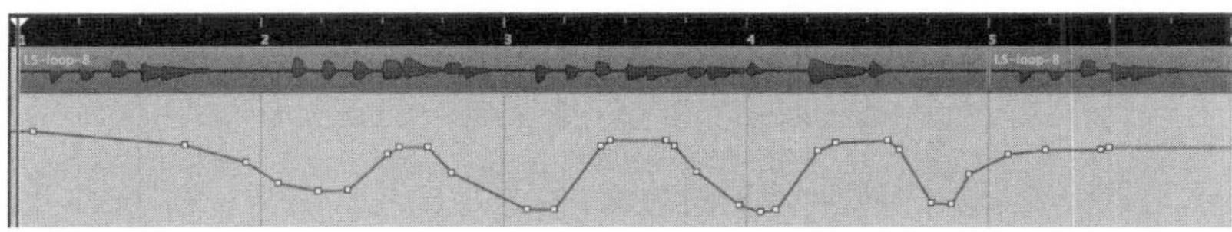

Figure 17.3

- The same volume curve after editing in Touch mode – use it for editing short sections of existing automation. Changes are made while the control is held (in this example, as far as bar 5).

Figure 17.4

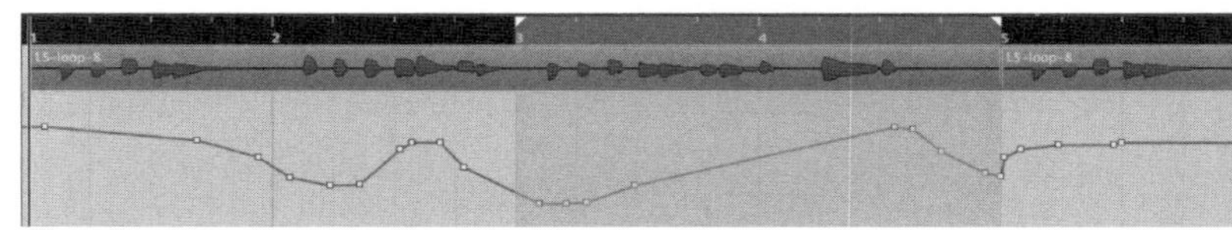

- This time the volume curve is edited in Auto-Latch mode – use it for writing longer sections. Last control position is used until the next stop action (in this example control was released at bar 4 and playback was stopped at bar 5.

Figure 17.5

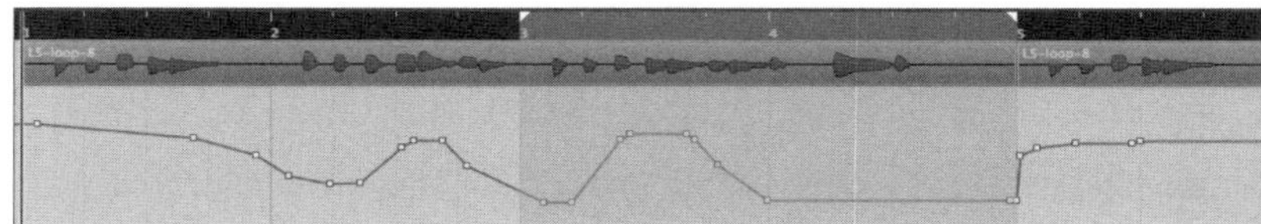

Several performance utilities are available on the Automation panel. One of the most useful is Trim. It works as follows:

- When Trim is made active on the Automation panel the fader is set to a centre position

Figure 17.5

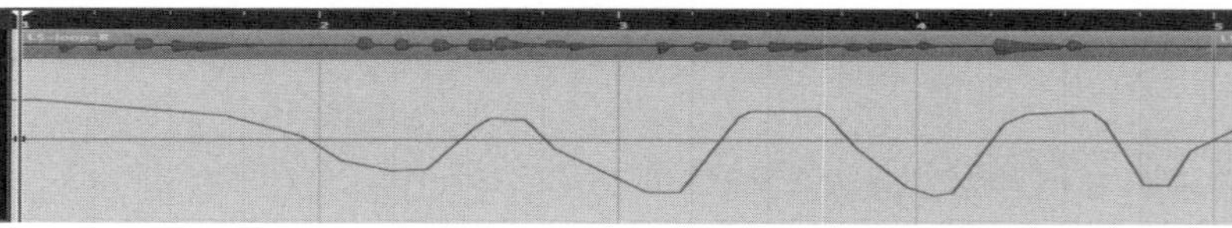

- In Stop mode – moving the fader up or down adjusts the curve.

Figure 17.5

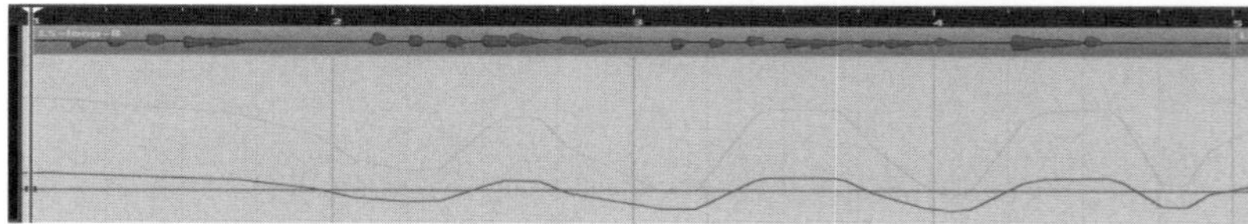

- In Play mode – moving the fader up or down adjusts the breakpoints as the project cursor moves across the timeline.

The above method of trimming is fine in many cases but if you need to scale a specific area, manual automation is often quicker and easier. Simply drag a rectangle around the automation you want to edit and use one of the 'smart spot' controls, in this case 'Move Vertically' (Figures 17.6 and 17.7).

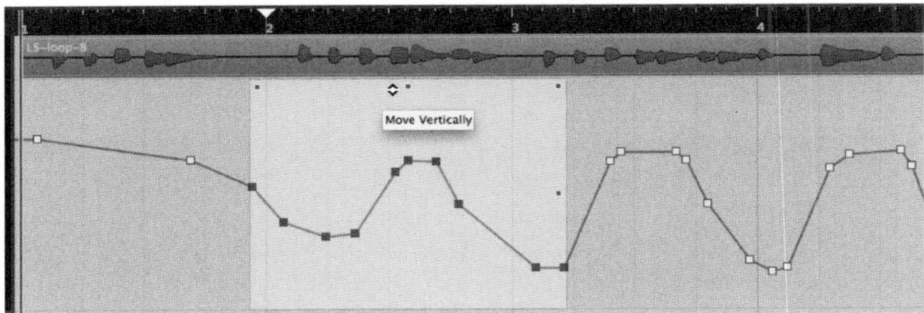

Figure 17.6
The selected automation data is about to be moved vertically with a 'smart spot' control

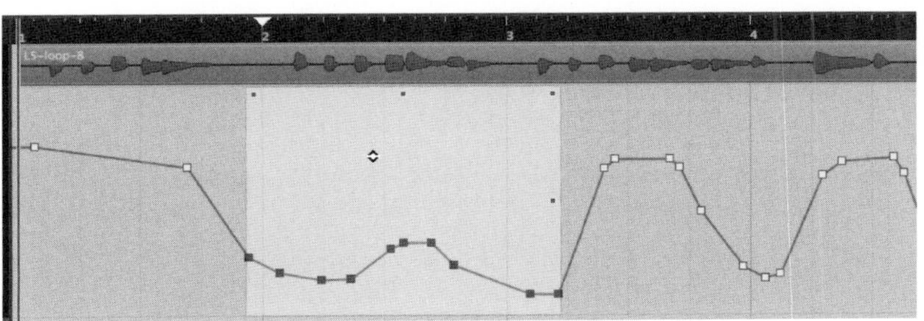

Figure 17.7
The selected automation after being moved vertically with a 'smart spot' control

The options to suspend automation parameters are very useful and the Operation Manual explains a couple of scenarios where you might want to do that (page 240). Also handy are the Show options, which allow you to view volume, pan, EQ, sends and inserts on all tracks with just a click of the mouse. This is so much quicker than opening automation subtracks manually and using the drop-down menus.

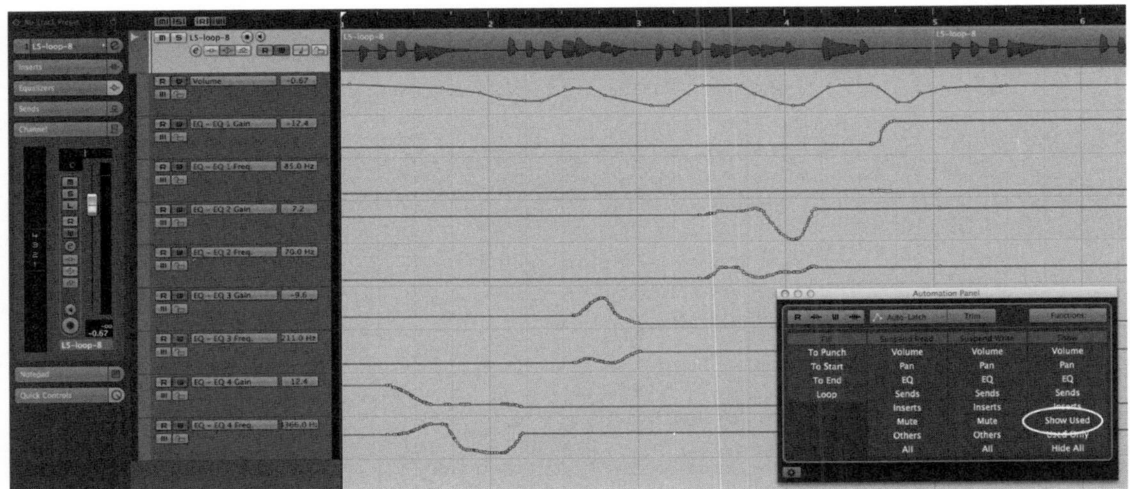

Figure 17.8
Viewing all used volume and EQ automation data by clicking Show Used on the Automation panel

To avoid an abundance of unnecessary breakpoints in your automation curves, experiment with the Reduction Level setting in the Automation Preferences (button is at the bottom left corner of the Automation Panel). I find that 25% usually gives me the results that I need.

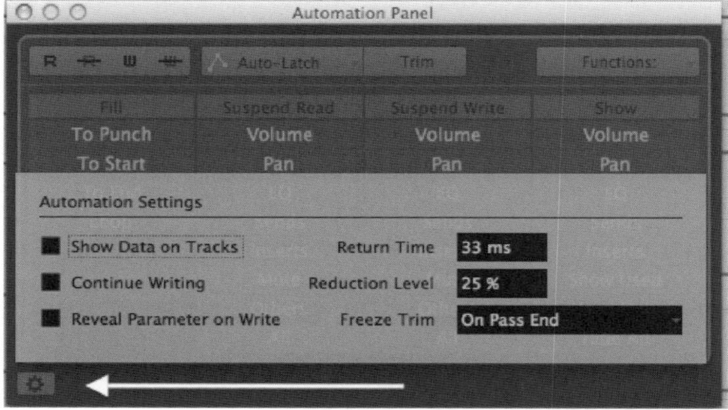

Figure 17.9
To access the Automation Preferences, press the button in the bottom left corner of the Automation Panel

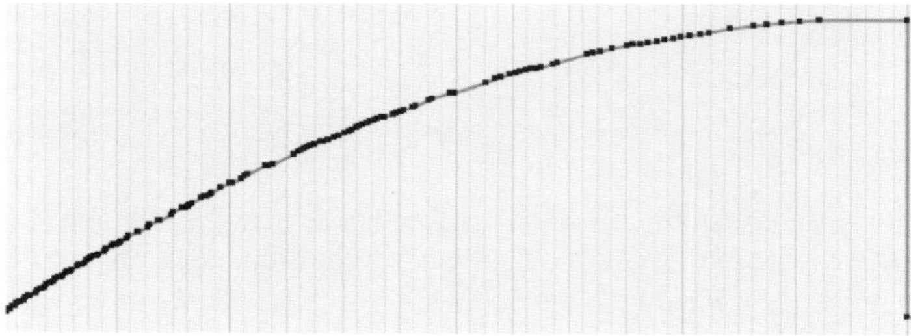

Figure 17.10
A volume curve without applying a Reduction Level

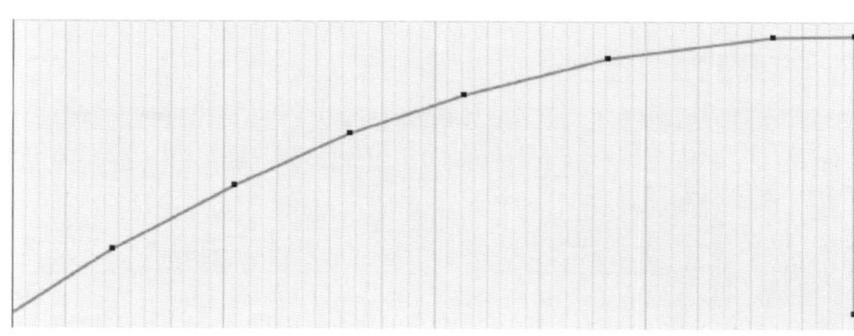

Figure 17.11
The same volume curve with a 25% Reduction Level

REVerence program switching

REVerence, the recently added Cubase convolution reverb plug-in, enables you to place your music inside sampled spaces such as rooms, studios, halls and even tunnels. It's conceivable, then, that you might want to switch reverb programs at specific points in a project, as a special effect perhaps. This is easily achieved in REVerence with the aid of two automation parameters, RecallPreset and Preset-Nr. With Write mode switched on, these can be recorded on-the-fly by double-clicking the program slots at the appropriate points.

In the following three screenshots you can see how REVerence has been automated to switch from program 1 to 10 at bar 5, and from 10 to 20 at bar nine.

Info

Two automation parameters are required to switch programs in REVerence - RecallPreset and Preset-Nr.

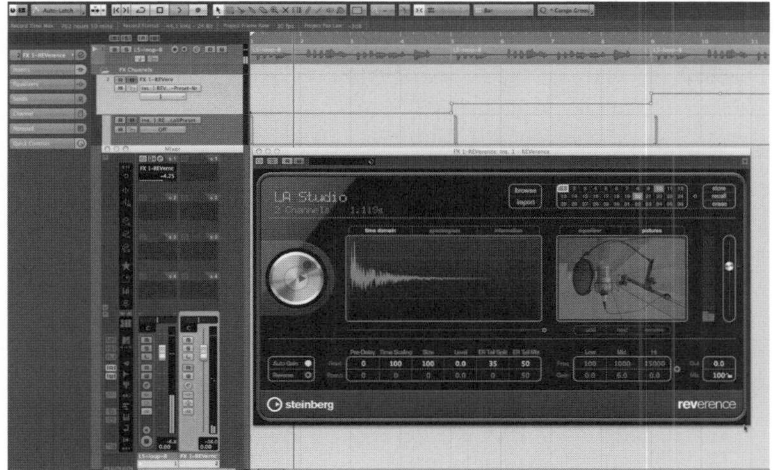

Figure 17.12
REVerence set to use program 1, LA Studio

Figure 17.13
By double clicking on program 10 in the matrix when the project cursor reaches bar 5, REVerence switches to an Exhibition Hall impulse response

Figure 17.14
By double clicking on program 20 in the matrix when the project cursor reaches bar 9, REVerence switches to a Music Academy impulse response

Quick tip

For successful on-the-fly automation it's necessary to double-click on the REVerence program matrix slot as the project plays.

Automatic gain riding

It's common practice in the modern recording studio to use a compressor to control peaks and lows on vocal tracks. However, although it may take longer to do, try using volume automation instead. This is akin to the 'old school' engineering practice, before compressors were widely available, and often yields a more subtle musical result.

Info

You can import your own impulse response files into REVerence but they must be either wave or aiff audio files and they must be no more than ten seconds long.

Merging MIDI Controller automation data

Because you can record MIDI controller data in two places – in a MIDI part or on an automation track – conflicts will inevitably occur if you record both data types at the same spot on the timeline. When this happens Cubase merges the part data and the automation data on playback according special rules. The rules, or Automation Merge modes, are selected in the Track list for the automation track.

Info

Setting up REVerence programs is described on page 39 of the Cubase 6 Plug-in reference found in the Help menu.

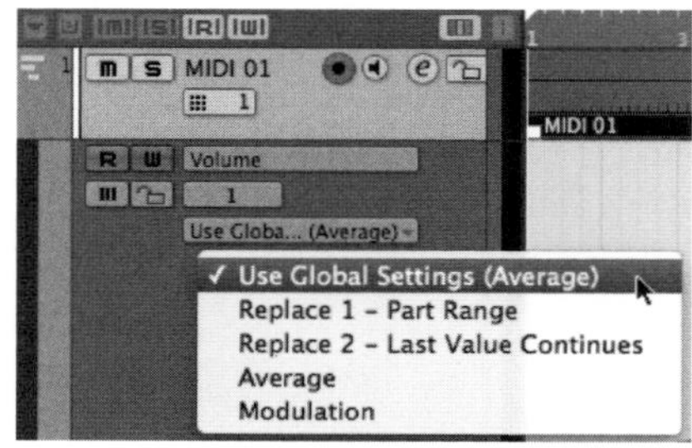

Figure 17.15
Automation Merge modes are selected in the Track list

The Average calculation is perhaps the most useful and is also the default setting. The following examples illustrate how the Average mode works.

- A four-bar volume ramp is recorded in a MIDI part.

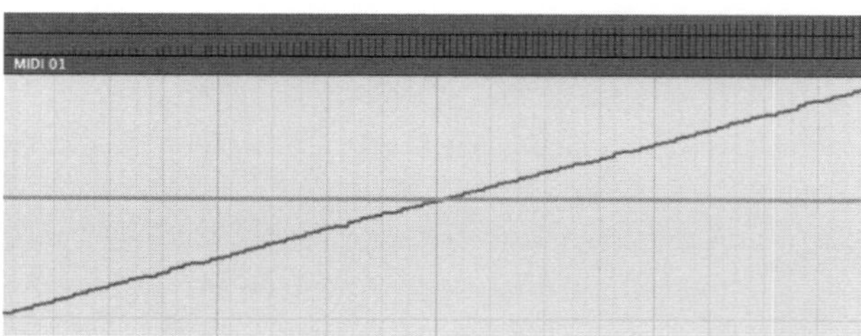

Figure 17.16

Info

You can specify how Cubase handles playback of existing MIDI automation in the MIDI Controller Automation Setup (MIDI menu > CC Automation Setup…).

- A volume curve is recorded on an automation track over the same four bars. Cubase works out the average values between part and track automation and modifies the ramp accordingly.

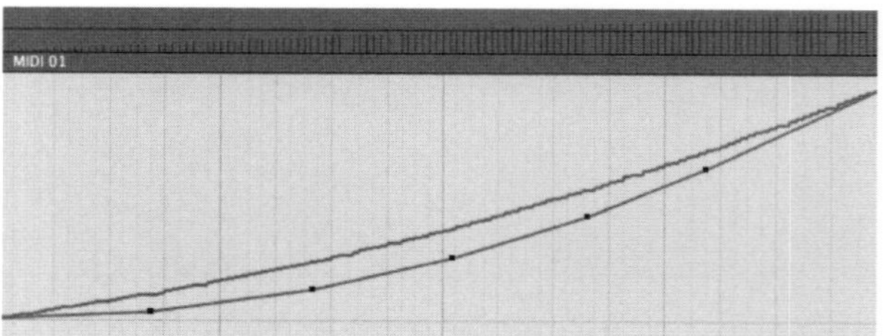

Figure 17.17

Convert MIDI part data into track automation data

It's a simple matter to convert existing MIDI part data into MIDI track automation data using the Extract MIDI Automation command.

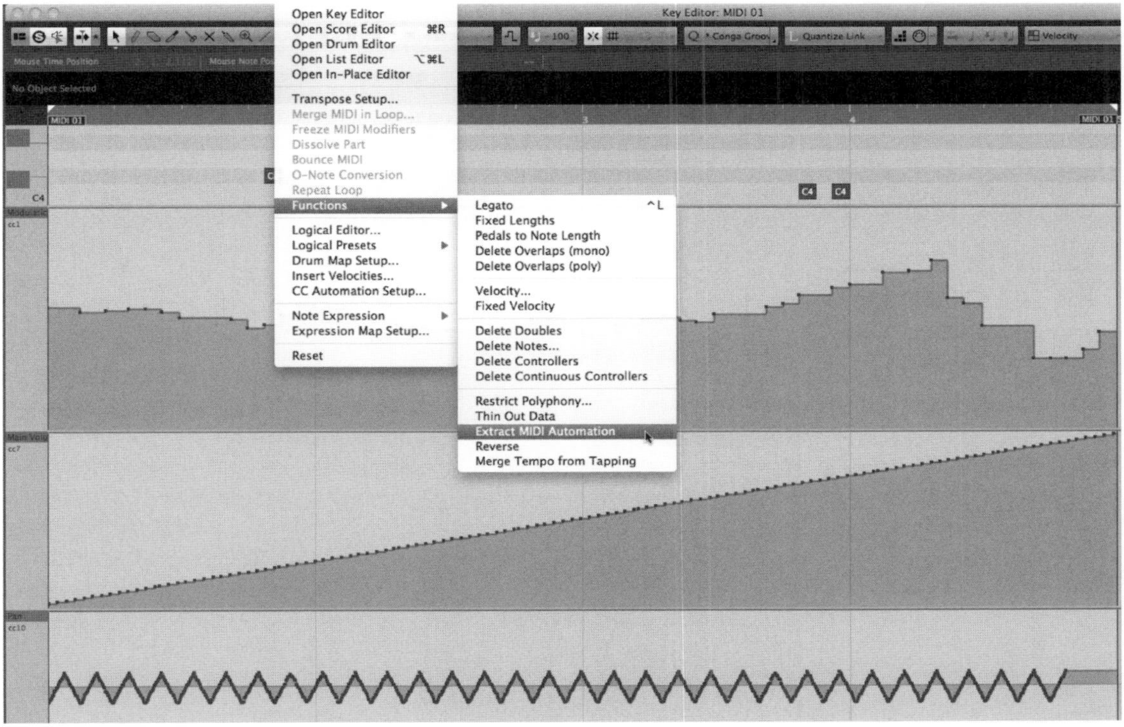

Figure 17.18

After executing the command the selected controller data will be removed from the controller lane (Key Editor) and automatically placed into newly created automation tracks (Project window).

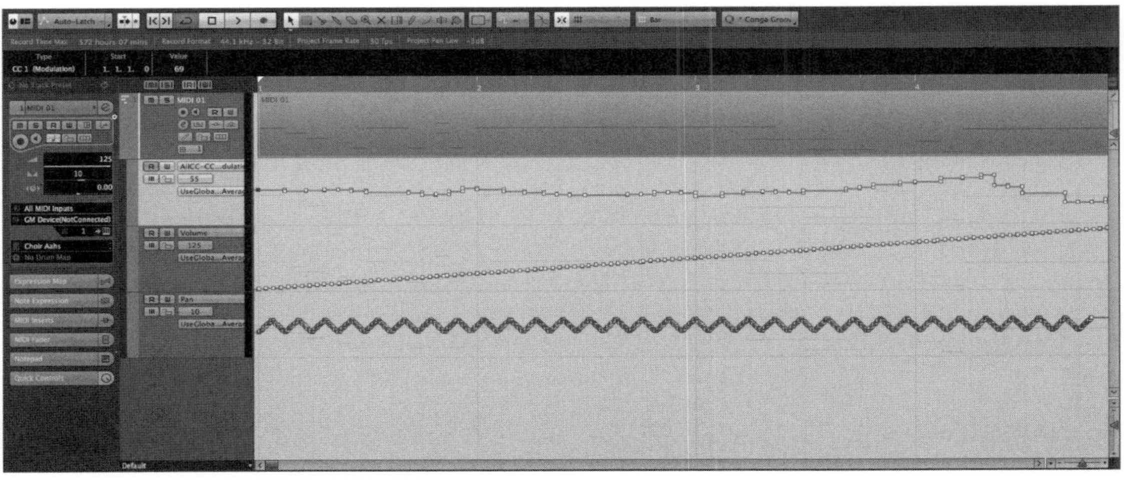

Figure 17.19

Info

After converting MIDI continuous controller data into track automation data remember to switch on the Read button otherwise you will not hear the result when it's played back.

Appendix 1: Key Commands

You can work very quickly with Cubase if you get to know the default key commands. It's a good idea to learn one or two new key commands each day. Most are logical and easy to remember.

You can add your own key commands using the Key Commands window (File > Key Commands...) and even alter the existing default set (although there seems little point in doing so).

Keep this list by you as you work. Your mouse will soon become redundant!

Audio

Option	*PC Key command*	*Mac Key command*
Adjust Fades to Range	A	A
Crossfade	X	X
Auto-Grid	Shift+Q	Shift+Q
Find Selected in Pool	Ctrl+F	Command+F

Automation

Option	*PC Key command*	*Mac Key command*
Toggle Read Enable All Tracks	Alt+R	Option+R
Toggle Write Enable All Tracks	Alt+W	Option+W

Devices

Option	*PC Key command*	*Mac Key command*
Mixer	F3	F3
Video	F8	F8
Virtual Keyboard	Alt+K	Option+K
VST Connections	F4	F4
VST Instruments	F11	F11
VST Performance	F12	F12

Edit

Option	PC Key command	Mac Key command
Autoscroll	F	F
Copy	Ctrl+C	Command+C
Cut	Ctrl+X	Command+X
Cut Time	Ctrl+Shift+X	Command+Shift+X
Delete	Del or Backspace	Del or Backspace
Delete Time	Shift+Backspace	Shift+Backspace
Duplicate	Ctrl+D	Command+D
Edit In-place	Ctrl+Shift+1	Command+Shift+1
Group	Ctrl+G	Command+G
Insert Silence	Ctrl+Shift+E	Command+Shift+E
Left Selection Side to Cursor	E	E
Lock	Ctrl+Shift+L	Command+Shift+L
Move to Cursor	Ctrl+L	Command+L
Mute	M	M
Mute Events	Shift+M	Shift+M
Mute/Unmute Objects	Alt+M	Option+M
Open Default Editor	Ctrl+E	Command+E
Open Score Editor	Ctrl+R	Command+R
Open/Close Editor	Return	Return
Paste	Ctrl+V	Command+V
Paste at Origin	Alt+V	Option+V
Paste Time	Ctrl+Shift+V	Command+Shift+V
Record Enable	R	R
Redo	Ctrl+Shift+Z	Command+Shift+Z
Repeat	Ctrl+K	Command+K
Right Selection Side to Cursor	D	D
Select All	Ctrl+A	Command+A
Select None	Ctrl+Shift+A	Command+Shift+A
Snap On/Off	J	J
Solo	S	S
Split At Cursor	Alt+X	Option+X
Split Range	Shift+X	Shift+X
Toggle Edit Group on Sel. Tracks	K	K
Undo	Ctrl+Z	Command+Z
Ungroup	Ctrl+U	Command+U
Unlock	Ctrl+Shift+U	Command+Shift+U
Unmute Events	Shift+U	Shift+U

Editors

Option	PC Key command	Mac Key command
Show/Hide Infoview	Ctrl+I	Command+I
Show/Hide Inspector	Alt+I	Option+I
Show/Hide Overview	Alt+O	Option+O

File

Option	*PC Key command*	*Mac Key command*
Close	Ctrl+W	Command+W
New	Ctrl+N	Command+N
Open	Ctrl+O	Command+O
Quit	Ctrl+Q	Command+Q
Save	Ctrl+S	Command+S
Save As	Ctrl+Shift+S	Command+Shift+S
Save New Version	Ctrl+Alt+S	Command+Option+S

Media

Option	*PC Key command*	*Mac Key command*
Open Media Bay	F5	F5
Open Loop Browser	F6	F6
Search Media Bay	Shift+F5	Shift+f5
Sound Browser	F7	F7

MIDI

Option	*PC Key command*	*Mac Key command*
Show/Hide Controller Lanes	Alt+L	Option+L

Navigate

Option	*PC Key command*	*Mac Key command*
Add Down	Shift+Down	Shift+Down
Add Left	Shift+Left	Shift+Left
Add Right	Shift+Right	Shift+Right
Add Up	Shift+Up	Shift+Up
Bottom	End	End
Down	Down	Down
Left	Left	Left
Less	Ctrl+Pad -	Command+Pad -
More	Ctrl+Pad +	Command+Pad +
Right	Right	Right
Toggle Selection	Control+Space	Command+Space
Top	Home	Home
Up	Up	Up

Nudge

Option	*PC Key command*	*Mac Key command*
End Left	Alt+Shift+Left	Option+Shift+Left
End Right	Alt+Shift+Right	Option+Shift+Right
Left	Ctrl+Left	Ctrl+Left Arrow
Right	Ctrl+Right	Command+Right
Start Left	Alt+Left	Option+Left
Start Right	Alt+Right	Option+Right

Project

Option	*PC Key command*	*Mac Key command*
Open Browser	Ctrl+B	Command+B
Open Markers	Ctrl+M	Command+M
Open Tempo Track	Ctrl+T	Command+T
Open/Close Pool	Ctrl+P	Command+P
Setup	Shift+S	Shift+S

Quantize

Option	*PC Key command*	*Mac Key command*
Iterative Quantize On/Off	Control+I	Control+I
Quantize	Q	Q

Tool

Option	*PC Key command*	*Mac Key command*
Delete tool	5	5
Draw tool	8	8
Drumstick tool	0	0
Glue tool	4	4
Mute tool	7	7
Next Tool	F10	F10
Play tool	9	9
Previous Tool	F9	F9
Range tool	2	2
Select tool	1	1
Split tool	3	3
Zoom tool	6	6

Transport

Option	*PC Key command*	*Mac Key command*
AutoPunch In	I	I
AutoPunch Out	0	0
Cycle	Pad//	Pad/
Exchange Time Formats	.	.
Fast Forward	Shift+Pad +	Shift+Pad +
Fast Rewind	Shift+Pad -	Shift+Pad -
Forward	Pad +	Pad +
Input Left Locator	Shift+L	Shift+L
Input Position	Shift+P	Shift+P
Input Right Locator	Shift+R	Shift+R
Locate Next Marker	N	N
Locate Next Number	Shift+N	Shift+N
Locate Previous Event	B	B
Locate Previous Marker	Shift+B	Shift+B
Locate Previous Hitpoint	Alt+B	Option+B
Locate Selection	L	L
Locators to Selection	P	P
Loop Selection	Shift+G	Shift+G
Metronome On	C	C
Transport Panel	F2	F2
Play Selection Range	Alt+Space	Option+Space
Recall Cycle Marker 1 to 9	Shift+Pad 1 to Pad9	Shift+Pad 1 to 9

Record	Pad *	Pad *
Retrospective Record	Shift+Pad *	Shift+Pad *
Return to Zero	Pad . or Pad ,	Pad . or Pad ,
Rewind	Pad -	Pad -
Set Left Locator	Ctrl+Pad 1	Command+Pad 1
Set Marker 1	Ctrl+1	Command+1
Set Marker 2	Ctrl+2	Command+2
Set Marker 3 to 9	Ctrl+ 3 to 9	Command 3 to 9
Set Right Locator	Ctrl+Pad 2	Command+Pad 2
Start	Enter	Enter
Start/Stop	Space	Space
Stop	Pad 0	Pad 0
To Left Locator	Pad 1	Pad 1
To Marker 1	Shift+1	Shift+1
To Marker 2	Shift+2	Shift+2
To Marker 3 to 9	Pad 3 to 9 or Shift+3 to 9	Pad 3 to 9 or Shift+3 to 9
To Right Locator	Pad 2	Pad 2
Use External Sync	T	T

Windows

Option	*PC Key command*	*Mac Key command*
Inline: Key Commands	Shift+F4	Shift+F4
Inline: Settings	Shift+F3	Shift+F3
Inline: View Layout	Shift+F2	Shift+F2

Workspaces

Option	*PC Key command*	*Mac Key command*
Workspace 1 to 9	Alt+Pad 1 to 9	Option+Pad 1 to 9
New	Ctrl+Pad 0	Command+Pad 0
Organize	W	W
Lock/Unlock Active Workspace	Alt+Pad 0	Option+Pad 0

Zoom

Option	*PC Key command*	*Mac Key command*
Zoom Full	Shift+F	Shift+F
Zoom In	H	H
Zoom In Tracks	Alt+Down	Option+Down
Zoom Out	G	G
Zoom Out Tracks	Alt+Up	Option+Up or Command
Zoom to Event	Shift+E	Shift+E
Zoom to Selection	Alt+S	Option+S
Zoom Tracks Exclusive	Z or Ctrl+Down	Z or Command+Down

Appendix 2: Tool summary

Here's a list of the main tools used in Cubase 6 - the ones you'll find in the 'right click pop-up tool box' plus a few more. Some of them vary from editor to editor. Their functions may vary too.

The toolbar in each editor is customizable and other icons and buttons can be added to it using the toolbar Setup (Ctrl click on the toolbar to open).

Project Window

Arrow tool - Use it to select, add, move, duplicate (hold down Alt key - on the Mac, Option key) resize and time stretch events.

Range tool - Use it to select whole areas of a project, ready for editing. Click tiny arrow for options.

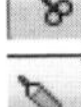

Scissors - Use it to split events.

Glue tube - Use it to glue events together.

Eraser - Use it to remove events.

Magnifying Glass - Click once to zoom in, drag to zoom in on an area. Hold down Ctrl (on the Mac, Command) to zoom out.

Mute tool - Use it to mute and unmute events.

Time Warp tool - Use it to adjust the Tempo track by dragging positions related to tempo to actual positions in time. Click tiny arrow for options.

Pencil - Use it to draw parts on MIDI and audio tracks and draw automation data on subtracks.

Line tool - Use it to draw automation data on subtracks. Click tiny arrow for options.

Speaker - Use it to audition audio events. Click tiny arrow for manual scrub option.

Color tool – You can override the default track colour for individual events and parts using the Color tool.

Key, List and Drum Editors

Arrow tool - Use it to select, add, move, duplicate (hold down Alt key - on the Mac, Option key) resize and time stretch events.

Pencil (Key and List Editor only) - Use it to add notes and alter their length. In the Key Editor, use it to create and edit controller. In the List Editor, use it to insert events.

Drumstick (Drum Editor only) - Use to create and delete drumbeats.

Line tool (Drum Editor only) - Use it to draw controller data. Click the tiny arrow for options.

Eraser - Use it to remove events.

Magnifying Glass - Click once to zoom in, drag to zoom in on an area. Hold down Ctrl (on the Mac, Command) to zoom out.
Mute tool - Use it to mute and un-mute events.
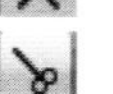
Scissors (Key Editor only) - Use it to split events.

Glue tube (Key Editor only) - Use it to glue events together.
Time Warp tool (Key and Drum Editors only) - Use it to tempo map freely recorded MIDI material. Click tiny arrow for options.

Trim tool – (List Editor only) Use it to divide notes. For example, an 1/8 note into two 1/16 notes.

Score Editor

Arrow tool - Use it to select, move and duplicate notes and objects (hold down Alt key - on the Mac, Option key).

Eraser - Use it to remove notes and objects.

Magnifying Glass - Click once to zoom in, drag to zoom in on an area. Hold down Ctrl (on the Mac, Command) to zoom out.

Note - Use it to insert notes and change their lengths.
Scissors - Use it to split tied notes (click on second note).
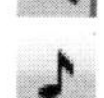
Glue tube - Use it to glue notes of the same pitch.

Q - Open Display Quantize box. Select note(s) first.

Hand - Graphic Move tool. Use it to move notes and objects without affecting playback (page mode).

Trim tool - Use it to divide notes. For example an 1/8 note into two 1/16 notes.

Export Tool – Use for selecting and exporting sections of a score as image files.

Sample Editor

Range Selection tool - Use it to select whole sections of an audio.

Magnifying Glass - Click once to zoom in, drag to zoom in on an area. Hold down Ctrl (on the Mac, Command) to zoom out.

Pencil - Use it to draw in the waveform display.

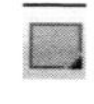

Speaker tool - Use it to audition audio.
Scrub tool - Use it to manually audition audio.
Time Warp tool - Use it to tempo map freely recorded audio.

Audio Part Editor

Arrow tool - Use it to select, add, move, duplicate (hold down Alt key - on the Mac, Option key) resize and time stretch events. Click tiny arrow for options.

Range tool - Use it to select whole areas of an audio part, ready for editing.

Magnifying Glass - Click once to zoom in, drag to zoom in on an area. Hold down Ctrl (on the Mac, Command) to zoom out.

Eraser - Use it to remove audio events.

Scissors - Use it to split audio events.
Mute tool - Use it to mute and unmute audio events.
Speaker tool - Use it to audition audio events.

Scrub tool - Use it to manually audition audio events.

Time Warp tool - Use it to adjust the Tempo track by dragging positions related to tempo to actual positions in time. Click tiny arrow for options.

Tempo Track

Arrow - Use it to select tempo events. You can also enter tempo events with the Arrow by holding down the Alt key (on the Mac, Option).

Eraser - Use it to delete tempo events.

Magnifying Glass - Click once to zoom in, drag to zoom in on an area. Hold down Ctrl (on the Mac, Command) to zoom out.

Pencil - Use it to draw and edit tempo events on the tempo grid display.

Index